Legends Never Die

To Dr.
Ward?
(Not on Amazon Orders)

Sports and Entertainment
Steven A. Riess, *Series Editor*

LEGENDS NEVER DIE

Athletes and Their Afterlives
in Modern America

RICHARD IAN KIMBALL

SYRACUSE UNIVERSITY PRESS

∞ The paper used in this publication meets the minimum requirements of the American
National Standard for Information Sciences—Permanence of Paper for Printed Library
Materials, ANSI Z39.48-1992.

For a listing of books published and distributed by Syracuse University Press,
visit www.SyracuseUniversityPress.syr.edu.

ISBN: 978-0-8156-3506-2 (hardcover)   978-0-8156-1086-1 (paperback)
978-0-8156-5405-6 (e-book)

Library of Congress Cataloging-in-Publication Data
Names: Kimball, Richard Ian.
Title: Legends never die : athletes and their afterlives in modern America / Richard Ian
    Kimball.
Description: First edition. | Syracuse, N.Y. : Syracuse University Press, 2017. | Includes
    bibliographical references and index.
Identifiers: LCCN 2017001141 (print) | LCCN 2017010234 (ebook) | ISBN 9780815635062
    (hardcover : alk. paper) | ISBN 9780815610861 (pbk. : alk. paper) | ISBN 9780815654056
    (e-book)
Subjects: LCSH: Sports in popular culture—United States. | Athletes—United States—
    Death. | Athletes—United States—Public opinion. | Athletes—United States—
    Biography. | Premature death—Social aspects—United States.
Classification: LCC GV706.5 .K56 2017 (print) | LCC GV706.5 (ebook) | DDC
    306.4/83—dc23
LC record available at https://lccn.loc.gov/2017001141

Manufactured in the United States of America

For My Pop

Contents

Illustrations

Acknowledgments

This project started over a meal at a Chicago pub with Elliott Gorn. At the time, he was soliciting chapters for an edited volume on Chicago sports. The only connection that I had to sports in Chicago was a vague memory about Kenny Hubbs, the Cubs second baseman who had died in a plane crash in 1962. Elliott encouraged me to pursue the story and I dug in. And I kept digging for the next ten years. It is a pleasure to step out of the deep shaft and recognize Elliott and others who inspired, corrected, edited, read, and supported *Legends Never Die*.

Steven A. Riess was also at the table in Chicago that afternoon and he has closely followed the project ever since. His interest in my work and his guidance through the process kept me inching forward when I did not really want to. Thanks, Steve.

Many of my colleagues in the history department at Brigham Young University helped me to hone my thinking, stay on track, and enjoy coming to work every day. Jay Buckley introduced me to the story of Lane Frost and kept reminding me about it. Friend and mentor Susan Sessions Rugh gave much-needed support and direction. Her help, while she wrestled with fierce challenges of her own, went the second mile and beyond. Others helped in countless ways, large and small: Julie Radle, Angie Thomas, Ignacio Garcia, Don Harreld, Paul Kerry, Matthew Mason, Shawn Miller, Jenny Hale Pulsipher, Jeffrey Shumway, Aaron Skabelund, and Neil York. Chris Hodson deserves special mention for reading the entire manuscript in one evening—and having pages of comments and suggestions. Mensch in every way. Dean Ben Ogles of Brigham Young University's College of Family, Home, and Social Sciences provided generous support for research and travel. David Lunt, professor of history at Southern Utah University, taught me about athletes and death in the ancient world.

The North American Society for Sport History has been a comfortable disciplinary home. For years, outstanding sports historians have commented on my essays and critiqued my ideas. Each made the book better. Special thanks to Mark Dyreson, Robert Pruter, Steven Riess, Maureen Smith, and Daniel Nathan. A timely dinner with William J. Baker introduced me to existential psychotherapy and encouraged me to no end. Bill epitomizes the scholarly gentleman.

Working with Syracuse University Press has been a true pleasure. Suzanne E. Guiod is a consummate professional who shepherded me through the process with grace and aplomb. It made a big difference to be kept in the know. I also benefited from the two reviewers who read the manuscript closely and were not afraid to offer suggestions. The reviews were blind and their contributions will be invisible in the text, but I know where they are and I deeply appreciate the reviewers' expertise. Thanks to Sara Cleary for a much-needed copyedit.

While I was researching and writing, the concept of podcasts came of age. I am not sure I would have made it without them. The regulars on Hang Up and Listen (Josh Levin, Stefan Fatsis, and Mike Pesca) as well as the cast of Culture Gabfest (Stephen Metcalf, Dana Stephens, and Julia Turner) gave me something to think about when I was not thinking about the things that I was supposed to be thinking about.

Finally, gratitude and love to my family. Bird, Abs, Solly, and Zadie Kae make my life worthwhile and fulfilling. I could not ask for more.

Legends Never Die

Introduction

Making Immortals

It all started with Achilles. Thousands of years ago, the story of Achilles supplied the template for the creation of a Greek hero—a mortal endowed with superhuman powers who accomplished incredible feats. According to Gregory Nagy, a scholar of ancient Greece, "heroes are mortals" and must die before immortality can be bestowed on them. "The hero can be *immortalized*," writes Nagy, "but the fundamental painful fact remains: the hero is not by nature *immortal*."[1] On the pages of the *Iliad*, Achilles faces his heroic dilemma: return home from Troy and live a long, peaceful life, or stay and fight the Trojans, face death, and win eternal fame. "If I stay here and fight at the walls of the city of the Trojans," Achilles reasons, "then my safe homecoming will be destroyed for me, but I will have a glory that is imperishable. Whereas if I go back home, returning to the dear land of my forefathers, then it is my glory, genuine as it is, that will be destroyed for me, but my life force will then last me a long time, and the final moment of death will not be swift in catching up with me."[2] By choosing everlasting glory over a long, fruitful life, Achilles entered the cult of heroes: mortals who were worshipped much like the Greek gods. Although his body died and was entombed, his soul was immortalized and lived in paradisiacal splendor in exotic locales including Elysium, the Islands of the Blessed, and the White Island. Achilles's choice to suffer a heroic death on the battlefield set the enduring standard for future heroic deaths in the Western world.

American athletes in the twentieth century who followed in Achilles's footsteps were also immortalized. They gained the glory and immortality that accompany the combination of athletic achievement and an early grave. Animated by the lure of unfulfilled promise, modern mythmakers lament the loss of athletes' untapped potential while celebrating their accomplishments and constructing their legacies. A good story helps, too. Achilles had Homer whereas heroic modern athletes are brought to life by sportswriters, filmmakers, family members, and even poets. Athletes pass away all the time, but, like Achilles, true legends never die.

Modern Muses

One of the first, and most influential, modern muses to link athletic greatness, early death, and immortality was the British poet A. E. Housman. Not an accomplished athlete himself, the poet nevertheless comprehended how the fleeting fame of athletic victors could be preserved in the amber of premature death. Housman's "To an Athlete Dying Young," published in 1896, underscores the attraction of an athlete's early grave:

> The time you won your town the race
> We chaired you through the market-place;
> Man and boy stood cheering by,
> And home we brought you shoulder-high
> . . . .
> Smart lad, to slip betimes away
> From fields where glory does not stay
> And early though the laurel grows
> It withers quicker than the rose.
> Eyes the shady night has shut
> Cannot see the record cut,
> And silence sounds no worse than cheers
> After earth has stopped the ears.
>
> Now you will not swell the rout
> Of lads that wore their honours out,
> Runners whom renown outran
> And the name died before the man.
> So set, before its echoes fade,

The fleet foot on the sill of shade,
And hold to the low lintel up
The still-defended challenge-cup.
And round that early-laurelled head
Will flock to gaze the strengthless dead,
And find unwithered on its curls
The garland briefer than a girl's.[3]

The "smart lad" in the poem was likely based on Moses John Jackson, Housman's classmate, roommate, and lifelong friend. Recalling Jackson's victory in the Quarter Mile Challenge Cup at the London Athletic Club in 1885, Housman may have imagined his friend's early death, which would have saved the poet from the pain of Jackson rejecting Housman's romantic overtures. Housman biographer Norman Page suspects that the poet may have found "consolation in death as a preserver of youth" and that he "might have been less unhappy if his friend had died young."[4] The primary themes of Housman's poem introduce one of the arguments of this book. First, Housman illustrates how an early death protects an athlete from the inevitable loss of skill, fame, and youth. Then the poem creates a narrative that reshapes the story to reflect the author's interests. The runner's death is fortuitous. He will never see his record broken nor strain to hear the fading cheers. The laurel surrounding his "unwithered curls" will remain green and vibrant—just like the town's memory of the athlete, perfectly preserved by the elixir of nostalgia.

Applying a modern varnish to Housman's elegy, British journalist Simon Barnes notes that "only the unfinished is perfect. There is more beauty in the Leonardo cartoon in the National Gallery than there is in his greatest completed masterpiece, because every completion is a kind of spoiling. A few lines of a lost great poem, a fragment of a sculpture: these things have a perfection that not even the greatest finished piece of work can ever rival. The reason is that we can fill in the gaps with ourselves. We can elevate the promise into an imagined perfection that can never, in the harshness of the real world, actually exist. . . . [W]e see an infinite potential, and convert it in our minds to perfection. It is a perfection that cannot be spoiled by anything save each passing second of time."[5]

Temporally unshackled, dead athletes live in an ever-present time-lessness, circumscribed only by the limits of our imaginations. Our minds can compose fitting, if imaginative, futures for our fallen heroes. Historian Garry Wills explains that "memory 'improves' sports to the heart's desired scale. Sports thus reverse the normal laws of optics, whereby things lessen as they recede from us. The farther off things are in the sports world, the larger they become."[6] And what could be farther away than an imaginary future based on a limited past? The black hole of unfulfilled potential magnifies the energy in the universe of memory.

Death, youth, and beauty form a potent combination in American society. One need only recall the nonstop coverage of the tragic acci-dents that killed Princess Diana and John F. Kennedy Jr. to appreciate the American obsession with celebrity death. When the death occurs during the prime of life the scope of the tragedy multiplies. Americans who had never met the celebrity mourn the loss as they would the death of a close family member. When the immortals are laid low, we are reminded of our own mortality. But the deaths of famous athletes are particularly poignant because unlike other celebrities, their physical gifts seem to transcend the imperative of the grave.

In cultural terms, some deaths matter more than others. When a cel-ebrated athlete dies unexpectedly, Americans mourn with unanticipated intensity. "People have a deeper and more abiding respect for sports fig-ures than almost anyone else out in the public because most people have played these games at some time in their life," describes journalist Harry Hammitt. "That is, in part, why [dying] athletes may get a stronger gut reaction. People can identify with them to a greater extent. We're very familiar with politicians, but we don't have a secret dream to be politi-cians. We do have a secret dream to be a star athlete."[7] When athletes die, our dreams die as well. And they go down hard.

What happens when athletic heroes die unexpectedly is the question at the heart of *Legends Never Die*. The death of athletes like Dale Earn-hardt, Lou Gehrig, and Benny Paret adhere to the American psyche with unusual attachment. Perhaps it is because athletes belong to entire communities. By playing in the public eye, athletes get integrated into the daily lives of countless fans. Perhaps it is because athletes who die young remain forever in their prime—the grainy footage of their physical exploits is never juxtaposed with pictures from their declining years. But early mortality alone does not transform athletes into immortals. That task is left to the living who revisit and refashion heroic accomplishments and construct legacies for the immortals. As novelist Margaret Atwood writes, "the past belongs to those who claim it, and are willing to explore it, and to infuse it with meaning for those who are alive today. The past belongs to us, because we are the ones who need it."[8]

The path toward immortality was unique for each of the athletes discussed in the following pages. Each lived and died in specific historical circumstances and their legacies were shaped by a broad group of interested parties, from family members to Hollywood producers to American presidents. Although the "immortalization" of each athlete occurred in its own setting, several similarities thread the stories together and help us to understand, at least in part, how and why athletes get remembered in certain ways by family members, fans, and American society.

The making of memories feels organic. Deep in our brains some chemical reaction imprints a moment on our cerebral cortex without our knowledge or consent. Things happen and we remember them whether we want to or not. But the process of shaping memories (or legacies) occurs at a much slower rate in conscious minds seeking to make sense of events or lives. In the case of athletes who die young, various groups including friends, families, and corporations seek to define the legacy of the athlete by constructing historical narratives centered on the concerns of the interested party. The myths and stories that emerge help survivors create meaning after tragic events. As Erika Doss reminds us, "our mourning rituals are devised to wrest order out of disorder, provide structure and give meaning to the ineffable, and prevent psychic and social anarchy."[9] The making of meaning, though, is a messy business full of differing priorities, perspectives, and needs. When Drew Gilpin Faust asserts that "the Dead became what their survivors chose to make them," she is describing a process of creation designed to comfort but also to persuade.[10] Power struggles do not end at the grave's edge. Survivors persistently manipulate the deaths of athletes to promote their own social, political, and religious purposes.

Throughout the course of the twentieth century, meaning-makers have used an array of technologies to broadcast their messages. Newspapers and magazines dominated the dissemination of myths early in the century when popular columnists played an outsized role in shaping an athlete's legacy by framing athletic accomplishments for readers. Just after midcentury, a new generation of reporters turned to the techniques of New Journalism and assumed a more critical stance toward athletic heroes. By reporting on the totality of an athlete's life, these journalists made mortal the once immortal. Conversely, Hollywood filmmakers revisited cherished American sports immortals. Portraying athletes like Lou Gehrig and George Gipp in heroic terms, the movies created lasting images of these athletes, virtually ensuring some form of immortality. Television, especially after World War II, played the primary role in creating athletic immortality by televising the deaths of athletic heroes in real time and immediately contextualizing tragedies in transcendent terms. Analysis of the roles played by mythmakers and their use of media form the foundation on which each chapter rests in this book.

Pierre Nora's theory of *lieux de mémoire* (sites of memory) undergirds much of our current understanding of how memories are created and preserved and how the process of memory-making has changed during the last two centuries. Sites of memory, Nora argues, "originate with the sense that there is no spontaneous memory, that we must deliberately create archives, maintain anniversaries, organize celebrations, pronounce eulogies and notarize bills because such activities no longer occur naturally." The "fundamental purpose" of sites of memory like cemeteries, monuments, and festivals is "to stop time, to block the work of forgetting, to establish a state of things, to immortalize death, to materialize the immaterial . . . in order to capture a maximum of meaning in the fewest signs." Sites of memory—and their meanings—constantly evolve to meet changing needs, tastes, and values. Such sites "only exist because of their capacity for metamorphosis, an endless recycling of their meaning and an unpredictable proliferation of their ramifications."[11]

Nora and other practitioners of "collective memory" tend to focus on the meanings of material memorial sites like cemeteries and monuments. Although material culture, statues, and halls of fame appear in *Legends*

Never Die, I have concentrated on how less tangible "sites of memory" are constructed and reconstructed. Following the ideas of Wulf Kansteiner, the "collective memories" analyzed throughout the book "originate from shared communications about the meaning of the past that are anchored in the life-worlds of individuals who partake in the communal life of the respective collective." Kansteiner describes three elements that make up collective memories: "the intellectual and cultural traditions that frame all our representations of the past, the memory makers who selectively adopt and manipulate these traditions, and the memory consumers who use, ignore, or transform such artifacts according to their own interests."[12] Although the consumers of collective memory have received short shrift in the scholarly literature, I have tried wherever possible to integrate all three aspects.

The incongruence of a *young* athlete's death, especially when it happens on the field of play, is particularly disturbing. It upsets the very order of things. Historian Joseph L. Price has written that the death of an athlete—young, strong, and often famous—stings more deeply than the death of a young soldier or singer. "[T]he shock about the reality that all will die becomes even more intense when observing that athletes die," writes Price. "When faced with the death of a physically fit or physically impressive athlete, we often experience a keener anxiety about our own mortality. For if an athlete can die in the midst of preparing to engage in sport, then how much more are we, who are less physically fit and often merely desirous of play, vulnerable not only to the certainty of death but also to its timing, its possible imminence?"[13]

To calm the cognitive dissonance that accompanies the unexpected death of a young athlete, fans create new belief systems that frame the athlete's death in positive, even transcendent, terms. The implementation of new safety devices or the anointing of an heir to continue the deceased's work helps fans reconcile the athlete's unanticipated death and return their psyches to a semblance of stasis. Memorials, scholarships, books, websites, decals on helmets, patches on sleeves, and retired numbers hanging in the rafters console fans and help push the horrifying reality to the back burners of consciousness.[14] Such efforts soothe grieving fans by attaching meaning to a seemingly senseless death. After athletes die, according to biographer Tony Castro, our memories "mold them into the collective image of the archetypal hero, interpreting their lives in a more spiritual way as a reflection of society's need for men and women who are a touch above ordinary, able to live on the plane of basic right and wrong, good and evil, heaven and hell. Sports is an obvious arena from which to draw candidates for this category of immortality, elevating their super-athlete's accomplishments on the field to an almost religious pitch and unwittingly interpreting their lives as expressions of unconscious projections of our own dreams."[15] An intriguing parallel connects how modern Americans treat the deaths of young athletes with how earlier Americans responded to the deaths of young soldiers in the Civil War. Historian Drew Gilpin Faust finds that "Death's significance for the Civil War generation arose . . . from its violation of prevailing assumptions about life's proper end—about who should die, when and where, and under what circumstances." To make sense of the nation's tremendous loss, families turned to religious narratives that stressed the providential timing of death for all Christians. Even the cult of the Lost Cause—the continuing celebration of Confederate memory—reinforced the idea that the soldiers had not died in vain, even in defeat.[16]

What happens when our athletic heroes die unexpectedly? Myths get created and movies get made. Statues and memorials appear. Journalists laud and decry the American obsession with sports. Family members create memorials to perpetuate the memory of their loved one. Fans build websites to share stories and grieve with other mourners in cyberspace. Corporations latch on to the advertising potential that remains after the athlete is gone. New policies and safety precautions get added to the rule books to ensure that similar tragedies never happen again. Each of these activities, and others, help the living to process their unexpected loss and to return a measure of normality to their lives.

· · ·

Legends Never Die is organized around case studies that cover much of twentieth-century America, although the content tilts toward the decades after World War II. No book could possibly include every prominent athlete who died young. Many athletic heroes have been left out. Roberto Clemente, Ray Chapman, Jack Trice, Hobey Baker, and Nile Kinnick receive brief mention at best.[17] If I have ignored your favorite player or most meaningful memory in this book, mea culpa. But painful decisions had to be made and countless worthy candidates were left for other historians to chase.

The subjects who appear in the book were chosen according to a loose set of criteria. If a particular story had already been well told, I decided not to replow existing furrows. I tried to include athletes and historical events that have received less attention or were ripe for reinterpretation. The subjects in each chapter illuminate a specific theme or deepen our knowledge of how myths get created and perpetuated. Several of the chapters consider prominent, timeless issues, and others are tied to a particular time and place but speak to larger concerns in American sports history. By analyzing examples from a variety of sports and eras, we can gain insight into how the deaths of young athletes have been used to create and manipulate meaning in personal lives and the national narrative.

Chapter 1 describes the psychological trauma caused by any unexpected death, but it focuses on the ruptures created when popular athletes die tragically. This chapter provides the historical and philosophical background for the remainder of the book. Furthermore, I examine the relationship between death and sports and argue that modern sports help Americans to suppress the fears associated with their own mortality.

The second chapter charts how the story of one athlete's death—Notre Dame's football star, George Gipp—was appropriated and manipulated by a series of individuals and institutions throughout most of the twentieth century. The power of Gipp's legacy endured, from Knute Rockne's "win one for the Gipper" speech, to the Hollywood biopic *Knute Rockne, All American* (1940), to Ronald Reagan's use of Gipper-speak throughout his political career. Although the dead may tell no tales, this chapter proves that the living more than make up for it.

Next the book turns to a comparison between two rodeo stars from different eras. The little-known cowgirl Bonnie McCarroll competed in rodeos during the 1920s until she was killed at the Pendleton Round-Up in 1929. Her death led to the prohibition of female riders in rough stock events and the virtual disappearance of women's rodeo for decades. Conversely, male bull rider Lane Frost's death at the Frontier Days Rodeo in

1989 catapulted bull riding into a golden age, which included the creation of the Professional Bull Riders tour complete with television broadcasts and million-dollar prizes. The gendered environment of rodeo initially allowed for female riders to flourish but the situation changed dramatically in 1929. Male riders have been consistently rewarded for taking risks and facing death.

Chapter 4 delves deeply into the 1962 title fight when Emile Griffith killed Benny Paret in the ring at Madison Square Garden and in front of a sizeable television audience. The fight itself is remembered for three things: Paret's death, Griffith's ferocity, and the gay slurs that Paret aimed at Griffith. This chapter goes well beyond the ring to analyze the international fallout after the match, including the calls to abolish boxing and the role that television played in stirring up the emotional reaction to the fight. Furthermore, Griffith's bisexuality and how it was treated in the press plays a major role in the chapter. Illustrating the arc of one LGBTQ athlete, Griffith's story offers insight into the sexual politics of boxing and how little attitudes have changed since 1962.

The fifth chapter homes in on how Dale Earnhardt's reputation transformed from the "Intimidator" to the "Good Shepherd" in the immediate aftermath of his fatal crash on the last lap at the Daytona 500 in February 2001. Commentators, journalists, and fans turned to the biblical tropes of evangelical Christianity to make sense of the death of NASCAR's most popular driver. Earnhardt's mourning fans took full advantage of the emerging technology of the Internet to create "cybermourning" communities where racing enthusiasts could gather virtually to share stories and comfort each other. Earnhardt's death even captivated the nation's intellectual cognoscenti who accorded NASCAR the status and respect of more traditional American sports.

Chapter 6 turns the book's approach on its head by considering athletes who died long after their careers had ended and their physical gifts had ebbed. Focusing on Joe DiMaggio, Mickey Mantle, and Ted Williams, the chapter showcases the role of New Journalists like Gay Talese who undermined the once-immortal heroes by portraying the totality of their lives beyond the ballpark. The fitting end to the book contextualizes the quixotic struggle undertaken by John Henry Williams to cryogenically preserve his father and, thus, assure his immortality.

. . .

It was a weekday game under the sun at Wrigley Field: Dodgers visiting the Cubs. Calling the action for Dodger fans on the coast, radio broadcaster Vin Scully offhandedly captured the existential crisis at the center of baseball and other modern sports. Scanning the injury report, Scully noted that Cubs outfielder Andre Dawson was "listed as day to day." Scully paused, then wondered, "Aren't we all?"[18] By focusing on athletic accomplishment, physical skill, and eternal youth, we make athletes into prime candidates for immortality.

Why Lou Gehrig Was Lucky

A Meditation on the Mortality of American Athletes

Lou Gehrig was right all along. When it came to leaving the spotlight of athletic stardom, he may well have been "the luckiest man on the face of the earth." Gehrig's retirement speech, delivered between games of a doubleheader at Yankee Stadium on July 4, 1939, became an instant sporting classic and then a celluloid classic three years later when Gary Cooper reprised the speech in *The Pride of the Yankees* (1942). Then, as now, watching the Iron Horse take his final bow raises a lump in the throat of even the flintiest fan.

At the time, the final scene of Gehrig's career played out as a tragedy. *New York Times* reporter John Drebinger described the farewell as a "pageant" as "colorful and dramatic . . . as ever was enacted on a baseball field." The spectacle of Lou Gehrig Appreciation Day started with an on-field reunion of the 1927 Yankees to honor their "former comrade-in-arms who had carried on beyond all of them only to have his own brilliant career come to a tragic close." The old-timers faced home plate as Gehrig "gulped and fought to keep back the tears." For several minutes, the crowd of 61,808 silently waited for Gehrig's valedictory. The speech was worth the wait. Gehrig's spontaneous response read like a Hollywood script. "Without doubt," according to Drebinger, "one of the most touching scenes ever witnessed on a ball field and one that made even case-hardened ball players and chroniclers of the game swallow hard. . . . [it was] an unforgettable day in baseball."[1]

Three years later, *The Pride of the Yankees* portrayed Gehrig as a tragic hero on the big screen. Standing alone behind a "galaxy of microphones,"

1. Lou Gehrig, the "Iron Horse," wipes away a tear while speaking during a tribute at Yankee Stadium on July 4, 1939. Gehrig's record-breaking career was cut short by neuromuscular disease. (AP Photo/Murray Becker)

Gary Cooper as Gehrig showed Americans how to act in the face of dire circumstances. Dignified to the end, Gehrig accepted his fate, delivered his speech, and walked slowly off the field. As the unsteady first baseman struggled down the steps of the dugout, the umpire's cry of "play ball" echoed throughout Yankee Stadium. If the messages about heroism had been lost on wartime moviegoers, the film's introductory frames (written by Damon Runyon) reinforced the moral: "[Lou Gehrig] faced death with the same valor and fortitude that has been displayed by thousands of young Americans on far-flung fields of battle. He left behind him a memory of courage and devotion that will ever be an inspiration to all men."[2]

Thirty years after Gehrig's farewell, in June 1969, another pinstriped hero said goodbye to Yankee Stadium. The theme of Mickey Mantle's swan song that afternoon harked back to Gehrig. Aware that he stood on the ground that had once been trod by Gehrig, Mantle reflected on the close of his own athletic career. "I always wondered how a man who knew he was going to die could stand here and say he was the luckiest man in the world," Mantle told the crowd. "Now I think I know how Lou Gehrig felt."[3] Mantle understood, as only an aging athlete could, that Gehrig *was* the lucky one—the athlete who died in his prime, whose legacy was secured in the sepulcher of death, safe from the ravages of age and poison-penned journalists. In athletic terms, the timing of Gehrig's death was not tragic at all. In fact, by dying young, he ensured that his memory and fame would live forever. Mantle seemed to envy Gehrig's good luck in exiting the athletic stage. The memory of Gehrig's good life would only be magnified by the lens of his timely death. In the end, Gehrig achieved the epitome of an athlete's "Good Death."

Since at least the early fifteenth century, the manner in which a person dies has been accorded significant meaning in Western societies. Techniques relating to the "art of death" (*ars moriendi*) appeared in published form by 1415. To qualify as a "Good Death," a man remained faithful to the end, shunning despair, spiritual pride, impatience, and avarice. Although the ways of living and dying changed considerably in the centuries between the Black Plague and Lou Gehrig's disease, the desire for a "Good Death" continued unabated, especially in times of uncertainty or strife like wars and outbreaks of epidemic disease. The art of dying for sports heroes, however, has never been cataloged. There are no nostrums to recite or questions to ask at an athlete's deathbed. But by looking closely at how American culture has responded to the deaths of young athletes in the twentieth century, we can begin to understand the significance of "when and where, and under what circumstances" a young athlete dies.[4]

Not surprisingly, the contours of the athletic art of dying emerged in the newspaper coverage of Lou Gehrig's farewell address. As previously mentioned, John Drebinger captured Gehrig's last curtain call at Yankee Stadium in all its tragic glory. In what must have been a throwaway line, however, Drebinger hinted at the idea that death might be a welcome alternative to the athlete who has outlived his physical skills. The rapid deterioration of Gehrig's baseball prowess was harrowing. The physical decline of his former teammates, accelerated by age and overindulgence, appeared pathetic and laughable. When his erstwhile teammates trotted out to the field to honor Gehrig, their names rung familiar—Tony Lazzeri, Mark Koenig, and Herb Pennock—but their physical appearances struck a dissonant chord. Drebinger wondered, could these "elderly gentlemen, some gray, some shockingly baldish" really have been the residents of Murderer's Row?[5] Even Babe Ruth ("robust, round and sun-tanned"), the greatest player of all, had "faded into retirement." Old soldiers might happily fade away, but athletes grow accustomed to burning bright. One way to avoid the slow fade toward death, ironically, is to die early. In essence, Neil Young's advice that it is "better to burn out than to fade away" applies as much to athletes as rock stars.[6]

.   .   .

"Death is the dark backing that a mirror needs if we are to see anything. Every perception causes a certain amount of death in us, and this darkening is a necessity," writes Saul Bellow in *Humboldt's Gift*.[7] Even the mirror we call sports receives its reflective power from the black backing of death. Every mirror's black rests largely unnoticed beneath the surface reflection but provides the contrast necessary to see clearly. Death, too, reposes in the background of our minds, pushed nearly out of our consciousness by the repression brought on by the fear of mortality. The mirror of sports helps us to understand societies and the black backing of death helps us to clarify the powerful attraction and passionate interest in sports in the modern world.

When contemporary thinkers turn to the question of death, the ideas of Sigmund Freud are never far behind. The father of psychoanalysis asserted that even when human beings claimed to recognize "that death was the necessary outcome of life" and was "natural, undeniable, and unavoidable," people quickly shifted that reality to the back corner of their unconscious minds. Because "our own death is indeed unimaginable" and "no one believes in his own death," Freud concluded that "in the unconscious every one of us is convinced of his own immortality." We spend our energy and resources running from the deep-seated fear of death. Using language redolent of the sporting world, Freud wrote that "whenever we make the attempt to imagine [our death] we can perceive that we really survive as spectators."[8] The imaginative projection of personal death fades to black yet the imaginer lives on.

Social structures and institutions exist to help people repress the fear of death by linking individuals to some type of transcendent power. According to cultural anthropologist Ernest Becker, this power "need not be overtly a god or openly a stronger person, but it can be the power of an all-absorbing activity, a passion, a dedication to a game, a way of life, that like a comfortable web keeps a person buoyed up and ignorant of himself, of the fact that he does not rest on his own center. All of us are driven to be supported in a self-forgetful way, ignorant of what energies we really draw on, of the kind of lie we have fashioned in order to live securely and serenely."[9] In short, human activities provide symbolic systems that divert our attention away from thinking about the ultimate reality of death.

Humans have to repress that greatest of fears to be able to function in the world. Montaigne asked in the sixteenth century, "If death frightens us how can we go one step forward without anguish?" He decided that "for ordinary people, the remedy is not to think about it."[10] Sports help millions of Americans not to think about death and have become one of the primary systems that scaffold the modern psychological constructions of immortality. Both athletes and fans benefit from the psychological prophylactic of sporting immortality. The deification of sporting heroes bestows immortality on the athlete and gives fans eternity by association. Fans hitch their mortal wagons to the rising stars of athletic heroes as they ascend toward immortality. Sports heroes, as Michael Oriard maintains, "infuse spirit into their world, and as such . . . [perform] an invaluable service for contemporary society." Loosened from the constraints of time, "the heroes of [sporting] contests [remain] unchanged after decades" and the games "attain the permanence of immortality."[11] Heroes like Babe Ruth, Jim Thorpe, and Wilt Chamberlain remain ever with us, roaming the earth as "deathless spirits," enabling others to look, if not quite see, past the grave.[12] Traveling to modern-day Valhallas in Cooperstown and Canton, fans reach out to touch the bronze faces of gods, a momentary but meaningful connection to sporting immortality.

A fan's attachment to an athletic hero often resembles religious devotion, with the athlete cast in the role of savior.[13] An oft-repeated (though apocryphal) anecdote told by Martin Luther King depicts one inmate's faith in heavyweight champion Joe Louis. In a southern state prison during the Great Depression, King related, a black inmate on the brink of execution importuned Louis from the gas chamber. "As the pellet dropped into the container, and the gas curled upward . . . came these words: 'Save me, Joe Louis. Save me, Joe Louis, Save me, Joe Louis.' . . . Not God, not government, not charitably minded white men," observed King, "but a Negro who was the world's most expert fighter, in this last extremity, was the [prisoner's] last hope."[14] Journalist David Margolick has since debunked the story, but King's version of the events nevertheless resonates with sports fans. Joe Louis's strength and skill could not extend the prisoner's life, but the convict's belief in Louis's transcendence gave him hope to the very end. Joe Louis might not save us from our sins, but we still have faith that his accomplishments in the ring can last forever.

Likewise, by playing sports, even the most amateur athlete can live forever. Bartlett Giamatti—Renaissance scholar, president of Yale University, and briefly commissioner of Major League Baseball—envisioned immortality at play in every open field. "In sports," wrote Giamatti, "some version of immortality is being sought whether by way of ritual or of record." Such leisurely pursuits led to "the occasional transcendence of death" and represented the "active engagement of a moment of immortality."[15] Even on the sandiest of lots, a touchdown pass or winning home run "offers the common man *immortality*," argues philosopher Howard Slusher. "The great performance is remembered and the man's name becomes a part of all the stages of time. The performance of the high school football team keeps man alive. It places him in *retrospect* to the unfolding history of time."[16] Eminent historian Allen Guttmann shows how sporting records provide a path toward immortality. "When we can no longer distinguish the sacred from the profane or even the good from the bad," Guttmann writes, "we content ourselves with minute discriminations between the batting average of the .308 hitter and the .307 hitter. Once the gods have vanished from Mount Olympus or from Dante's paradise, we can no longer run to appease them or to save our souls, but we can set a new record." Record holders are rewarded with "a uniquely modern form of immortality."[17] The existence of records compresses time and allows for the comparison of players across generations. The most famous records acquire a numeric shorthand that defines greatness (Joe DiMaggio's fifty-six-game hitting streak; Lou Gehrig's 2,130 consecutive games played; Babe Ruth's sixty home runs in a season). Just ask Roger Maris about the difficulty of ascending the peaks that house the gods of sport and their sacred records.[18]

Exercise and the pursuit of physical fitness do not explicitly promise immortality but they do cast the lure of a longer life. And Americans have taken the bait. In the 1950s, reacting to a "cardiac crisis," deskbound American executives turned to health guides, exercise programs, and lifestyle changes to stem the growing tide of heart attacks. Other middle-class men joined the fitness movement in the 1970s when fitness clubs became popular.[19] One historical account of the 1980s describes how "millions of joggers, runners, swimmers, cyclists, tri-athletes, walkers, weight-lifters, and aerobic dancers had convinced themselves that exercise preserved youth and postponed death. It was the yuppie panacea; 'working out' made them immune to the ravages of time."[20] The fortification of exercise protected the body—and, perhaps more importantly, the psyche—from unwelcome thoughts of death. When physical fitness is understood as an immortality project, obsessive exercise becomes comprehensible as a psychic defense against the fear of death.

The seasonal cycles of sport mark the passage of time, but in "sport time" every season's end is simply prologue to the next. Cries of "wait 'till next year" reverberate almost immediately following a season's final play. Hot stove leagues in baseball and preseason football drafts fill the empty off-season hours with the promise of future prosperity. The green fields of spring gradually lose their splendor over the long, hot summer but return resplendent with the sunshine again. Every new season starts fresh; even Cubs fans feel optimistic in the springtime.

Ernest Hemingway's romantic depiction of Spanish bullfighting, *Death in the Afternoon*, suggests that fans could acquire immortality by watching the death struggle in the ring. In Hemingway's view, the master bullfighter not only stares down death but shares his victory over mortality with the throngs packed into the arena. The bullfighter becomes an athletic Beatrice, leading followers on a tour of the afterlife and bringing them safely back. "[T]he essence of the greatest emotional appeal of bull-fighting," Hemingway wrote, "is the feeling of immortality that the bull-fighter . . . gives to the spectators." While performing his "work of art," the matador tempts death, "bringing it closer, closer, closer, to himself, a death that you know is in the horns because you have the canvas-covered bodies of the horses on the sand to prove it." The bullfighter then "gives the feeling of immortality" to his followers in the crowd. "Then when [the feeling of immortality] belongs to both of you, [the matador] proves it with the sword," killing the bull and symbolically slaying mortality. Should the matador fall prey to the bull's powerful horns, no matter. Once shared, the feeling of immortality remains. "Even if you saw [the matador] killed it would not be you who would be killed, it would be more like the death of the gods."[21]

A season reads like a life, according to essayist Roger Rosenblatt: slowing as it ages, but never quite giving in. Reflecting on the close of one baseball season, Rosenblatt mused, "The beauty of the game is that it traces the arc of life. Until mid-August, baseball was a boy in shorts whooping it up in the fat grass. Now it becomes a leery veteran with a sunbaked neck, whose main concern is to protect the plate. In its second summer, baseball is about fouling off death. . . . The batter cannot know what is coming. He can go down swinging or looking and be made to look the fool. Yet he has a bat in his hands. And if all goes well and he can accomplish that most difficult feat in sports by hitting a 90-m.p.h. sphere with a heavy rounded stick, well then, fate is thwarted for a moment and the power over life is his."[22]

The fact that athletes, like freshman students, never seem to age similarly suggests the possibility of immortality. Sports are the province of the young, strong, virile, and ambitious. The names of dominant athletes change, but their average age perennially hovers in the twenties. Time passes right by them. Possessing a full complement of skills and physical abilities, athletes seem to have found the fountain of youth, or at least general managers have. Athletes on the field never age—even those who die are quietly replaced by younger models. When athletes compete beyond their prime, such as Muhammad Ali, fans become disproportionately unsettled. Watching a broken-down Ali enter the ring reminds us of our own physical decline—that we too are merely shadows of our former selves. The aging athletic hero turns from an idealized projection of our-selves into a doppelgänger, a ghostly harbinger of death. British journalist Simon Barnes describes the wistful denouement for athletes who outlive their physical gifts: "[S]ometimes the very best are remembered not as themselves, but as the people they once were—the greying, ever heavier, ever more boozy shell a living embarrassment to the mythologies of his own past."[23]

Athletic halls of fame offer perhaps the most striking example of the link between sports and immortality. They exist to ensure that the exploits of sports heroes transcend time. For example, the Alabama Sports Hall of Fame in Birmingham advertises itself as a place "where heroes and their memories live forever." The hall "immortalizes the glory of Alabama's most famous champions," from Jesse Owens to Bo Jackson.[24] In sculpture, plaque, photograph, and other forms of memorabilia, these athletic Alabamians appear in timeless poses, never to age, decay, or die. Halls of fame traffic in "cosmic specialness," the faith that certain accom-plishments will outlive one's allotted three-score and ten.[25] Former Los Angeles Dodgers manager Tommy Lasorda summed up the purpose of baseball's hall of fame with uncharacteristic brevity: "[T]he Hall of Fame is eternity."[26] More than merely housing relics of bygone days, halls of fame testify that athletic excellence paves the way to immortality.

Visitors to the National Baseball Hall of Fame approach, almost sacra-mentally, the immortals whose "miraculous performances" are preserved there. Although too much has been made of baseball as America's civil religion, Roberta Newman rightly argues that the hall of fame is "base-ball's Vatican, baseball's Canterbury Cathedral, baseball's Mormon Tab-ernacle." Baseball's hall stands as "a central place, open equally to every worshiper, no matter what his or her local affiliation may be." Just as countless religious pilgrims gather at temples and shrines, "so too do they flock to Cooperstown, to observe the relics of baseball's saints and mar-tyrs." Generations of fans respond to the "spiritual magnetism" emanat-ing from the hall in much the same way that Christians are compelled by the shrine at Santiago de Compostela and Mecca beckons Muslims.[27] Each place offers access to the transcendent and links worshipers to generations of the devout. At first glance, Babe Ruth's cleats and the remains of St. James seem to have little in common, but both provide their worshipers a tangible connection to their immortal heroes.

Other sacred sites dot the American sporting landscape. Stadiums likewise bathe in the holy waters of memory, nostalgia, and hope. The site of wins, losses, joy, and heartbreak, the arena represents lived religion—where communities form and reform, rituals are observed, and enduring ties created. If the National Baseball Hall of Fame is a cathedral, then Lambeau Field, Fenway Park, and the Los Angeles Coliseum are meetinghouses, defined by local interests and regular participation. Broadcaster Bob Costas recalls the first time he visited Yankee Stadium as a seven-year-old in 1959. The game proved largely forgettable: the Yankees lost; Mickey Mantle did not play. After the last out, Costas and his father walked along the outskirts of the field, along the warning track, toward the bullpen exits. Surrounded by thousands of other fans, but lost in his own world, the walk became a quasi-religious pilgrimage as Costas experienced a spiritual connection to the Yankees. Holding his father's hand, Costas regarded the field as a shrine, though one where he did not need to remove his cap. Costas remembers being

> careful not to disturb anything. [I] looked down at the red clay on the warning track, but it wasn't my place to kick it, and to move it around. I was a visitor. I was being allowed to see this. And we got out to dead center field, where the monuments to Ruth, and Huggins and Gehrig were. And I stood there, and seven years old, I started to cry. . . . I really thought that these guys were buried there. I thought that this was a sacred Yankee burial ground and surely when DiMaggio passed away, when Mantle passed away, they'd be buried there too. And my father tried to explain to me, yes, these men are dead but they are buried someplace else. I would have none of it. I was convinced that that was their tombstone.

The ambiance of the stadium and its history deeply impressed Costas but his memories of the day are profoundly personal. For a son who shared little in common with his father other than baseball, that trip to Yankee Stadium remained Costas's "happiest memory" of his father, even four decades later.[28]

Fans sanctify objects related to their athletic heroes even if the mementos never reach the hall of fame. It might be a talisman baseball card rubbed by a Little Leaguer before every crucial at-bat or a fan's lucky autographed jersey worn ritualistically on the day of every big game. Each embodies a little piece of immortality. For the family of one funeral home director in the 1940s, Joe DiMaggio's discarded clothing and gear became objects of worship, reminiscent of the past but capable of shaping the future, too. Biographer Richard Ben Cramer asserts that the "treatment of Joe's relics was the surest sign of his . . . saintly status." Geta and Bina, daughters of DiMaggio's friend and funeral park owner Jerry Spatola, worshipped the ground beneath the center fielder's feet. On one occasion, after a spot of wine stained DiMaggio's shirt, he gave it to the girls "as a remembrance of me." The shirt was the family's first emblem sanctified by Joe D. Soon, the sisters acquired "the shoes Joe wore during the Sacred Streak—or as Geta insisted upon calling them, 'The Spikes.'" Jerry's coffin-maker "fashion[ed] a beautiful encasement for The Spikes, which would then rest, in perpetuity, on rolled and tufted velvet, such as is seen in only the finest coffins. From time to time, over the years, the girls would bring out the velvet-lined encasement, so that Little Leaguers or Legion ballplayers (who were playing for the Spatola Funeral squad) could rub The Spikes for good and godly effect." Most of the time, the shoes remained in a family closet, resting next to a perfectly preserved piece of the cake served at DiMaggio's wedding in 1939.[29] Even in a funeral home, a stained shirt, some holy cake, and a pair of golden shoes signified the immortality and virtual divinity of Joe DiMaggio.

.   .   .

Names and relics *might* last forever, but athletes do not. Even "the luckiest man on the face of the earth" eventually gave his final curtain call. When an athlete dies tragically, the psychological fabric of repression is rent, revealing our illusions of immortality. Because athletes can simultaneously have personal relationships with millions of fans, the psychological disruption is amplified across society. Consider the case of Sanford, a fan of the Pittsburgh Pirates throughout his childhood in the 1950s and 1960s. In an oral history, Sanford characterized his relationship to the players in familial terms: "They were ours, you know; they were our Pirates, as our cousins were our cousins and our uncles were our uncles . . . they were family." But in the very same breath, Sanford could not imagine the players were "mere people. . . . They were like gods. Wearing a baseball uniform made them superhuman to me. Superman wore his uniform, and [Bill] Mazeroski and [Roberto] Clemente wore theirs, and there wasn't all that much difference. . . . I saw them as the equivalent of Greek gods. Yet at the same time," he recalled, "they were like members of the family." That multilayered relationship—with players that he had never met or spoken to—may have been the most important of his young life. On the day that Roberto Clemente died, Sanford "walked into [his] parents' bedroom and saw [his] mother, sitting on the bed, crying. And it didn't seem strange. It didn't seem excessive."[30] The effects of Clemente's death on Sanford beggar description. He lost an athletic idol, a family member, a superhero, and a god in one heartbreaking moment. Sanford's intense connection to the Pirates of his youth is not unusual. Fans feel like they "know" their favorite athletes and are therefore affected by their deaths in profound ways.

Freud averred that in encountering the undeniable death of others, a reality that breaks down the fictional bulwark of personal immortality, men and women quickly set about to repair the chink in their psychic armor. "Our habit," wrote Freud, "is to lay stress on the fortuitous causation of the death—accident, disease, infection, advanced age; in this way we betray our endeavour to modify the significance of death from a necessity to an accident."[31]

Nineteenth-century British poet Gerard Manley Hopkins illustrates the wrenching realization of mortality in his description of a young woman contemplating the falling leaves in "Spring and Fall":

Márgarét, áre you gríeving
Over Goldengrove unleaving?
. . . .
Now no matter, child, the name:
Sórrow's spríngs áre the same.
Nor mouth had, no nor mind, expressed
What heart heard of, ghost guessed:

It ís the blight man was born for,
It is Margaret you mourn for.[32]

For many Americans, the death of an athlete awakens them from the slumber of repression much like the falling leaves shook Margaret from the comfortable moorings of youth. Journalist Christopher Lehmann-Haupt had his "Margaret moment" while watching the televised reports about the death of baseball star Thurman Munson, who was killed in an airplane crash in 1979. Although Munson had been an All-Star catcher on Lehmann-Haupt's favorite team, the Yankees, the reporter struggled to understand the depth of his emotional response as he sat alone in a hotel lobby glued to the television. Lehmann-Haupt discovered that in mourning Munson, he was grieving something much bigger than a hole in the Yankees' batting order: "The truth was, we were all of us—or those of us over forty, at least—in a continuous state of grief over our mortality, and public deaths offered occasions for public mourning, a ritual outlet for our sorrow. Though you had to feel anguish for the sake of his family and friends, it wasn't Thurman Munson in particular we were mourning; it was the death of a young athlete. It was the loss of youth."[33] In the end, it is not about the athlete or the falling leaves. In lamenting the loss of Margaret or Munson, we mourn for ourselves. While our eyes look skyward and trace the paths of falling leaves or falling planes, our mourning turns inward and we weep at our own earthbound mortality.

Anthropologist Katherine Verdery claims that dead bodies have political lives and continue to influence society and morality through their legacies and the reinterpretation of those legacies by the living. Athletes have posthumous lives as well. By recalling the lives of sporting heroes past, the living cannot unbury the dead, but they do use their memories to create meaning for a new generation of athletes and fans. Verdery concludes, "No matter which conceptions of cosmic order, ancestors, space, and time we human beings employ, it seems our dead . . . are always with us. The important thing is what we do with them."[34]

Eighteenth-century French philosopher Voltaire remarked caustically that "if God did not exist, it would be necessary for men to invent him."[35] Three centuries later, Yankee broadcaster Mel Allen, no Voltaire he, updated the couplet by proclaiming that if Mickey Mantle had not lived, someone would have invented him.[36] As it turned out, both happened— the Yankee center fielder did live and Americans invented a Mickey Mantle to meet their social and psychological needs in the twentieth century. And a Gipper. And a St. Dale Earnhardt. Mickey Mantle may have been mortal like the rest of us, but we need him and other sports heroes to be so much more. Our legends never really die. Although they are mortal like Achilles, the glory of their accomplishments remains forever on the lips of the Muses and in the minds of their fans.

The Gipper Wins One for the Gipper

George Gipp, Knute Rockne, and Ronald Reagan

During his halftime speech at the Army–Notre Dame football game in 1928, coach Knute Rockne created the most enduring legend in American sports history when he implored his team to go out and "win one for the Gipper."[1] The heart of Rockne's motivational speech related the story of George Gipp, the All-American running back for the Fighting Irish who died tragically of pneumonia at the close of his triumphant 1920 season. Part of Rockne's story was "true," according to the conventional definition of the word. George Gipp *had* played magnificently for Notre Dame and he *had* died in December 1920. But when Rockne described Gipp's deathbed plea that some future team win a game in his memory, the story strayed from the verifiable historical record and entered the realm of mythmaking.

From one sentence to the next, Rockne transformed the flesh-and-blood George Gipp into the immortal, legendary "Gipper," a new character whose story provided a creation myth for Notre Dame and college football, cemented Rockne's place at the pinnacle of American coaches, and wrote the script from which Ronald Reagan built two careers—one on film, the other in politics. That must have been one unforgettable speech.[2]

Russell Baker, the longtime "Observer" columnist for the *New York Times*, captured the power of the Gipper tale in his column on Super Bowl Sunday in January 1971. Baker's "child's history of football, for women" placed the Fighting Irish at the center of the modern sport. "To bring football into the 1970s," he wrote, "it was first necessary to invent Notre Dame. This was done by Grantland Rice and Pat O'Brien, but Notre Dame might

26

never have seen the light of day if it had not been for the great George Gipp, whose ability to run, pass and kick helped invent Ronald Reagan. With the creation of Notre Dame, Gipp and Reagan, football seemed to have reached its acme."[3] Invention piled upon invention, and soon the art became the truth. Gipp's death spawned Rockne's story, which led to Reagan's portrayal of the myth on the silver screen, which paved the way for the actor's future political success.

Examining George Gipp from the historian's vantage point, at least four versions of his life emerge. First, the life and times of George Gipp, the supremely athletic young man who starred on the football field and at the poker table before he was cut down tragically by strep throat and pneumonia in 1920. Later in the 1920s, the second version of the story came to life when Rockne resurrected Gipp and transformed him into "the Gipper," the patron saint (or avenging angel) of Notre Dame football. Rockne's well-publicized halftime speech cemented Gipper's place in the pantheon of heroes, but the imaginative reframing of the story reveals more about Rockne than Gipp. A dozen years later, the Hollywood biopic *Knute Rockne, All American* (1940) reformulated the myth of the Gipper again. Starring Pat O'Brien as Rockne and Reagan as Gipp, the movie's key scenes center on Gipp's now famous deathbed request and Rockne's emotional retelling of the story. By the time of the film's release, Gipp had been dead for twenty years and Rockne had died in a plane crash nearly a decade earlier. For generations of movie watchers, Pat O'Brien became Rockne and Reagan *was* the Gipper.

Capitalizing on the popularity of the movie, Reagan later updated the Gipper legend by combining the myths of Gipper and Rockne to create the political persona, which proved vital to his political success. Reagan dressed up in Gipper's imaginary uniform and stormed the political field, harnessing the power of the Gipper myth and inserting himself into the story. When Reagan left the White House in 1989, a generation of Republican politicians sought to inherit Reagan's mantle, at times even referring to themselves as the Gipper. More than two decades have passed and Reagan's heir has yet to be crowned—and the University of Notre Dame still waits for the national championship crown that has eluded it since Reagan was in the Oval Office.

The "Real" George Gipp

Let's start with George Gipp before he became the Gipper. This is not as easy as it sounds. Penetrating the clouds of myth that surround Gipp's name, let alone his character, seems challenging enough. How can we separate the flesh-and-blood version from Rockne's legendary version and both from the cinematic version? Is the real George Gipp in there somewhere? By peeling back layers of myth, can we get closer to the true story? Not surprisingly, such daunting tasks have not stopped intrepid historians from trying to capture the "real" George Gipp. Writers have ranged from those who knew or had played with Gipp to historical revisionists focused on the nitty-gritty of Gipp's life on and off the field to counter-revisionists in rose-colored glasses seeking to restore Gipp's reputation.[4]

This much we know. George Gipp was born on February 18, 1895, to Matthew Gipp and Isabella Taylor in Laurium, Michigan, in the mining country of the Upper Peninsula. A remarkable athlete, Gipp excelled in baseball and basketball but avoided the football field altogether. Through a series of connections made on the diamond, Gipp received a scholarship to play baseball at Notre Dame. Although he came from a strict Protestant home, Gipp had few options after graduating from high school and did not hesitate to enroll at the Catholic school in South Bend, Indiana. At Notre Dame, he played center field for the baseball team in addition to spending four years on the varsity football squad. On the gridiron he became a superstar, leading the Irish to a 27–2–3 record (19–0–1 in his final twenty games). Gipp led the team in rushing and passing yards in each of his final three seasons, and his career rushing yardage of 2,341 yards stood as the school record for more than fifty years. Following the 1920 season, Walter Camp named Gipp to his All-American team, the first Notre Dame player to gain that honor. The statistics do not quite tell the whole story, though.[5]

Most historians agree that George Gipp was a bit of a rakehell who knew every gambling establishment within a day's drive of South Bend. Even sympathetic biographer George Gekas concedes that "gambling was a preoccupation with Gipp. It was his great love, perhaps more than football, baseball or other sports. Gipp seemed to like wagering on games

2. George Gipp (c. 1920), All-American halfback for the University of Notre Dame from 1917 to 1920. (University of Notre Dame Archives)

of chance. During his career at Notre Dame, Gipp would find a way to place bets on just about every game."[6] An oft-repeated story reveals Gipp's style and attitude. At halftime of the Army game in 1920, after a lackluster performance by the Irish, Rockne questioned the commitment of the cigarette-smoking Gipp. "What about you, Gipp?" Rockne yelled. "I don't suppose you have any interest in this game?" "On the

contrary, Coach," Gipp replied. "Look, Rock . . . I got four hundred dollars [of my own money] bet on this game and I'm not about to blow it."[7]
Gipp certainly did not blow it; he directed a second-half comeback that
secured a victory and protected his investment. Even this description of
what we might consider Gipp's gambling "addiction" paints him less as a
ne'er-do-well professional gambler and more as a supremely confident, if
somewhat detached, football hero. He only bet on himself, right? Stories
like these, which have circulated for generations, capture the moral ambi-
guity that resides in the shadow of Gipp's athletic talents. Father Charles
O'Donnell, an English professor at Notre Dame during Gipp's days and
later president of the university, admitted that "[Gipp] was an enigma
that we never solved."[8]

Almost by acclamation, commentators and historians have placed
Gipp at the heart of Notre Dame football, a spot close to the center place
of college football itself. Paul Hornung, who starred in the Irish backfield
thirty years after Gipp and won the Heisman trophy in 1956, called Gipp
"perhaps the greatest football hero who ever played for the University of
Notre Dame." But Gipp's influence extended beyond the football field, even
during his collegiate days. Biographer Gekas boasts that "Gipp, through
his brilliant play, was able to turn-on the South Bend area as no other
player had ever done. He became more than a player on the Notre Dame
football team. He was Notre Dame."[9] Not bad for a running back, even
the All-American Gipp. Rockne's biographer Ray Robinson, less prone to
exaggeration than George Gekas, contends that Gipp "remains the most
durable icon in Notre Dame's crowded pantheon of legends. He was the
greatest all-around athlete in the school's history" and possessed the "talent that ultimately was to set him apart from all Notre Dame mortals."[10]
Rockne claimed that he knew "from the first time he spotted Gipp, that he
'was a perfect performer who comes along only once in a generation.'"[11]
Notre Dame alum and Pulitzer Prize winner Walter "Red" Smith invoked
religious imagery to describe Gipp: "Of all the names on the roll of Notre
Dame sports, Gipp is the holiest."[12]

The word "immortal" appears almost reflexively in any description
of Gipp. Here, though, the line between Gipp and the Gipper disappears
in the haze of hagiography. It was Gipp's very mortality that secured his

legendary status. In 1960, *Los Angeles Times* columnist John Hall teased that Gipp exhibited the "timing that helps make immortals" by dying in the afterglow of his All-American season in 1920. Hall's version of Gipp "wasn't all quite that lovely." In reality, "Gipp was a loner, an individualist who seldom took part in practice, a hero who admittedly loafed on defense and who didn't like to make a tackle. . . . [H]is off-campus activities were a constant source of worry." Hall knew "the real George Gipp" but could not fully resist the powerful pull of the myth. Even the scoffing columnist admitted that, above all, "it's a beautiful legend."[13] Like the celluloid Wild West of *The Man Who Shot Liberty Valance*, "when the legend becomes fact, print the legend."[14]

Following his death but before Rockne's invention of "the Gipper," George Gipp's spirit lived on among the students at Notre Dame. And not just in memory or verse. "It was not long after the death of George Gipp," according to the *Notre Dame Alumnus* magazine of January 1932, "that the series of inexplicable events occurred which gave rise to the tale of the Ghost of Washington Hall." Stories circulating at the time of Gipp's death claimed that the star had contracted his fatal case of pneumonia after spending the night on the steps of the Gothic-style theater building, the consequences of a late night on the town. Although Gipp lived in a hotel room in South Bend during most of his time at Notre Dame, he apparently developed a posthumous soft spot for Washington Hall and returned to it soon after his death. Students reported that lights turned on and off without cause and voices echoed in the hallways. One resident witnessed the spirit of Gipp astride a white horse ascending the stairs of Washington Hall. These sightings began in the 1920s and continued for decades. To contextualize the otherworldly visitations, the *Alumnus* magazine reasoned that "whatever the truth concerning the origin of the ghostly visitations may be, the fact remains that the ghost of Washington Hall has become the character about which many fanciful tales have been woven during the time-honored 'chin-fests'" popular with college students. "The tale of the Spirit of Gipp [note the capitalization] will go down to student posterity as long as one stone of Notre Dame remains upon another."[15] Gipp's spirit continued to influence Notre Dame students long after he left the football field.

More than Gipp's ghost haunted campus in the 1920s. The presence of his final playing uniform, according to at least one undergraduate's recollections, provided grist for the mill of Gipp's legend. Thomas Lawrence Doorley tried out for the freshman football team in 1929 and unwittingly became the "second Gipper." As one of the last to arrive at the oversubscribed tryout, Doorley suited up in the pants and jersey that George Gipp had worn during his final game in 1920. Fifty years later, Doorley remembered the scene: "I ended up wearing a rock hard, stalactite infested pair of football pants that felt like a coat of mail left over from the Third Crusade but which had actually belonged to the immortal George Gipp. . . . And Gipp's jersey wasn't much better; tore, tattered, moldy, mud-caked." Eugene "Scrap Iron" Young, trainer and equipment manager, filled Doorley in on the history of his uniform. "We didn't wash it," Scrap Iron told him. "Didn't touch it. That mud came from Dyke Stadium at Northwestern. Poor old George." But lucky young Tom. Instructed not to tell anyone about the provenance of his gear, he was to treat the uniform like "hallowed relics, like St. Peter's bones in Rome."[16]

Doorley had Gipp's uniform, but not his speed, size, or athletic versatility. On the first day of practice, All-American running back Marchmont Schwartz plowed over Doorley, split his nose open, and forced the freshman to take a quick trip to the infirmary. Patched up by the nuns, Doorley returned to the practice field just in time to be cut from the squad. Even holy relics have their limits. But the story did not end when Doorley returned the uniform. Later that week at the dining hall, Doorley listened to "a skinny, little runt of a redhead proudly proclaim that he had worn George Gipp's last uniform for the first two days of practice, before being cut. Another student overheard him and disputed that claim, insisting that he had worn Gipp's uniform. Later on, somebody took a count of the second Gippers on the initial freshman squad and came up with twenty-seven." Gipp's uniform, like the biblical fishes and loaves, multiplied to feed the egos of dozens of football hopefuls at Notre Dame.[17]

But Doorley saw through the claims of his classmates. "I knew better," he wrote, "although, as promised, I kept quiet. How was I so sure? I had worn the uniform to the infirmary where the dear old sister who administered to me had given me a beatific smile and said; 'Well, a wounded warrior, eh. And wearin' the sainted Gipper's very own uniform. . . . I hope you'll be half the man The Gipper was.'" Doorley's experience was legitimate, he asserted, because "in those days nuns didn't lie. They still don't." Unless Doorley's story is fiction (of which there is no indication), something happened at Notre Dame that fall. Perhaps it was a well-organized practical joke. Or maybe Scrap Iron and the women in the infirmary believed in the power of holy relics, whether they belonged to St. Peter or "the sainted Gipper." Might they have indulged in some storytelling that burnished the legend of George Gipp while building confidence in nervous freshmen? We'll never know. But Doorley knew. And probably another two dozen freshmen who visited the infirmary that week believed that they knew the truth as well.[18]

Not all of the posthumous stories about George Gipp enhanced his reputation or that of Notre Dame. In the weeks after Gipp's death, Fielding Yost, the football coach at the University of Michigan, publicly accused Notre Dame of saddling Gipp's family with the bulk of his funeral expenses.[19] A longtime rival of Rockne's, Yost likely propagated the scandal looking to gain a recruiting advantage. The story spread throughout the nation. One fan of Notre Dame, Joseph P. O'Rourke, was troubled enough by the rumors that he turned to Rockne for an explanation. Writing from Providence, Rhode Island, O'Rourke feared that residents of New England would get the wrong impression about the university and the football team. He wrote, "The story that is widely circulated . . . is that George Gipp, was stricken with pneumonia while playing for Notre Dame, and that he died before the season ended and that the University shipped his body home in a cheap wooden casket and that his parents had to obligate themselves greatly to defray the funeral expenses." Such shabby treatment undermined the very foundations of the Catholic university. O'Rourke did not believe "one word" of the accusations but needed Rockne's help to reclaim the university's good name. "I have heard [the rumors] so often," he wrote, "that I have taken this liberty to ask you to furnish me with some tangible [*sic*] proof so that I may vigorously and honestly deny all accusations against the great name and traditions of Notre Dame."[20] The coach's reply implicated Michigan's Yost, whom Rockne said "ha[d] always been very anti-Notre Dame." The accusations against the university were "absolutely without foundation in any shape, manner or form. . . . This story is just like many others you hear by everybody that are gotten out by people who just like to tell nasty stuff against someone they don't like. It is not true and is like many of the other stories that Mr. Yost sends out."[21] Years before Rockne would think to take advantage of Gipp's death, Fielding Yost had already shaped the story to meet *his* needs. The facts, as Rockne attests, were not on his side, but Yost sought publicity, not veracity.

Rockne and "the Gipper"

After Rockne's halftime performance in 1928, trying to disentangle the real George Gipp from "the Gipper" feels like a fool's errand. Rockne so masterfully tied the two together that the gossamer line between reality and myth vanished. Rockne fictionalized Gipp, removing him from the day-to-day banalities of college athletics and successfully situating him alongside the distinguished characters of American sports fiction. As late as 1987, James J. Whalen, president of Ithaca College, nonchalantly began his essay "Purging College Athletics" with an appeal to the classic characters of college football: "George Gipp, Dink Stover, Frank Merriwell—legendary names that conjure up the image of the college athlete as moral hero."[22] Gipp, Stover, Merriwell—three peas in a heroic pod. The trio tripped naturally from his pen. Little or no distinction was noted among the three heroes; no lengthy introductions needed. But Stover and Merriwell came to life on the pages of books and played only fictional games. Gipp's contests played out in reality where bone crushes bone and disease strikes down even the strong-hearted. Whalen was not the only one comfortable equating the Gipper with fictional legends. More than a half-century earlier, Knute Rockne showed the same predilection when describing Gipp's record-setting sixty-two-yard dropkick field goal in his first game as a freshman against Western Normal (now Western Michigan University). "This Frank Merriwell finish was so poetically right that I thought Gipp too good to be true," Rockne remembered.[23]

Rockne may never have appreciated his own role in making the Gipper too good to be true. Put simply, Knute Rockne invented the Gipper. He took what history had given him, dressed it up in a holy shroud, set the final scene on a deathbed, and unveiled it at Yankee Stadium during the biggest game of the college football calendar in 1928. A version of Rockne's speech appeared in *Collier's* magazine two years later and seems to be substantively accurate, though not verbatim. Gipp, on his deathbed, turned to Coach Rockne:

> "Some time, Rock," [Gipp] said, "when the team's up against it; when things are wrong and the breaks are beating the boys—tell them to go in there with all they've got and win just one for the Gipper. I don't know where I'll be then, Rock. But I'll know about it, and I'll be happy."[24]

Following the speech, fortune swung Notre Dame's way in the second half and the Irish defeated the Cadets, 12–6. *Chicago Tribune* sportswriter (and Notre Dame publicist par excellence) Arch Ward told the world that "Gipp's ghost" had beaten Army. This was virgin territory for American sports: the creation (virtually ex nihilo) of an immortal athletic hero. George Gipp became the Gipper. And for Rockne's reputation, generations of sportswriters, and Ronald Reagan, this was the Gipp that kept on giving.

Rockne's speech motivated his moribund team that afternoon and later became a powerful marketing tool for Rockne and Notre Dame football. The story crowned the sainted Gipper's career while forever connecting Rockne to the Gipper myth and the Gipper myth to Notre Dame. The Gipper character merged Rockne and Gipp into a single entity. Without Rockne's halftime dramatics, Gipp would be remembered as an unlucky All-American rather than as the Gipper, the centerpiece of the most enduring myth in college athletics.[25] After all, no one runs onto the field shouting, "win one for Nile Kinnick" or for Hobey Baker—equally gifted athletes who died tragically. Kinnick and Baker lacked a key element that Gipp had: a first-rate storyteller to popularize his legend.[26] Rockne preached the importance of tradition in building a strong football program. In his handbook on coaching published the year after the Gipper speech, Rockne referred to the long-term value that came from Gipp's deathbed plea. "The history or traditions of the school are a great thing to excite your team, and to keep before them," he instructed. Perhaps remembering his own halftime performance the previous fall, Rockne

3. Football coach Knute Rockne in uniform on Cartier Field at the University of Notre Dame in South Bend, Indiana (c. 1920s). (University of Notre Dame Archives)

told coaches to "exaggerate these [traditions] as much as you can, and set a somewhat exaggerated standard to emulate. A school without traditions will find it very hard to build up a successful football team."[27]

Rockne may have created the character but the legend of the Gipper blossomed in the writings of the "Fighting Irish network" of journalists including Arthur Daley, Red Smith, and Arch Ward. Arthur Daley, the "Sports of the Times" columnist at the *New York Times* from 1942 to 1974, led the way.[28] A graduate of Fordham University, but besotted by the Irish, Daley took every opportunity to invoke the memory of Rockne and polish the image of the Gipper. A close reading of Daley's columns helps to explain how the legend of the Gipper remained vibrant during the middle decades of the twentieth century, long after Gipp and Rockne had left the scene.

In January 1945, prompted by the publication of Arch Ward's *Frank Leahy and the Fighting Irish*, Daley made his case for reprising the Gipper tale. Although the story was two decades old, Daley wrote that "it can bear repeating because it symbolizes the tremendous hold Gipp had on the affections and esteem of all Notre Dame men." Daley portrayed Gipp as "a tragic youth whose relatively brief but meteoric career immortalized him at South Bend. It has been a long parade of super-stars who have marched through that capital of the gridiron world but at the head of that parade and greatest of them all was Notre Dame's beloved Gipper. Even in death he was to win at least one game for his alma mater." Daley's Gipper had become an immortal—beloved and capable of scoring touchdowns from the grave.[29]

In the summer of the same year, the Gipper entered Daley's column again in the wake of Jack Chevigny's death at the Battle of Iwo Jima. Chevigny had scored the tying touchdown against Army following Rockne's Gipper speech in 1928 and went on to coach the NFL's Chicago Cardinals and at the University of Texas. Daley contrived a scene in which Chevigny, facing a barrage of Japanese artillery, raced from a foxhole to a nearby command post, just like he had dashed against Army on the playing field. This time, however, he never reached his destination. Chevigny, in Daley's imagination, spent his last minutes thinking not of his family, or fiancée, or comrades-in-arms, but remembering the fallen Gipper. Disguising his fiction as a newsman's fact, Daley reported that "the dying words of an almost legendary Notre Dame athletic hero [Gipp] had been his inspiration for most of his adult life, and Capt. Jack Chevigny of the Marines undoubtedly went to his death with those same words on his lips. At least they were in his heart." No Hail Mary. No Our Father. Chevigny's last thoughts were of the Gipper, presumably a man he had never met. In Daley's estimation, though, the fallen Marine and Gipp led similar lives. Chevigny exchanged a stateside assignment for the danger of the front lines—"just as the Gipper himself would have done," suggested Daley.

Chevigny was one of "those Notre Dame men" who outdid themselves on the gridiron and in life. They will "always be winning 'one for the Gipper' as long as the Golden Dome peers majestically over the campus."[30] Chevigny gave his life on Iwo Jima, but the Gipper somehow played the hero in Daley's story.

The annual clash between Army and Notre Dame consistently brought the Gipper back to Daley's columns—no more so than when the rivalry drew to a temporary close in the late 1940s. Daley crowned the games "the greatest single attraction in sport,"[31] and the end of the series in 1947 felt "almost like losing someone near and dear. It brings with it a wrench at the heart-strings." As the final game neared, Daley turned once again to "the immortal Gipper" who had led the way to victory many years before.[32] He was not the only one thinking of the Gipper. At halftime, under the reflection of the Golden Dome, the Irish marching band formed two patterns. The first, "1913," memorialized the year of the inaugural game in the rivalry (when Rockne and Gus Dorais employed the little-used forward pass to beat the Cadets). The band then formed the word "GIPP" to honor, in Daley's words, "the immortal George Gipp, who undoubtedly smiled down from on high with Knute Rockne at his side."[33]

When Daley invoked the Gipper, Rockne was never far away. The legend bound them together by the Gordian knot of immortality. In 1946, on the fifteenth anniversary of Rockne's death, the columnist revisited "the gridiron's game's outstanding personality" in all his glory. "Sheer genius to the ultimate degree," Daley's Rockne stepped straight out of a Horatio Alger story. The young Norwegian immigrant ascended the ladder of American success with luck, pluck, and style. Emblematic of Rockne's success, of course, was his canny use of the Gipper story. Rockne told the story "in tones of simple pathos" and the master motivator "didn't miss a trick as, tears in his eyes, he wound up dramatically" and willed his team to "win one for the Gipper."[34] On the twentieth anniversary of Rockne's death, Daley reminded readers that the Notre Dame coach was "genius in its purest form" and that "any schoolboy exposed for a single second to the magnetic charm of this dynamic man was forever lost. Every kid in the country dreamed of playing football for Rock."[35] The pied piper of South Bend, Rockne's charms lured a steady stream of talented athletes to his door, and Daley's reimagining kept Rockne and Notre Dame football at the center of the college football world.

Daley was far from alone in publicizing the invented traditions of Notre Dame football. Father John Cavanaugh, president of Notre Dame from 1946 to 1952, wrote the postscript to Rockne's autobiography and held nothing back in his praise. Cavanaugh compared Rockne favorably to some of the preeminent figures in world and Christian history. Dismissing naysayers who claimed that "his field of achievement was too trivial and limited to warrant his canonization among the immortals," Cavanaugh asserted that Rockne "was vastly more than merely the incomparable coach." In fact, "there was a touch of Napoleon" in the coach. The two shared a love of combat, strategy, and an ineffable genius. Cavanaugh then detected "something of Lincoln in the little immigrant from Norway." Lincoln's assassination secured his legacy just as "Rockne's fame and influence may ultimately grow into a myth of epic proportions because tragedy smote him in the strength and splendor of his noonday." Straying from the world of politics, Cavanaugh claimed that "innumerable parents . . . recognized in the great coach the David of their deliverance, the David who with the simple pebble in the country boy's sling was to lay low the turgid fatness of Goliath." Rockne had taken the "small pebble" of Notre Dame football and struck down the powerful universities of the East, giving Catholics something to cheer about and delivering them from the "turgid fatness" of American higher education. Finally, putting all football accomplishments aside, Cavanaugh proclaimed that "merely as a moral teacher," Rockne "deserves to be, like Saul, among the prophets!"[36] Could higher praise fall from the lips of an educated priest?

The Gipper myth took on a life of its own. Notre Dame fans latched on to the idea of the Gipper's immortality and refused to let go. The inimitable Jimmy Breslin, firebrand and longtime columnist at *Newsday*, delved into the Gipper's hold over Notre Damers in his sardonically titled essay, "The Man Who Died for Notre Dame." An acolyte of the New Journalism movement, Breslin penetrated the myth but also recognized its power in people's lives. Notre Dame needed the Gipper. According to Breslin, "George Gipp is a guy who hasn't died as far as Notre Dame is concerned because he played the game as everybody around the nation takes for granted that Notre Dame always plays. As a runner, he was a three-gaited, shifty, hard-boned guy who always had the big play in him. As a passer, he was a specialist. And his kicking was something to see." Gipper's heroic stature described the faith of Notre Dame fans more accurately than the reality of the institution. The Gipper (not Gipp himself) represented an ideal version of all things Notre Dame and therefore he was too important to die. "You can try to batter the Gipp legend down to nothing," concluded Breslin. "You can try to explain him away as part of the ever-expanding legend of the Roaring Twenties. But as long as there is a Notre Dame, you won't be able to. As long as there really was a Gipp, there is no sense trying."[37] The Gipper is, was, and will be Notre Dame. Rockne's creation lived on because it had to. The Gipper became the North Star by which Notre Dame navigated the past and charted the future. Notre Dame football coach Frank Leahy, who was a player in the locker room during Rockne's classic speech, appreciated the significance of the myth to his alma mater: "[The Gipper] is still one of us, a very real part of our winning tradition. . . . No—the Gipper didn't die."[38]

Rockne's version of the Gipper was equal parts coach and player. Because they plied their trades at Notre Dame, both were bathed in religious light, even glory. We have already witnessed the posthumous creation of St. Gipp, but the canonization of Rockne began during his lifetime. The man was undoubtedly accomplished. As a player, he brought the forward pass into the mainstream. As a coach, he perfected the famed Notre Dame shift, which bedeviled opposing coaches until the college football rules committee outlawed the tactic. Rockne's eminence only increased after his unexpected death in 1931. "Dramatic in everything he did, even to his death," reported Robert F. Kelley in the *New York Times*, "Rockne became a god to the boys who played for him."[39]

Sportswriter Wells Twombly likewise used religious imagery to praise Rockne's gifts. To Twombly, Rockne rivaled the biblical prophets in power and majesty. "On the Notre Dame calendar of feast days," he gushed, "the holiest is November 12. It commemorates that afternoon when Rockne walked quietly into the dressing room at halftime of the Army game and moved from player to player, offering only small scraps of advice and encouragement. . . . Like a great preacher, Rockne was building slowly to the greatest sermon of his career." The locker room became a cathedral as Rockne reached the high point of his homily. "Gently, Rockne began to talk. The machine-gun-fire voice had all but disappeared. He acted like a man who could not find the proper words easily. He glanced toward the ceiling hesitantly, while gripping a cigar in his hand. He seemed like a man who had seen a vision of the Holy Grail and was all but transfixed by it." Rockne found the words and delivered the stirring speech, imploring his team to win one for the Gipper. Many players, including future Notre Dame coach Frank Leahy, wiped tears from their eyes. Former New York Mayor Jimmy Walker "sobb[ed] convulsively" and even the hardened policemen in the room bit their lips. The atmosphere "fairly crackled" and a great change—a conversion—swept over the team. "These weren't football players" anymore, noted Twombly, "but holy zealots." Jack Chevigny, "a crusader with a strong emotional streak," gathered the team and "reminded them that they had a sacred obligation to win."[40] Rockne's halftime testimony had willed it. Whether the story was founded on fiction, emotional manipulation, or real events, the moment felt sacred to observers and subsequent scribes. At that moment, Rockne assumed the mantle of a prophet and Gipp became the patron saint of college football.

"The Gipper" on the Big Screen

In the film *Knute Rockne, All American*, Hollywood's mythmaking machine essentially picked up where Rockne left off. The film starred Pat O'Brien as the eponymous coach and Ronald Reagan as George Gipp. Screened in theaters, for soldiers during World War II, in church basements, and on late-night television, the movie transformed these characters into larger-than-life heroes and preserved their saintly status.

Edward "Moose" Krause, football player and later athletic director at Notre Dame, asserted that *Knute Rockne, All American* was "the most important movie ever made" about college sports because it "set up the ideal for coaches and players."[41] The film also ranks as one of the most important political films of the twentieth century because it certified Ronald Reagan as a movie star. Reagan took to the role of George Gipp so completely that "the Gipper" came to define his political persona. According to Sperber, Reagan "capitalized on this idealized image of the Notre Dame player. Reagan's

Gipp embodied the American virtues that the politician cherished and constantly invoked."[42] Politically, Reagan willed himself to become the Gipper and eventually tapped into the vein of virtue immortalized in *Knute Rockne, All American*. The transformation was so thorough that it became difficult to tell where "the Gipper" ended and Ronald Reagan began.[43]

The Gipper was not just the role of a lifetime for the young actor; it was a role that Reagan played for the rest of his life. The film's success catapulted him to Hollywood stardom. If it strains credulity to claim that Reagan *became* the Gipper, it is less debatable that by the end of the twentieth century, "the Gipper" *became* Ronald Reagan. Reagan's retelling of the story folded the legends of Rockne and Gipp together—the wise, psychologically savvy coach and the eminently talented young man who valued the success of the team more than individual accomplishments. What better message for an American politician trying to lead an ideological revolution? Through an adroit use of the tools of modern media, Reagan manipulated the myth of the Gipper to create a fictive narrative that cast himself as a strong, heroic American icon.

Reagan's fascination with Gipp started early in his career when he told Gipp's story to fill air time while working at WHO radio in Des Moines, Iowa, in the 1930s. When Reagan moved to Hollywood, he took the Gipper with him and shopped around for a studio willing to make a movie based on Gipp's story. He had no luck selling it, but Warner Brothers was already casting for Rockne's life story, featuring Reagan's pal Pat O'Brien in the lead role. Reagan finagled a screen test and, making the most of his football-playing days at Eureka College, won the part of Gipp. The role was "a nearly perfect part from an actor's standpoint," Reagan wrote. "A great entrance, an action middle, and a death scene to finish up." Shooting the climactic death scene, Reagan "had a lump in [his] throat so big [he] couldn't talk." Reagan's memory of the film, however, became clouded by nostalgia, and his rendition of the events changed as he discussed the film over the years. In 1970, for example, Reagan recounted the first screening of the movie: "Suddenly there I was on the screen playing the scene, and I was as unmoved as if I had a cold in the nose. It was a terrible letdown and I went home thinking I was a failure. Actually, if I'd only been aware of it, the rest of the audience had the sniffles" because of his moving portrayal

4. Ronald Reagan as George Gipp in the 1940 film, *Knute Rockne, All American*. (Ronald Reagan Presidential Library)

of Gipp.[44] Twenty years later, after his presidency, Reagan remembered the film's impact quite differently. "As the picture began to unreel in the dark theater," he wrote in 1990, "I sensed a glow radiating from the audience like a warm fire." Following Gipp's deathbed soliloquy, "men and women in the audience started pulling out their handkerchiefs. Then, from the back to the front of the theater, I heard sniffles, making me wonder if this was the breakthrough I'd been waiting for."[45] It was.

Whatever Reagan felt when he walked out of the theater that night, the film had created an enduring connection between the future president and the University of Notre Dame. Reagan wrote that "Rockne and Gipp are very much alive in the tradition that plays such an important role at Notre Dame, and everyone connected with the university was very willing to transfer their affection, for the moment at least, to Pat [O'Brien] and myself as proxies."[46] The "moment" lasted nearly fifty years and the university's affection transferred so completely that eventually the institution hardly differentiated between Reagan's "Gipper" and George Gipp. Insiders at Notre Dame, like athletic ticket manager Bob Cahill, considered Reagan a "Notre Damer" because of his role in *Knute Rockne, All American*, and he regularly provided tickets for Reagan, especially for the annual game against the University of Southern California.[47] Reagan felt deep affection for Notre Dame as well. Patrick J. Buchanan, who worked as the communications director in Reagan's White House, noticed that when Reagan traveled to South Bend, "He's going home. In his heart, that's where he thinks he went to school."[48] It was as if real life became fiction became real life again. Reagan, according to one historian, "merged his on- and off-screen identities" by "making active efforts to obtain certain roles and escape others."[49] Leo E. Litwak captured Reagan's talent for transformation on the screen and the political stage: "Careers are often discovered while play-acting. Perhaps you can become a George Gipp by pretending to be him."[50] Reagan and many at Notre Dame would agree.

Notre Dame did its part to turn the concept of Reagan-as-Gipper into reality. On several occasions, without a hint of irony, the university embraced Reagan as a conquering hero. In May 1976, on the eve of the Republican primary in Indiana, Reagan spoke to a crowd of more than 2,500 at the Notre Dame field house. Underneath a red, white, and blue banner that read "Welcome Back, Gipper," school officials presented the candidate with a Rockne-era leather helmet (which he later wore for photographers).[51] Reagan managed to eke out a primary victory in the Hoosier state, though Gerald Ford ultimately won the Republican nomination.

Reagan and Notre Dame combined their mythmaking skills during Reagan's first presidential visit to the university in May 1981. Two months earlier, Reagan had been shot in the chest by would-be assassin

John Hinckley Jr. The trip to Notre Dame marked Reagan's first public appearance since the shooting, and graduation at the University of Notre Dame provided the perfect backdrop for the return of the Gipper. Reagan warned the audience that "if I don't watch myself this may turn out to be less of a commencement than a warm bath in the nostalgic memories." Of course, most of those memories were made on celluloid and had little to do with the university itself, but Reagan reveled in the connections nonetheless. Once again at the side of Pat O'Brien, who received an honorary doctorate from Notre Dame, the scene harked back to a movie made forty years earlier about an event that happened twenty years before that. It was a lineage of curious workmanship, to say the least, but it was no less real to Notre Dame leaders like University President Theodore Hesburgh. As Reagan entered the field house, Hesburgh told the cheering crowd: "We welcome the President of the United States back to health, we welcome the President of the United States back into the body of his people, the Americans, and lastly here at Notre Dame, here in a very special way, we welcome the Gipper at long last back to get his degree." Reagan as politician, Reagan as actor, and Reagan as Gipper all crowded the dais, and even President Hesburgh could not tell them apart.[52] David Gergen, who worked in the Reagan White House, believed that the public did not recognize Reagan's "heroic character" until the assassination attempt "made the Gipp legend 'much more poignant' in the public mind and fused the image of the President, and the actor, together."[53] Seven years later, on Reagan's final presidential trip to Notre Dame, the confusion remained. Visiting South Bend to issue a postage stamp celebrating the 100th anniversary of Knute Rockne's birth, Reagan was greeted by a large banner reading "Notre Dame Welcomes the Gipper." Athletic director "Moose" Krause told the crowd, "Never in our wildest dreams did we think that George Gipp would be President of the United States."[54] Even in hindsight it is difficult to decipher exactly who Krause had in mind—the president, the movie star, or the former Notre Dame football player.

Ronald Reagan essentially began his presidency at the Notre Dame commencement and ended it by hosting the Fighting Irish national championship football team at the White House in January 1989. Just two days before leaving Washington, the president met coach Lou Holtz and the team in the Rose Garden. "My life has been full of rich and wonderful experiences," Reagan told the team, "and standing near the top of the list is my long and honored association with the University of Notre Dame and its legendary hero Knute Rockne. So, I want you [to] know [that] . . . George Bush's election [was] important, but having the Fighting Irish win the national championship is in a class by itself." Reagan then turned to the heavens. "Right now," he said, "I can't help but think that somewhere, far away, there's a fellow with a big grin and a whole lot of pride in his school. And he might be thinking to himself that maybe you won another one for the Gipper." As an expression of the university's abiding relationship with Reagan, Notre Dame President Edward Malloy presented Reagan with George Gipp's original monogrammed Notre Dame sweater. "I think that's a great sacrifice by the university," the president responded, "but believe me, no one could have it and treasure it more than I will."[55] It must have felt like he had it all along. Ronald Reagan was literally costumed in the clothes of the Gipper. Surely Reagan treasured the sweater like it was his own. Reagan's chief of staff Ken Duberstein remembers that there was "not a dry eye in the Rose Garden as Reagan walked into the twilight."[56]

In addition to invoking the images of the selfless athlete and the legendary coach, Reagan-as-Gipper updated the most famous speech in American sports history and changed the contest from football to politics. When Reagan asked followers to "win one for the Gipper," he did not mean George. In Reagan's parlance (and estimation), *he* was the Gipper. The rhetoric of the Gipper nicely paralleled one of Reagan's "larger myths" based on "a nostalgic view of America, rooted in small-town values of hard work, patriotism and neighborhoods."[57] Historian John Sayle Watterson asserts that Reagan's Gipper-speak "reaffirmed the pieties of his midwestern past, or perhaps became a denial of the realities of that time period when poverty hovered over the Reagan household."[58] The Gipper became a powerful two-edged sword in Reagan's hands: one edge to return American society to midcentury norms and the other to rewrite his personal history.

Reagan, who viewed political speeches as "pep talks," returned again and again to Rockne's halftime speech.[59] The examples pile one on top of the other:

1. An advertisement in the program of the Notre Dame–Navy football game in 1980 instructed, "Win one for the Gipper! Reagan for President."[60]

2. In a congratulatory phone call to coach Bill Walsh of the San Francisco 49ers in 1982, Reagan applauded the Super Bowl champions. "And you might tell Joe Montana [a former Notre Dame quarterback himself] and the fellows that they really did win one for the Gipper," Reagan said.[61]

3. In denouncing Democratic Congressional leaders slow to pass Reagan-sponsored legislation, he gave them a "flash from the Gipper: They're not going to win now."[62]

4. On the eve of the 1984 Olympic Summer Games in Los Angeles, Reagan tried to inspire American athletes by revisiting the halftime speech he knew best: "Go for it! For yourselves, for your families, for your country. And you can forgive me if I'm a little presumptuous—do it for the Gipper."[63]

5. In countless stump speeches for himself and other Republican candidates, Reagan rallied the troops by asking them to win one for the Gipper. It was a surefire applause line.[64]

Perhaps the most dramatic political rendering of the famous line occurred at the 1988 Republican National Convention when Reagan passed the baton of party leadership to Vice President George H. W. Bush. According to Robert Brustein, artistic director of the American Repertory Theater in Cambridge, Massachusetts, the central character at the convention was the Gipper:

> [Reagan] has been playing George Gipp for more than 40 [years]. Using the New Orleans Superdome as a Warner Brothers set for the Notre Dame football field, the Republicans staged a series of heart-rending goodbyes to the Gipper that had the mostly white, middle-aged stadium audience leaking with nostalgia. Jack Kemp, whose nostalgia is so powerful he wants to restore the gold standard, recalled how Knute Rockne asked Reagan to run for a touchdown.
>
> Then the legendary quarterback himself appeared . . . to speak of his pride in Nancy [Reagan], his "sweet country," and Bush, who was urged to "win one for the Gipper."

Performances like these suggested "why Reagan will be so difficult to replace."[65] The Republicans have yet to find the Gipper's true political heir.

Reagan could tailor the Gipper story to fit a variety of situations because he cared more about the speech's message than its historical accuracy. He realized that "Gipp was in reality a slothful fellow who bet heavily on the team's games," and he recognized that Gipp had never voiced the famous deathbed request. But the moral of the story mattered more than the specific details. "For Ronald Reagan," presidential aide Pat Buchanan asserted, "the world of legend and myth is a real world."[66] Reagan praised Rockne's use of the story, even if the coach had fabricated the original tale. "It was natural that Rock would one day use the story of Gipp's death to inspire a Notre Dame team," Reagan recorded in his autobiography. "To me the great significance was that Rock saved the story for eight years, and then didn't use it just to win a game, but used it to inspire a team that was losing mainly because of bickering and jealousy. For at least one half he gave this team, torn with dissension, the knowledge of what it was like to play together, and to sacrifice their individual quarrels for a common goal."[67] The whole of the story, then, was much greater than the sum of its parts—to Reagan's mind, anyway.

When Reagan died in 2004, the flood of posthumous tributes from prominent politicians illustrated just how deeply the myth of Reagan-as-Gipper had penetrated American political culture. Congresswoman Juanita Millender-McDonald observed, "Today, for millions of Americans, the legends of George Gipp and the man who portrayed him on film have become inextricably linked." For Representative John B. Larson, Reagan-as-Gipper overshadowed Gipp-as-Gipper. "Millions remember Reagan as 'the Gipper,'" Larson claimed, "and far fewer remember George Gipp." Former President George H. W. Bush noted that Reagan-as-Gipper had won one for the peace of the world by working with Soviet leader Mikhail Gorbachev to end the Cold War. Representative Robin Hayes of North Carolina appealed to the ultimate source to validate Reagan's Gipper. Echoing the biblical parable of the talents, Hayes pictured Reagan at God's elbow. "I rejoice knowing that he has met his Maker, and his Maker is looking him in the eye and saying, President Reagan, the Gipper, you are a good and faithful servant."[68] If so, perhaps somewhere in the heavens, one Gipper was smiling at another Gipper who was smiling down on us. And, presumably, Knute Rockne was not far away.

Although Reagan had been eulogized and the Gipper put to rest, Reagan's legacy continued to shape the Republican Party into the twenty-first century. "In politics," wrote Watterson, "George Gipp didn't die," and the quest to be the next Gipper began the moment Reagan departed the Oval Office.[69] George H. W. Bush tried to transform his wimpy image by borrowing the Gipper's verve but never quite measured up. In 1996, Republican presidential hopeful Robert Dole promised to "be another Ronald Reagan, if that's what [the electorate] want[s]," and he referred to the Gipper in his acceptance speech at the Republican convention.[70] After winning the 2000 election, Republican George W. Bush worked assiduously to become the Gipper for a new generation. Bush's attendance at Reagan's funeral inspired *New York Times* columnist Maureen Dowd to wonder about Bush's political paterfamilias. "At every opportunity as the extraordinary procession solemnly wended its way from California to the Capitol," Dowd wrote, "W. was peeping out from behind the majestic Reagan mantle, trying to claim the Gipper as his true political father."[71] Alas, it was not to be. In the campaign to replace Bush in 2008, the Republican candidates still clamored for "any way to identify with Mr. Reagan," according to political analyst Stuart Spencer. Even Democrat Barack Obama "called down the spirit of St. Ronald . . . to bless" his candidacy.[72] Each aspirant, regardless of political party, failed to capture the myth so carefully cultivated by Reagan-as-Gipper. "Those who would sanctify the Gipper have about as much chance of success as those who try to impersonate him," warned Reagan's biographer Edmund Morris in 2003.[73]

When informed about the production of a new feature film about George Gipp, Reagan viewed the project with "mixed emotions." Although he wished the filmmakers well, another part of him "hate[d] to think of anyone else being the Gipper."[74] The myths surrounding George Gipp sprung to life on his deathbed, found a persuasive publicist in Knute Rockne, and then catapulted a B-list actor to political stardom. George Gipp became Rockne's Gipper and Rockne's Gipper became Ronald Reagan. The power of this legend shaped the history of college football and propelled Ronald Reagan into the White House.

Only Cowgirls Get the Blues

Bonnie McCarroll and Lane Frost

Tragedy marred the Pendleton Round-Up rodeo in September 1929. Bonnie McCarroll, an accomplished bronc rider, became entangled in her stirrups and was dragged to her death. Sixty years later, the scene looked much the same at the Frontier Days rodeo in Cheyenne, Wyoming, where former world champion bull rider Lane Frost died after being gored in the back by a bull named Taking Care of Business. As similar as these scenes appeared, the reactions to the deaths of the two rodeo stars differed dramatically and changed the trajectories of women's and men's rodeo. The key difference between the two incidents was that a cow*girl* was killed at Pendleton and a cow*boy* died at Cheyenne. As gender theorist Joan Scott reminds us, "gender is a primary field within which or by means of which power is articulated."[1] Rodeo rings have been one of the fields where power was defined and deployed by the men who controlled the professional sport. For all practical purposes, McCarroll's death led to the prohibition of women's rodeo for a generation and ended women's participation in rough stock events for good. Frost's death, on the other hand, marked the start of the meteoric rise in popularity enjoyed by bull riding in the 1990s. Professional bull riders, many of whom were Frost's closest friends, capitalized on his death by transforming bull riding into a stand-alone sport, separated from other rodeo events. In the changes that shaped and reshaped rodeo life in the twentieth century, being a cowgirl or cowboy made all the difference. Only cowgirls, it seems, got the blues.

Cowgirls in the Rodeo

Rodeo cowgirls worked in the most gender-transgressive sport of the early twentieth century. Other female athletes, like swimmer Gertrude Ederle and tennis champion Helen Wills Moody, enjoyed widespread popularity during this time; their sports were considerably more "feminine" than competitive rodeo. Tennis, swimming, and even field hockey were played by upper-class women in country clubs and private schools and were deemed acceptable to critics of female sport.[2] Rodeo, on the other hand, was never genteel, private, or traditionally feminine. But it was popular, especially in the West. By 1904, when Bertha Blancett became "history's first cowgirl bronc rider" at the Cheyenne Frontier Days rodeo, women had been riding wild horses on cattle ranches for decades. Blancett faced no lack of competition as the popularity of female bronc riding expanded in the two decades following her historic ride. Along with bronc riding, roping, trick riding, bulldogging, and relay races rounded out the women's events in rodeos, "stampedes," and "Wild West shows." Roman races, in which each rider straddled two horses with one foot in each saddle, were especially popular.[3]

From the 1890s through the 1920s, rodeo "offered great opportunities for cowgirls, who could and did compete directly against men in steer roping, trick roping, trick riding, and Roman racing. Rodeo was the first, and perhaps the only, sport in which men and women truly competed as equals." According to rodeo historian Mary Lou LeCompte, "Even with the growth of special cowgirl contests in bronc riding, trick riding, trick roping, and relay and cow pony races, women continued to compete successfully against men in a variety of events, and still enjoyed the respect and friendship of the cowboys." Compared to life on the ranch, rodeo work was exhilarating without threatening gender expectations. "Professional athletic careers provided talented ranch girls an exciting alternative to unending drudgery, while apparently posing no threat to their perception of their own femininity," details LeCompte.[4]

Despite growing popularity, rodeo remained concentrated in western states with occasional forays across the Mississippi River. A relic of frontier days gone by, rodeo provided exotic entertainment, especially when petite cowgirls worked the ring. "By 1910," Renee M. Laegreid explains, "the spectacle of women riding broncs and roping steers was still a novelty, one that captured the imagination of townspeople who watched as the cowgirl athletes rode into town in a blaze of fanfare. The women wowed the crowd with their stunts, then galloped off in search of another town, another performance, another chance to win the prize money."[5] The gender-based fears of urban audiences in the 1920s—that respectable middle-class girls would follow the siren song of the cowgirl chorus—were allayed by the unique skills required of female rodeo performers. Bonnie McCarroll and other female riders never faced sharp denunciations from physical education advocates or opponents of women's sports because neither group felt threatened by this brand of female athlete. The lifestyle of competitive cowgirls appeared so alien to most American young women that "running away to the rodeo" was beyond contemplation, let alone a cause for serious concern. So far removed from everyday life, this "separate sphere" was more a novelty than a peril to established gender norms.

Bonnie McCarroll Enters the Ring

Mary Ellen Treadwell, known as Bonnie or "Dot," was born in 1897, in High Valley, Idaho, about fifty miles north of Boise. She spent her early years working summers at her grandfather's 2,000-acre ranch in High Valley and attending school in Boise during the winter. The view from horseback became one of her earliest memories. "I've ridden all my life," Bonnie told one correspondent. "My mother, although never a professional rider, used to ride range and break broncos with the best of them. When I was just a baby she used to take me with her on horseback, carrying me in her arms. My training started then."[6] At age ten, she began to ride horses on her own, and by fourteen she "could sit most broke-in horses." No longer challenged by tame steeds, she soon braved her first bronc. "I mounted," she recalled, "the boys let go, and the broncho began to behave like a wild cat. I held [on] for about five seconds and then all at once I seemed to grow wings. Up I soared, and turned a sumersault [sic], and the earth seemed about ten miles below. Then I went to sleep and woke in bed." Although some gaps marred her memory of the dismount, she had fallen hard for this dangerous new pursuit.[7]

In 1913, Bonnie entered her first rodeo at the Idaho State Fair. She rode "Bear Cat" but, more importantly, she met Frank McCarroll, a twenty-year-old professional cowboy who had just established the world record time for bulldogging. Two years later, Frank and Bonnie married and hit the professional rodeo circuit together. In 1915, Bonnie took top honors at the Pendleton Round-Up in Oregon, one of rodeo's premiere events. She followed that with a second place finish in Vancouver, British Columbia. For the next dozen years, Frank and Bonnie split their calendar between rodeos in the summer months and resting during the winter in Boise, a seasonal schedule reminiscent of Bonnie's childhood.[8]

Considering the amount of travel required of early rodeo athletes, a winter of rest was well deserved. When Bonnie and Frank returned home in November from an especially long 1924 season, a Boise newspaper reported that "both look well and in excellent condition, though they admit possession of sore places a-plenty." Bonnie "walk[ed] a little gamely from the effects of injuries received at the [Madison Square] Garden" and Frank had "two fingers that look like young hams as the result of dislocations." The McCarrolls expected some "bumps and breaks" from the six-month-long season, but felt "lucky to be all shipshape, with all our joints and bones."[9] "'Big league' broncho riders and round-up performers" like Frank and Bonnie could not avoid the injuries, pains, and seasonal cycles that were as much a part of competitive rodeo as big belt buckles and long, dusty train rides. The McCarrolls considered the sport a "calling" that gave them a "life in the open, daily excitement, a good livelihood, and a few broken bones now and then."[10]

Although it is difficult to reconstruct a day-by-day itinerary for any particular season, creating a "composite calendar" from the remnants of several years in the early 1920s illustrates that cowboys and cowgirls lived on the road, constantly on the move. The dawn of the 1920 season found Frank and Bonnie traveling with fellow competitor Rose Smith from Boise to Mason City, Iowa, for the summer's first rodeo. From there, they competed at the fair in Oskaloosa, Iowa, and then decamped for Chicago and the nine-day-long round-up in early July.[11] As the summer wore on, a typical season might include stops in Joplin, Missouri; St. Paul, Minnesota; Colorado Springs and Pueblo, Colorado; Fort Worth, Dallas,

Waco, and Wichita Falls, Texas; Weiser, Idaho; Phoenix, Arizona; Ogden, Utah; and Binghamton, New York. Exhibitions in Twin Falls and Idaho Falls, Idaho, permitted the McCarrolls to spend a day or two at home before heading to the round-up at Pendleton, Oregon, or Frontier Days in Cheyenne, Wyoming. Not all rodeos were held in one-stop cow towns, though. By the mid-1920s, rodeo fans in Detroit, Cleveland, Philadelphia, and New York City enjoyed annual visits from the touring competitors. Visits to Madison Square Garden by the Wild West shows of Buffalo Bill and others had set the stage for genuine cowboys and cowgirls to entertain urban audiences.[12]

Both Bonnie and Frank were bona fide stars on the rodeo circuit—headliners who lured fans to the arena year after year and spent enough time in the winner's circle to be admired for their skill and courage. For example, as the time neared for the Pikes Peak rodeo, residents of Colorado Springs eagerly awaited the first sighting of the McCarrolls. "To the close follower of rodeos and horse shows in the country," the arrival of Frank and Bonnie "mean[t] that two champions, the best in their specialties, are planning to add prestige to the Pikes Peak Rodeo by displaying their prowess against 'bad horses' at the show next week."[13] As the local paper pointed out, Bonnie and Frank's participation "in the rodeo will draw enthusiasts in the sport here from long distances." Their presence in town would "guarantee success to the show."[14] Advertisements for the Elks Roundup in Twin Falls contained a large photo of Frank and Bonnie and announced special daily trains and a "big parade" on the Fourth of July, in addition to $5,000 in cash and prizes.[15] Frank and Bonnie were "one of the principal attractions" that led to the "biggest crowd [the] town ha[d] ever seen" over the course of the three-day western carnival.[16] Bonnie occasionally received top billing as a "world's champion woman bronco rider" and a "distinguished representative" of the rodeo.[17]

Bonnie earned every accolade that appeared in her advance press; or, in the words of one wide-eyed scribe, "the many honors [that] have been showered and flowered upon her."[18] In 1922, she captured the "world's championship in the cowgirls' bucking contest" at Cheyenne Frontier Days, the most venerable rodeo in the West. Ben F. Davis, president of the Cheyenne rodeo, celebrated Bonnie's accomplishment: "She won as a result of her combined skills, nerve and horsemanship in competition over a large field of girl riders [eleven in all]. The judges in this event were unanimous in placing her first, as were the thousands of people who saw her ride [in Cheyenne]. This little lady is entitled to a world of credit for her world's winning."[19] Most notably, in 1924, Bonnie received the Lord Selfridge trophy for winning the ladies' bronc riding championship at the First International Rodeo at Empire Stadium in Wembley, England. Over the course of her rodeo career, Bonnie won titles at rodeos in St. Paul, Waco, Fort Worth, Ogden, and Chicago, among others. In the summer of 1927, Bonnie even performed for the vacationing President Calvin Coolidge at Belle Fourche, South Dakota. At the end of each season, she and Frank had banked enough winnings to ensure that they did not need "to worry about the price of coal" during the cold winter in Boise.[20]

The highlight of the rodeo circuit in the early 1920s was the late season competition held in New York. The first exhibition had convened at Madison Square Garden in 1922 and the event later moved to Yankee Stadium. The New York publicity machine played on the incongruity of horse-riding westerners visiting the big city. "The rodeo invaded Gotham this year and literally swept the inhabitants off their feet," wrote one journalist. New Yorkers "took to bucking-horse riding and steer-busting like a kid takes to candy." Focusing on the female competitors, the author declared that a "nice feature of the round-up is the girls. Beautiful damsels ride twisting, plunging steers with a grace that would shame an English riding master and make him want to poison his horse."[21] Despite the supposed tension between urban and rural Americans in the decade of the Scopes Trial and the new Ku Klux Klan, New Yorkers could not get enough of their western guests. Bonnie made a splash on the rodeo's opening day by parading down Broadway alongside her competitors, dressed to the hilt in full cowgirl regalia.[22] The cowgirls, all "expert horsewomen," stole the hearts of New Yorkers and each had her "special groups of rooters"; their performances in general "seem to have especial attraction for the spectators." Bonnie clinched the title of champion cowgirl bronc rider with "a spectacular and dangerous ride on Mohawk Black." Other winners included Mabel Strickland and Donna Glover. The large crowd in Madison Square Garden "went wild" at the crowning of the cowgirl champions.[23] In 1923, after the rodeo moved to the larger environs of Yankee Stadium, Bonnie pocketed more than $1,700 by winning the bronc riding competition and finishing near the top in several trick riding contests.[24]

The cowgirls and cowboys did not spend all of their time locked in competition. Dropped into the center of the Great White Way, rodeo folks attracted attention from an array of entertainers in Manhattan. Cinema idol Douglas Fairbanks invited the McCarrolls and others to view his newest feature film, *Robin Hood*. The Lyric Theater installed special hitch racks along the sidewalk to accommodate the seventy-five horses that transported the rodeo stars down Broadway. Double takes and dropped jaws must have followed right behind. The cognitive dissonance caused by the convoy "almost caused a riot . . . from some of the New Yorkers who had never seen a cowboy before." The rodeo competitors made the most of their regional garb and dressed in their "cowboy clothes" while in the city. When cowboys paused on the streets "for a minute's time," crowds gathered and blocked the sidewalk. Will Rogers, who used his own cowboy skills to achieve stardom in the big city, invited the westerners to the follies where they were entertained in true western style. Real cowboys and cowgirls dressed in authentic apparel watched a Native American (Rogers was more than one-quarter Cherokee) dressed in the costume of a vaudeville cowboy perform roping and riding tricks for their entertainment. Later, Rogers was entertained by cowboys in their costumes who performed roping and riding tricks in the rodeo arena.[25]

On the heels of the New York rodeo in 1924, promoter John Van "Tex" Austin took his troupe across the Atlantic for a two-week engagement at the British Empire Exposition. Held at Empire (later renamed Wembley) Stadium in London, this was the first full-scale, competitive rodeo held in Great Britain. The British government had sponsored the exhibition to gather the nations of its far-flung empire and celebrate the cultures of the dominion. Although the Americans had long since left the British Empire, the western cowboys and cowgirls did bring an unfamiliar form of American culture with them.

Nearly 100 rodeo performers, with 233 horses, sailed for London aboard the SS *Menominee*. The group showed little interest in the seagoing life. Throwing dice initially helped to pass the time, but disputes among the players shut down the games before any real violence could erupt. Competition moved from the gaming table to the dining table, where cowboys loosened their belt buckles in pursuit of "records as the world's heaviest eaters." One hungry diner consumed five puddings and others requested "that the courses should be repeated till further orders." Bursting at the seams, some cowboys slept all afternoon while others "wander[ed] restlessly from deck to deck with hat and boots donned ready to go ashore." Anxious for any form of excitement, one cowboy from Wyoming heard the call for a boat drill and exclaimed, "Thank God we're sinking." Singing provided the only reliable "relief from the strain of pent-up energy" onboard the "sea-going ranch." Cowboys and cowgirls gathered nightly to "roar out pathetic ballads, mostly of love and death," accompanied by "sketchy . . . banjo chords."[26] Once in port, an energetic crowd welcomed the rodeo performers, who arrived fully decked out in western finery. Several cowboys mounted their horses and galloped down the gangplank.[27]

Huge crowds attended the rodeo at the exhibition. Opening day drew 80,000 spectators to Empire Stadium and one Saturday exhibition entertained more than 100,000 visitors, including Rudyard Kipling. "Soft June sunshine flooded the vast arena when the cowboys and cowgirls rode out like gladiators parading to do battle before Imperial Rome," effused one thrilled correspondent.[28] According to one account in the *Daily Chronicle*, attendees at the "first Rodeo ever held in Europe" learned that the sport was "the most exciting, thrilling, breathtaking and virile outdoor spectacle ever 'staged' in [England], with the entertaining attributes of a circus thrown in as a relief to the almost too tense struggle for mastery between men and beasts that is the real soul of Rodeo."[29]

Bonnie McCarroll, who looked "so gentle and feminine in small poke hat and fawn-coloured wrap that she might have been a dairymaid," took command of center stage when the rodeo competition started.[30] She may have looked like a dairymaid, but she rode like an old cowhand. Bonnie assured English readers of the *Illustrated Sunday Herald* that she was a bronc rider *and* a lady. She described how she fell for her husband Frank like a steer for a bulldogger. The first time she spied Frank he was diving from the saddle "to the head of [a] steer and went through the motions of bulldogging it. And inside thirty seconds flump went the bull." Flump, too, went Bonnie's heart. Soon they were married and she "learnt that he was a slave to this habit of bulldogging. There was no holding him. One day he wrestled steers all one afternoon at Cheyenne, and then came in and threw the best wrestler in Wyoming out of sheer exuberance of spirits." Bonnie was not alone in her admiration of strong cowboy types. Most "women seem to like this bulldogging," she claimed, because "it appeal[ed] to the primitive Eve in them." Mother Eve, transgressive in her own right, did not hesitate to grab a good thing when she saw it. Neither should her modern daughters.

Bonnie showed a softer side as well. At season's end, her thoughts turned to things domestic and her "wonderful home in Idaho." "Our home is so nice that when we get back to it, Frank and I, we decide we'll never leave it again. But when May comes around, and the rodeos start, and we hear the boys yelling: 'Whoopee! Ride 'im, cowboy!' well, something just leaps in us and we make tracks for the cowboy ring again." While at home, Bonnie handled a few wild horses and practiced racing and roping, in addition to "darning and cooking." At night, however, she loved to "go and dance away the evening," though it occasionally proved difficult to shift gears from the lively tempo of the ranch to the "languid, witching-wave jazz" style popular in nightclubs. On the road, Bonnie did not travel with a "trunkful of Paris models" like some continental beauties, but she admitted to keeping "quite a range of fancy riding breeches, because, somehow, you know, one does like to know one's looking one's best even at the moment when one's being bucked off the back of a wild-cat steed." Bonnie recognized that she had a "good life" and could ask for little else. An occasional craving to "try [her] hand at a little bulldogging" crept into her conversations, but Frank "put his foot down." And, she reported, "It's a large foot!" In a day's work, Bonnie tamed broncs, darned the socks, danced the Charleston, and kept up with the latest European fashion trends. But, at the end of the day, she reminded her British readers, husband Frank could still rein her in.[31]

Female rodeo athletes lived and worked on the outer edges of social acceptability in the early twentieth century. By softening their masculine images with details of domestic life, cowgirls stoked interest among fans:

exotic enough to be attractive, tame enough not to intimidate. During the decade in which American society spawned its first generation of celebrities, Bonnie McCarroll harnessed the powers of publicity and advertising to further her career and spread the popularity of her sport.

Bumps, Bruises, and Broncos

Cowgirls knew how to straddle the fine line between grace and strength but bucking broncs did not. After Bonnie won the Selfridge trophy in London, the Prince of Wales asked her if he could learn to ride a bronco. No, she "replied honestly. 'I'm afraid you aren't strong enough.'"[32] A wild horse did not care if a "demure, bobbed-haired blue-eyed girl" or Prince Edward clung to its back. When the chutes opened and the horse reared, a successful ride depended on athletic skill, strength, and experience. But failure was never far behind, even for a champion like Bonnie. Injured countless times, Bonnie shrugged off the bumps, bruises, and broken bones.[33] A cowgirl had an image to maintain and could not be seen shrinking away from the consequences of life in the ring.

Throughout her career, serious injuries threatened Bonnie's health and even presaged her death. While battling a bucking steer at the Coliseum in Fort Worth, Texas, Bonnie "barely missed death." After the animal's fourth jump, "a crack like a pistol shot" pierced the air but went largely unnoticed by the large crowd. The "trained rodeo men," however, knew immediately that the sound was Bonnie's forehead slamming into the bull's horn. Blood, "redder than the costume she wore," coursed down her face as cowboy rescuers lifted her from the bull's back and carried her to safety. Three stitches closed the wound and before long Bonnie was seated in the audience.[34] On another occasion, quick thinking and physical dexterity saved Bonnie from "being kicked to death" in Detroit. After completing a bronc ride, Bonnie lost her balance and was thrown from the back of the horse. During her dismount, Bonnie's foot got tangled in a stirrup and the horse dragged her across the arena floor. Exhibiting "presence of mind," Bonnie "caught the bronk's tail and pulled herself high enough" to avoid the steed's deadly hooves.[35] A few years later, this scene would be repeated in Pendleton, but without the happy ending.

5. Idaho cowgirl Bonnie McCarroll being thrown from a horse named Silver during a bucking contest at the 1915 Pendleton Round-Up. (DeGolyer Library, Southern Methodist University, US West: Photographs, Manuscripts, and Imprints)

Most of Bonnie's female competitors preferred riding with their stirrups "hobbled," or tied together beneath the horse's belly. Cowgirls believed that this technique provided more stability and led to longer rides.[36] Bonnie, when possible, rode "slick" using her leg strength to keep the stirrups tight around her mount. Bonnie's insistence on riding slick was a matter of gender equality. "We cowgirls have butted in on a so-called strictly man's game—and if to 'play' on the hurricane deck of a sunfishin', whirlly-giggin', rearin-up, fallin-over-backward, squallin', bitin', strikin', buckin', roman-nosed cayuse ain't a he-man's game, there never will be one—still, as I say, we cowgirls that like the game well enough to play it should play it just like the cowboys do."[37] Although less popular, riding slick was the safer technique. A rider's foot was more likely to get caught in a hobbled stirrup and the rider dragged behind the horse, much like Bonnie's experience in Detroit.

Journalist Marjorie Wilson, writing about cowgirls like Bonnie, described the possible consequences of competitive rodeo in clear, certain terms: "Deaths at roundups are frequent. So are accidents. To be a cowboy or a cowgirl is to be a human being without fear. Without fear of fate, of death, of maddened beasts."[38] Such western stoicism played well in the paper, but did not necessarily describe life on the ranch or in the rodeo arena. Confronting beasts that can weigh 2,000 pounds and shift direction on a dime, rodeo athletes tried to mitigate risk with skill, experience, and concentration. Still, accidents happened. At least six rodeo cowgirls died in the first decades of the twentieth century. More often than not, however, the deaths occasioned little or no backlash. According to historian Mary Lou LeCompte, a different gender standard applied in rodeo, permitting women in the rough stock events to incur injuries that would have been unacceptable for other female athletes. For example, when a female runner collapsed after the 800-meter run at the 1928 Olympics, the International Association of Athletics Federations barred women from competing in future races. Conversely, after Tillie Baldwin collapsed following the Roman race at the Winnipeg Stampede in 1913, she was commended for rising out of her hospital bed and returning to action against her doctor's wishes. "Women were rarely criticized for participating in dangerous [rodeo] events," LeCompte notes. "Even the few cowgirl fatalities, like those of cowboys, were taken in stride by both competitors and the press until 1929." Bonnie McCarroll's death changed that.[39]

At the twentieth annual Pendleton Round-Up, an atmosphere of "bustle, rush, action and color" greeted visitors who had come to see their rodeo heroes, make a fast buck, or pick a few pockets. Amid the smells of fried onions and meat emanating from the temporary hamburger joints, rodeo stars mingled with movie stars (Hollywood star Mary Duncan had been the queen of the Round-Up the previous year) and public officials. Detectives from several cities prowled the streets keeping an eye out for more nefarious types. Beggars sat on street corners, blind "troubadours" serenaded in alleyways, and native groups exhibited wares made from beads, buckskin, eagle feathers, and elk teeth.[40]

Some menacing characters may have populated the streets of Pendleton, but the real risk was in the arena. "Danger was rampant," reported *Billboard* magazine, and "escapes from sudden death came half a dozen times, with fate lurking in the hoofs of vicious bucking horses, or in racers on the track." Not everyone escaped, however. During a bronc-riding exhibition, Bonnie McCarroll flew "from her mount [Black Cat] as it pitched forward, and the animal turned a somersault on her."[41] Fellow rider Reba Perry Blakely described the chilling scene: "Once all the way over, Black Cat did the instinctive thing, he leaped to his feet and continued his bucking while Bonnie McCarroll, so obviously knocked out in that fall, head hung down, her body limp and one left foot still caught in the stirrup. For six more horrible leaps and bucks Black Cat's weight literally shook the ground and at each leap Bonnie's head banged on the earth with sickening repetition, until mercifully that boot came off and she lay limp upon the ground."[42] Ollie Osborn ran to her injured friend but "Bonnie was out just colder than a wedge. . . . Everybody just stood still they were speechless when it happened cause we all knowed she was hurt bad."[43] Bonnie's lifeless body was gathered up and transported to Anthony Hospital, where she spent the next eleven days battling a severe spinal injury and pneumonia. Her husband and family stood vigil at her bedside, but Bonnie never regained consciousness and died on September 29, 1929.[44] She was buried wearing a diamond brooch in the shape of a steer's head, and her casket was decorated by the pearly sombrero she wore during her final ride and a pair of riding boots with spurs.[45]

Bonnie's death struck a ferocious blow to the performers, producers, and fans of rodeo. The pain was compounded because the Pendleton Round-Up was Bonnie's swan song on the rodeo circuit. Following her last go-round, she and Frank planned to retire to Boise and a new life, close to the land but far from the competitive arena. According to one report, Frank had wanted to hang up his boots before the Round-Up but Bonnie had persuaded him to attend.[46] Adding to the grief, Bonnie's injury might have been avoided if she had ridden "slick," as she preferred. Instead, as required by Round-Up regulations, she dutifully tied her stirrups around Black Cat's belly and then could not dislodge her boot when she lost control of the wild horse. Who knows what would have happened had her stirrups hung loose.

Nearly every historian of women's rodeo concludes that Bonnie's death changed the nature of her sport almost immediately. Andrea Mugnier notes that Bonnie's "horrifying death . . . caused organizers around the country to reconsider women's bronc contests," including the elimination of the event.[47] Michael Allen affirms that the "public and peer reaction to the violent death of a woman rider seems to have been strong enough to eliminate female participation in the sport."[48] The board of directors of the Pendleton Round-Up, according to Joan Burbick, "decided that their rodeo would never again include the ghastly death of a woman. Men could be hurt and even killed," she writes, "but no woman would be allowed to ride a bucking horse or bull again."[49] Historian Renee M. Laegreid posits that Bonnie's death, along with the formation of the Rodeo Association of America and the stock market crash, struck women's rodeo with a nearly fatal triple whammy in 1929. In the wake of those events, the sport changed dramatically as more traditionally feminine rodeo queens took center stage, judged according to "who had the best horse, most attractive outfit, and most admirable horsemanship." Women's competitive rodeo essentially disappeared until after World War II.[50] Bonnie McCarroll's plaque in the Cowgirl Hall of Fame agrees that "her tragic death at the 1929 Pendleton Round-Up changed the face of women's rodeo when rodeo officials began exercising more scrutiny on rules and regulations for women in bronc riding."[51] Today most major rodeos continue to bar women from rough stock events like bull and bronc riding.

Most of the prominent rodeos turned away from female bronc riding without delay though smaller rodeos more slowly phased out the rough stock events for cowgirls. Fans of female rodeo resisted the changes by using the little leverage that they had. On the pages of the "The Corral," the section in *Billboard* magazine devoted to rodeo, letter writers sprang to the defense of female bronc riders and lamented their absence. When rodeo entertainer W. V. "Buckskin Bill" Snethen learned in February 1930 that some rodeos planned to bar cowgirl riders, he questioned the change. "What is nicer than looking around a rodeo grounds and seeing a good-looking girl on a prancing horse?" asked Snethen. "It looks good to me—if I am getting a little 'silver' in my hair."[52] Sexist, even misogynistic, Snethen unapologetically recognized the sex appeal of cowgirls, though he only dimly recognized their skills. Nevertheless, he wanted more than a beauty pageant rodeo queen who offered little in the ways of horsemanship and grit. In a more emphatic vein, Nora E. Wells wrote that she hoped "to see cowgirls contesting everywhere in bronk and steer riding, as well as in saddle riding. Of all the sports," Wells claimed, "rodeo is the only one in which the girls do not get a square deal." She admitted that "there is no cowgirl who can ride like the boys" but nevertheless, cowgirls deserved "an even break." A competitive bronc rider herself, Wells spoke from experience and from the heart. "Listen, you rodeo promoters and cowboys, aren't you proud of your cowgirls? . . . And, big boys, this is 1930, not 1800. So snap out of it, you promoters and contest men! Don't let the promoters with 'old-maid' hearts get you to thinking ways of 1800 and put the cowgirl bronk riders out on the fence! Yunno, the cowgirls must eat and wear clothes just the same as the men do!"[53] Turning the promoters' argument on its head, Wells contended that the rodeo code demanded equality, not patriarchal protection, for helpless women. Act like real cowboys, she insisted, by letting women be real cowgirls. One male rodeo fan—W. "Cowboy" Fortier of Albuquerque, New Mexico—agreed with Wells, noting that his local rodeo was "seemingly colorless because we had no 'wimmen' busters." Fortier liked to "see the gals come out of the chutes" and "to holler [his] lungs almost out in encouragement of them. I have seen some good girl riders," Fortier wrote, "and they always get good hands from the PAY section—which are really the ones to be entertained." It was good business to promote cowgirl events, and promoters should have listened to fans who supported female rodeo with their cheers and their wallets.[54]

Two months later, Nora Wells sharpened her argument in a follow-up letter to "The Corral." She described rodeos that were advertised as "open to the world" where she was not allowed to compete because "the promoter . . . was afraid that [she] would get hurt, that he didn't have lady bronk riders at his shows, as he thought that riding a bronk was no place for a woman, and that she should be baking bread for some man." Wells denounced the "'hero' promoter who would be afraid the cowgirl might get her 'little head' scratched if he let her ride. . . . Give me the real promoter," she continued, "who gives the girls a chance and is tickled pink to see her ride—even if the bronk flops her all over the arena."[55] It was hard enough for cowgirls to earn a living in Depression-era America without paternalistic promoters turning them away at the gate. And the reaction to Bonnie McCarroll's death closed nearly all of the gates to female rodeo competitors for decades.

Our Heroes Have Always Been Cowboys

The death of Lane Frost sixty years later, on the other hand, ushered in a golden age for male bull riders who found legions of new fans and opportunities to win fame and fortune on the grandest scale. Whereas Bonnie McCarroll's death had foreclosed the future for women's rodeo, Frost's death spurred the beginning of a separate bull-riding circuit (a specialized splinter organization not affiliated with the Professional Rodeo Cowboys Association, or PRCA) that threatened to undercut traditional rodeo events. Frost's death inspired his fellow bull riders to showcase the thrills and violence of the most exciting eight seconds in sports without sharing the spotlight with other performers. Bull riders became athletic superstars in their own right and turned their sport into a stand-alone, television-friendly event within a decade of Frost's fatal ride at Cheyenne in 1989.

The story of Lane Frost, rodeo cowboy and world champion bull rider, sounds almost too good to be true. Part John Wayne, part Pecos Bill, and part Tom Joad, Frost had a life of athletic accomplishments in the rodeo ring that culminated in the most memorable death in rodeo history. By most accounts, Frost minded his mother, married his sweetheart, and always had time for every little kid who lined the back alleys of rodeos from Amarillo to Honolulu. His life, combined with his tragic and well-publicized death, has become the stuff of western legend. The story of Lane Frost illustrates that when a male athlete dies in the arena, the cultural significance of the athlete's memory grows in the fertile soil of an early grave.

Lane Frost's life appeared charmed from the beginning. Born October 12, 1963, to Clyde and Elsie Frost in La Junta, Colorado, Lane combined the champion rodeo skills of his bareback-riding father and the disposition of his mother. Even as an infant, as the story goes, rodeo caught the young cowboy's attention. His mother recalled that when he was just a few months old Lane slept "through most of the rodeo, but when the bull riding would start he would wake up and really start watching what was going on." On one occasion, Elsie "got up to go when there were still four or five bull riders left. . . . As we walked out of the seating area, Lane started to cry and looked back toward the arena. I thought, 'He acts like he wants to stay and watch the bull riding.' . . . Just to see what he would do, I turned around and walked back in where he could see the arena and what was going on. He stopped crying immediately." Before his first birthday, the myth of Lane Frost had already begun to assemble.[56]

As Frost matured, his attraction to bull riding intensified. At two years of age, he walked in his sleep down the stairs and out the front door, bull rope in hand. Just two years later, Frost climbed aboard the family's dairy calves, started kicking, and held on with all his might. In short measure Frost jumped to the junior rodeo circuit where he cut his competitive teeth. High school rodeo was next, and Frost won the bull-riding championship at the 1981 National High School Finals in Douglas, Wyoming. After his high school graduation, Frost immediately joined the professional rodeo tour and found early success. Though he failed to reach the National Finals in his rookie year, he managed to finish sixteenth in the world standings.

Fortune smiled on Frost during most of the 1980s. He steadily worked his way into the sport's upper echelon and won the title of World Champion Bull Rider at the National Finals Rodeo in 1987. His place in the pantheon of rodeo heroes secured, Frost burnished his reputation by riding Red Rock, a feat of courage and skill that many considered the rodeo equivalent of pulling the mythical sword from the stone of Arthurian legend. The 1987 "bull of the year" had never been successfully ridden in 309 tries (a cowboy must stay aboard the bull for eight seconds to receive a score). During the summer of 1988, the champion cowboy and the unrideable bull dueled in a seven-ride series dubbed the "challenge of the champions." Bucked off in his first two attempts, Frost conquered Red Rock in four of the last five matches. With the champions challenge in hand, Frost acceded to the rodeo throne and earned the title "king," a moniker that his traveling companions had already attached to him.

Although Frost rose to the top of the rodeo world, it was his tragic death that seared his memory into the consciousness of rodeo buffs and lured new fans to the sport. Emerging from one of the worst slumps in his career, Frost had high hopes going into the Cheyenne Frontier Days Rodeo in July 1989. Working his way through the early rounds at the "daddy of 'em all," Frost seemed poised to make a run at another world title. In the championship round on Sunday, July 30, he scored an impressive 85 (out of 100) aboard the bull Taking Care of Business. Lane's dismount, however, landed him squarely in the bull's path and the bull's horn struck Frost in the back, breaking several ribs and severing a major blood vessel. Following the blow, Frost rose to his feet, called for help, and crashed to the ground. Within seconds, the king of rodeo was dead at the age of twenty-five.

Professional bull riders are no strangers to injury. Concussions, torn ligaments, and pulled groin muscles plague nearly every rider on the circuit. Bull riders and their family members reflexively repeat the adage that "in bull riding, it's not when you get hurt, but how bad." In fact, bull-riding accidents result in about half of all injuries in professional rodeo.[57] Due to the ubiquity of physical violence, cowboys acknowledge debilitating injury and death as distinct possibilities. But the impact of Frost's death extended well beyond the expected response to a cowboy's passing. Maybe it was because he was just twenty-five, or maybe it was his charm, or good looks, or his unparalleled skills. Or maybe it was his limitless future. Whatever the reason, Frost's death struck his fellow cowboys with unexpected force. As bull-rider Cody Lambert related, "When someone who's one of the best, if not the best ever, has a perfect ride and gets off in good shape and then gets killed, it makes you realize how dangerous it is." "There's been deaths before, sure, but they've been mostly young kids," Lambert continued. "You don't think of it happening to a world champion in the prime of his career."[58] Along the same lines, another bull rider who had learned the ropes from Frost recalled: "Lane's death was hard. . . . In my eyes he was immortal. He was a champion above and beyond the arena. In my mind, he was pretty much untouchable, and [his death] drove home that nobody's untouchable."[59]

Shaping Lane's Legacy

Rodeo changed dramatically after Frost's death. The charismatic Frost had introduced rodeo into America's living rooms through his appearances on the syndicated television program *George Michael's Sports Machine*, and his death supercharged the sport's popularity. As one rodeo historian describes, Frost's death "made bull riding more popular because of the romantic legacy of a great one felled before his time."[60]

Monuments to Frost's legacy and memory sprung up straightaway. Soon after the accident, *George Michael's Sports Machine* aired a video montage of Frost's career, the first coordinated attempt to shape Lane's legacy. According to George Michael, thousands of viewers requested videotapes after the show aired.[61] At the National Finals Rodeo later that year, Frost's closest friend and longtime traveling companion delivered perhaps the most poignant memorial to his friend. After Richard "Tuff" Hedeman finished the ride that secured him the bull-riding championship, he remained aboard the bull for an extra eight seconds to honor Frost. Hedeman requested that both of their names be engraved on the winner's coveted buckle. In performing such a public tribute to his fallen friend, Hedeman linked his career to Lane's memory. But the quest to secure and shape Frost's romantic legacy was just getting started.

Posthumous honors poured in. In 1990, Frost became the youngest member inducted into the Professional Rodeo Hall of Fame. He would have been twenty-six years old. Red Rock, his erstwhile nemesis, was inducted into the hall that year as well. Three years later, the Frontier Days Park in Cheyenne unveiled a larger-than-life memorial sculpture of Frost atop a bucking bull. This ensured that future rodeo competitors and fans at the annual Cheyenne rodeo would remember Frost's life and his death.[62] The statue celebrated the cowboy's heroism more than it mourned his tragic loss.

Perhaps the most complex and enduring memorial to Frost appeared on the Internet tribute site http://www.lanefrost.com. A digital labor of love by creator Sharon Mahrley, the site contains hagiographic descriptions of Frost's personal talents and professional triumphs. The website's structure is typical, if extensive, containing quotes from friends and family, chronologies of his life, and many pictures. But the site contains much more. For example, Frost's parents used the site to highlight their son's spiritual devotion in the hopes that others would follow his example and be born again in Christ. Elsie Frost clarified her primary interest in keeping her son's memory alive: "If people remember one thing about Lane we want it to be that he was a kind person and knew Jesus."[63]

6. Statue of Lane Frost on the grounds of the Old West Museum in Cheyenne, Wyoming. Frost's death at the Frontier Days Rodeo in 1989 presaged the growth of the Professional Bull Riders tour. (Courtesy of Chris Navarro. Photo reprinted with permission of the author.)

To perpetuate Lane's legacy and his parents' personal ministry, the Frost family sold "Cowboy Bibles" for three dollars in the website's merchandise section. The paperback Bibles include a New International Version of the New Testament adorned with a drawing of Frost riding a bull in front of a large cross. The back cover contains several small drawings of rodeo scenes surrounding a portrait of an oversized championship-style belt buckle inscribed with a cross and the words, "Champion of Champions. Jesus Christ. He is Lord." Beneath the buckle—squarely between renderings of a bareback rider and a bull rider—appears the dedication: "This Bible is given in memory of Lane Frost, 1987 PRCA World Champion Bull Rider. Born 1963. Born again 1988. Died 1989." In case the message had not been clear enough, Clyde and Elsie explained their intentions inside the front cover: "We all have an eternal destiny. It may be an eternal life in hell or an eternal life in heaven. Lane chose a heavenly home by accepting Jesus as his personal Savior. This New Testament has come into your hands with our prayer that you will make that choice also." Lane was not just a cowboy, he was a Christian cowboy. At least according to the version of Frost's story shaped by his parents.[64]

The website http://www.lanefrost.com further sanctified Frost's memory by displaying photographs of "holy relics" that had been attached to his life and career. Prominently featured are Frost's bronze medal from the 1988 Olympics, championship belt buckles, and close-up shots of Frost's ring that commemorated his posthumous entrance in the Professional Bull Riders' "ring of honor." No images on the site, though, are more evocative than those that show the glove Frost wore during his last ride and the rope that had been tied around the bull that day. Rosin, not blood, stains the glove, which transports the viewer back to that tragic day in Cheyenne. Such memento mori, reminiscent of the holy relics of Christendom, obscure the line between fandom and worship.

However, not all of the content on the website is so otherworldly. A section of the site entitled "Memories of Lane" perpetuates and shapes Frost's legacy by selling merchandise decorated with the bull rider's image or name. Interested consumers can purchase photos, posters, collectible cards, videos, belt buckles, and exact replicas of Frost's bull-riding glove. Available T-shirts include some that contain Biblical quotes alongside pictures of Frost in action. Baseball caps remind purchasers that Frost "Won't Soon Be Forgotten" and that "Legends Never Die"—at least not if the living have anything to do with it.

The most widely recognized tribute to Frost materialized in 1994 when a feature film based on his life appeared in theaters across the nation. Titled *8 Seconds*, and starring teen heartthrob Luke Perry as Frost, the film found modest success at the box office and provided Americans outside of rodeo circles with a memorable sketch of Frost's life. The film welcomed Frost into the club of cowboys who became screen legends. A novelization of the film captures its main point: "[Frost's] biggest challenge was learning to live in the shadow of his larger-than-life image, but Lane faced it with style and went on to become a contemporary Western legend."[65] *8 Seconds* elevates Frost from a western hero to an archetypal symbol. The film's final scene shows Frost, arms outstretched like the Christus, waving to his wife Kelli across the divide of mortality. On film, at least, legends can live forever.

Bull-Riding Boon

Unlike Bonnie McCarroll's death, which sent women's rodeo into a tailspin, Frost's death occurred on the cusp of an explosion in the popularity of rodeo, especially bull riding. Frost's star shone like Venus on the horizon, heralding the constellations of modern rodeo superstars who rose in the 1990s. Much of the sport's newfound prominence traces back to Frost's death that soggy afternoon in Cheyenne. The characters who surrounded him then—Tuff Hedeman, Cody Lambert, Ty Murray, and others—built on Frost's legacy and revolutionized bull riding, transforming it into a stand-alone sport suitable for television. The two decades following Frost's accident became a golden age of professional bull riding. Not a single rodeo organization called for the prohibition of bull riding or channeled cowboys toward less violent events. Although sixty years separated McCarroll and Frost, they were worlds apart in how gender expectations shaped their legacies.

In 1992, Frost's bull riding buddies, including Hedeman, Murray, and Lambert, banded together and broke away from the Professional Rodeo Cowboys Association. Twenty-one cowboys each anted up $1,000 toward

the creation of the Professional Bull Riders (PBR), an association dedicated solely to bull-riding competitions. The tour grew from eight events
and $660,000 in prize money in 1994 to eighteen competitions and $2.2
million three years later. By 2002, the tour awarded $10 million in prizes,
and major networks like CBS and CBS Sports Network televised several
events each season. In 2015, PBR World Champion J. B. Manney received
a $1 million bonus. For comparison, in Lane's best year on the PRCA cir-
cuit, he pocketed $105,697. Overall, his six years on the tour netted him
less than $500,000.[66]

From day one, the PBR capitalized on the violence of the eight-second
ride. PBR executives, recognizing that bull riding and stock car racing
shared the same core demographic audience, followed NASCAR's well-
worn path from regional attraction to global marketing power. "If casual
race-car fans might start watching NASCAR in hopes of seeing a crash,"
PBR officials reasoned, "casual bull-riding fans might well be drawn in by
the chance that a 2,000-pound animal decides that the little man he has
just tossed to the ground needs some stomping." The most cantankerous
bulls gained fame as "the bringers of death and destruction."[67]

The fact that bull-riding accidents often seriously injured or killed
riders gave pause but no remorse to the athletes and promoters of the
PBR. Rather, such tragic events legitimized the sport and the cowboys
who climbed aboard the penned-up bull to face "enormous danger . . .
in the coffin-shaped metal cage." Apparently, PBR marketers believed
that "coffin-shaped" enclosures would attract more attention than simple
rectangular chutes. In 2009, the PBR published a historical and promo-
tional paean to the "toughest sport on earth." The possibility of grave
injury shows up on page one of the glossy picture book, where readers
learn that bull riders will "risk everything they've known—their homes,
families, indeed, their very lives—for one eight-second ride." Pages later,
Dr. Tandy Freeman, the physician who runs the PBR's sports medicine
program, soberly reminded readers that "every time these guys go out
there to ride . . . there is a realistic risk of being maimed or killed." The
ubiquitous risk of death creates an environment that cultivates "immortality." These death-defying cowboy "legends live forever. They are men
whose accomplishments transcend mere numbers and statistics, who are

on a level all their own." The PBR immortals include Chris Shivers, Justin McBride, and Adriano Moraes. Lane Frost did not make the cut, perhaps because his career preceded the formation of the PBR, even if his death inspired its creation.[68]

The risk of death hones a cowboy's performance and keeps the audience glued to the action. Bull riding connects to something primordial, an atavistic strand stretching back to a time when human–animal interactions were more unpredictable and violent. John Growney, renowned stock contractor of bulls including Red Rock, believes that "bull riding is one of those things for a modern man who understands that death is wrong but still gets excited about seeing that guy die or almost die." The "rush" of bull riding comes from knowing that "you're going to cross the line, and death awaits you over there. You cross the line, and then you get back."[69] Ty Murray, crowned by *Sports Illustrated* in 1990 as "the best danged rodeo cowboy of 'em all" and an original investor and later president of the PBR, knew firsthand that death rode alongside every bull rider.[70] Murray was standing just twenty feet away from Frost's lifeless body in Cheyenne. Later, he witnessed the fatal injury of Brent Thurman in 1994 and the death of PBR rider Glen Keeley in 2000. Nevertheless, Murray insisted that the thrill of bull riding outweighed the risks. "I think the guys that do it, especially at the professional level, understand the danger of it as good or better than anyone," reasoned Murray. "It's part of what makes up the sport. A big part of why people enjoy the sport is because of how extreme and how dangerous it is."[71] The virtue of a fatal final ride has been integrated into cowboy culture. Boxers do not revel in the romance of a ringside death but cowboys cling to the idea that sitting atop a bucking bull is a noble way to ride off into the sunset. Country singer and former world bareback riding champion Chris LeDoux fantasized about how he wanted his life to end. "I'd be at the height of my glory," he dreamed, "maybe I could be riding Cheyenne—and a horse would throw me off and kill me."[72] LeDoux never realized his fantasy (he died in 2005 from complications related to liver disease) but his ashes were scattered over Frontier Park Arena in Cheyenne.

Bonnie McCarroll and Lane Frost both met death in the rodeo ring. Both had been world champions. Both left grieving families and fans behind. Both had limitless futures. As similar as their situations appear on the surface, the worlds of rodeo reacted in opposite ways following their deaths. McCarroll's death hastened the demise of women's rodeo, a once-thriving institution that offered women an unorthodox occupation and lifestyle. Frost's death catapulted bull riding into a new stratosphere of popularity; after his death the rough stock event became a stand-alone sport. Gender and time separated McCarroll and Frost. One was a cowgirl, the other a cowboy. And that made all the difference.

Who Killed Benny Paret?

Faggot. Just like that. Whispered in Spanish—*maricón*—into Emile Griffith's ear as he stood on the weigh-in scales in front of reporters and others in a room at Madison Square Garden. No one else reacted to the provocation. "I'm nobody's faggot," thought Griffith as he lunged toward Benny Paret to answer the invective; Griffith's manager and others jumped between the fighters to stave off an early knockout punch, thrown before the television cameras started rolling.[1] Welterweight champion Paret reunited with Griffith several hours later under the hot lights of boxing's main arena and the klieg lights of ABC's *Saturday Night Fights*. Far from forgotten, Paret's not-so-silent accusation may have cost him his life.

On the evening of March 24, 1962, with the welterweight crown on the line, Emile Griffith pounded Benny "Kid" Paret senseless before a raging crowd at Madison Square Garden and a national television audience. Battered by nearly thirty unanswered punches in the twelfth round, Paret's body slumped in a corner, comatose and still. Ten days later, he died in a New York City hospital, a victim of the violence inherent in combative sport. Paret's death was a personal tragedy for his pregnant wife and two-year-old son, but the aftershocks of his death shook the sport of boxing to its core and prompted an extended examination of the sport from all corners—politically, culturally, philosophically, and even artistically.

The boxing ring is a violent workplace. Boxers die. If a victim is relatively famous, commentators remark on the brutality of the sport briefly and move on. "In the boxing ring, even in our greatly humanized times, death is always a possibility," writes Joyce Carol Oates. "A statistically rare possibility like your possible death tomorrow morning in an automobile accident or in next month's headlined airline disaster. . . . Spectators at 'death' fights often claim afterward that what happened simply seemed to happen—unpredictably, in a sense accidentally. Only in retrospect does death appear to have been inevitable."[2] Every few years, almost ritualistically, a redeemed boxer, trainer, or journalist argues for the abolition of the sport. The charges typically fail to stick. But, in the early 1960s, with the image of Paret's pounding fresh in the minds of millions, the call for boxing's reformation reached its highest pitch in the modern history of the troubled sport. The 1960s were a time of rapid cultural and social change, and boxing was swept up by the swirling currents of reform. Paret's death pushed boxing away from the shore and into a maelstrom of controversy.[3]

Who Killed Benny Paret?

Six weeks after Paret's televised tragedy, Norman Cousins, the influential editor of the *Saturday Review*, returned to the question that had vexed doctors, reporters, fight fans, and reformers. "Who Killed Benny Paret?" rang out the headline. Though no single answer prevailed, the mélange of explanations indicted nearly everyone involved—boxers, trainers, fans, television. A culture built on bloodlust, spectacle, and greed paved the way to Paret's grave.

Who killed Benny Paret? Acknowledging that the fighter was "killed because the human fist delivers enough impact, when directed against the head, to produce a massive hemorrhage in the brain," Norman Cousins argued that "the primary responsibility lies with the people who pay to see a man hurt." Cousins described an interview with prizefight promoter Mike Jacobs a quarter century earlier. When Cousins asked about the key to successful promotion, Jacobs did not hesitate. "You put killers in the ring and the people filled your arena," he said, "you searched for the killers and sluggers and maulers—fellows who could hit with the force of a baseball bat." Whatever the year, bloodthirsty boxing crowds demanded violence and mayhem in the ring. "The crowd wants a knockout. It wants to see a man stretched out on the canvas. This is the supreme moment in boxing," wrote Cousins. "No crowd was ever brought to its feet screaming and cheering at the sight of two men beautifully dodging and weaving out of each other's jabs. The time the crowd comes alive is when a man is hit hard over the heart or the head, when his mouthpiece flies out, when blood squirts out of his nose or eyes, when he wobbles under the attack and his pursuer continues to smash at him with pole-axe impact." Promoters and boxers simply gave the people what they wanted—modern-day gladiatorial spectacles that showcased the violence and death of strangers fighting in a ring. A vicarious pleasure that posed no threat to savage-minded consumers. The social norm that regarded prizefighting as an acceptable "vehicle of entertainment" bore the brunt of the blame for Paret's death.[4]

Twenty-five years later, Joyce Carol Oates helped to contextualize Cousins's conclusions by comparing ancient spectacles with modern boxing. Oates found that little had changed over the centuries. "When the boxing fan shouts, 'Kill him! Kill him!' he is betraying no peculiar individual pathology or quirk but asserting his common humanity and his kinship, however distant, with the thousands upon thousands of spectators who crowded into the Roman amphitheaters to see gladiators fight to the death. That such contests for mass amusement endured not for a few years or even decades but for centuries should arrest our attention." At its finest, boxing demonstrated the "body's dialogue with its shadow-self—or death."[5] Something communal surrounded the grisly scenes of a sporting death. Crowds urging athletes to fight without ceasing slaked a thirst for blood, power, or excitement. The attraction of the bloody canvas was less an atavistic remnant of antiquity than a common thread across the millennia. Critics of sports, not just boxing, had long highlighted the violence inherent in sports. Writing in the 1930s, social commentator Lewis Mumford expressed concern about the imperative toward violent death in modern sports. "In the latest forms of mass sport, like air races and motor races, the thrill of the spectacle is intensified by the promise of immediate death or fatal injury," wrote Mumford. "The cry of horror that escapes from the crowd when the motorcar overturns or the airplane crashes is not one of surprise but of fulfilled expectation: is it not fundamentally for the sake of exciting just such blood lust that the competition itself is held and widely attended?"[6] Norman Cousins could not have said it better.

Who killed Benny Paret? The "who" in this case is a "what": two subdural hematomas. Articles describing Paret's treatment at Roosevelt Hospital read more like medical textbooks than postfight analyses as sportswriters and fans received a crash course in neurophysiology. Dr. Howard Rusk, writing in the *New York Times*, described Paret's condition in the antiseptic terms befitting medical science. "Hemorrhage under the dura results when the meningeal vessels are torn on its undersurface," wrote Rusk. "As a result of this bleeding, blood clots, known as subdural hematomas, form, exerting pressure on the brain."[7] Griffith's pounding fists had slammed Paret's brain against his skull, causing bruises and brain damage. Doctors immediately tried to decrease the swelling by removing the bruises and excess fluid through four holes bored in Paret's head, but the operation did not offer much hope. Paret's brain injury, exacerbated by a bout with pneumonia, proved fatal. What had killed the twenty-five-year-old boxer was obvious, if difficult to pronounce. The questions of who had killed him, and why, remained beyond the reach of even the most advanced medical practitioners.

Who killed Benny Paret? Despite his reputation as the best in the business, veteran referee Ruby Goldstein initially received the lion's share of the blame for letting the fight continue too long.[8] Five years earlier, journalist Gay Talese had written that "his job as the ring's third man has made Ruby Goldstein possibly the most lonely guy in boxing."[9] After Paret's death, Goldstein received more attention than ever. Criticism of the referee began before Griffith's final onslaught of unanswered punches. "Long before Griffith had completed this cyclonic sortie," wrote Robert L. Teague in the *New York Times*, "many in the crowd of 7,600 were begging Referee Ruby Goldstein to intervene." Goldstein, however, "was not moved to pity" until Paret's lifeless body could make no defense at all.[10] In the days following the fight, Paret's manager Manuel Alfaro repeated the charge against Goldstein. "I lost a champion because of negligence on the part of a referee," Alfaro said. "Paret will never be able to fight again if he lives." Goldstein, for his part, defended his hesitance by claiming that "lots of fighters put their heads between the ropes that way to avoid punches.... They do that, and roll with the punches, and many times they don't get hit as hard as some people think." From the referee's perspective, the crafty Paret may have been playing possum, awaiting an opening in the fistic barrage. "I knew Paret as a tough fellow," Goldstein said.

"Sometimes, in the first part of a round, he doesn't do too well. Then he comes out of it and starts fighting."[11]

As the third person in the ring that night, the fifty-six-year-old Goldstein played his part flawlessly in the pas de trois that makes up boxing's hypermasculine core. A former lightweight and welterweight boxer (known as the "Jewel of the Ghetto" during his fighting days), Goldstein had refereed several championship bouts by 1962. In two earlier fights—a 1957 middleweight match between Randy Turpin and Sugar Ray Robinson and a heavyweight title fight pitting Floyd Patterson and Ingemar Johannson two years later—Goldstein had been criticized for ending the fights prematurely. "I'm usually accused of stopping fights too soon. . . . My first thought is always for the fighter's safety," explained Goldstein. Concerns for safety, however, had to be tempered by the magnitude of the bout. "But this [Paret–Griffith] was a championship fight. I believe the champion should get the chance to lose his title on his back, not on his feet."[12] Although all parties prefer that a fight be stopped too soon rather than too late, boxing's unwritten code stipulates that champions are allowed to defend their crowns without regard to physical punishment. In defining their physical limits, seasoned fighters deserved the benefit of the doubt. Earlier in his career, accusations of a quick trigger finger had stung Goldstein and raised questions about his willingness to let fights play out to the finish. Goldstein carried these concerns with him into the ring at Madison Square Garden and they may have kept him from stepping in sooner. Defending his delayed reaction, Goldstein dissected his handling of the Turpin–Robinson fight five years earlier: "I stopped it when Robinson was smashing Turpin at the ropes. . . . The British complained afterward that Turpin wasn't getting hit hard and that there was only eight seconds left to go in the round. I didn't know how much time was left, and I wouldn't have cared anyway. I thought it was time to stop it, and I did."[13] Did Goldstein let the Paret fight continue so that he would not face such criticism again? Did a shadow of doubt from the Robinson–Turpin fight momentarily cloud Goldstein's ability, or desire, to see the extent of Paret's injuries?

Goldstein maintained that his performance in the ring that night was unimpeachable. "What I am saying," Goldstein told *The Ring* magazine in August 1962, "is that for every single thing I have done as a referee, I have had a reason that satisfied me at the time as being logical and fair to all concerned—the fighters, the public, the commission." The logic behind his decision not to stop the Paret–Griffith fight emerged out of Goldstein's familiarity with Paret's fighting style. Because "Paret was a strong boy who had come back from trouble in almost every important fight he had," Goldstein hesitated to step in before Paret gained his second wind. Moreover, as the final flurry of punches assailed the Cuban boxer, Goldstein reasoned that Paret's response befit his style. "Don't forget, Paret did not fall into the ropes. He went into the corner on his own. That had been a favorite move of his, both in other fights and in this one," the referee insisted. Although Goldstein understood the public's desire to make him into a scapegoat, he felt no personal culpability for the bout's tragic conclusion. "I came out of the Paret fight grieving for that poor unlucky boy," Goldstein recalled, "but also high in spirit because I knew I had made no mistakes in handling the fight."[14]

While Paret lay unconscious at Roosevelt Hospital, members of the New York State Athletic Commission absolved Goldstein and other officials of any responsibility for the tragic accident.[15] Alfaro, who had harped on Goldstein's incompetence, eventually conceded that it was "the custom to give a champion some 'extra consideration.'"[16]

Who killed Benny Paret? A host of commentators focused on the destructive link between boxing and television. In the early years of broadcast television, boxing promoters and TV executives worked hand-in-glove to deliver content to the growing number of television sets in American homes. According to historians Randy Roberts and James Olson, "During the late 1940s and 1950s, boxing forged the strongest ties with television. It was the ideal sport. The actions involved only two men in a small area. Easy and inexpensive to televise, boxing also had an undeniable attraction for sponsors. It was a manly sport, just as razor blades, beer, automobiles, and cigarettes were manly products."[17] The pauses between three-minute rounds provided ample opportunity for advertisements, and the unscripted action in the ring provided genuine drama on the small screen. Television demanded action, and boxing filled much of that need during the 1950s—Monday nights on ABC and the DuMont Television Network,

Wednesdays on CBS, and Friday nights with featured fights from Madison Square Garden on NBC's *Gillette Cavalcade of Sports* program. On Saturday, ABC aired additional matches.[18] The ring was the thing. Boxing shaped the viewing habits of TV watchers, and the demands of television likewise influenced behavior in the ring. Artful, disciplined, scientific boxing fell victim to the public's preference for "wild hooks and haymakers" rather than more controlled jabs and crosses. Advertisers, promoters, and broadcasters responded by focusing on middleweights and heavyweights by the early 1960s. "Style and technique now gave way," writes Richard O. Davies, "to a simple, mindless brutality with emphasis on the sensational knockout punch."[19] Boxing may have been the original "reality" show: an unscripted drama playing out in real time. Journalist Pete Hamill, who covered the Paret–Griffith fight for the *New York Post*, underscores the magnetism of the genuine action in the ring: "At its glorious best, a prize-fight was not a movie, in which every action was choreographed and the good guy always won. When we saw a fight, we knew that the damage was real. The blood was real. The pain was real."[20] The death was real, too.

Commentators noted that the Paret tragedy was not produced by boxing alone, but by boxing and television combined. In part, Paret's death could be explained by the free-swinging, slugger mentality that emanated from the box in the corner of American living rooms. The fact that an estimated fourteen million viewers tuned in to the championship fight and unwittingly invited the dreadful scene into their homes magnified the impact of the event and ensured that the image of the lifeless Paret would linger in American minds. *Time* magazine reported that "seldom has a nationwide TV audience been treated to so shocking a reminder of boxing's basic brutality."[21] Along the same line, sportswriter Arthur Daley acknowledged the irony of a new broadcast technology being used to display the atavistic brutality of the boxing ring: "It was the inexorable eye of the camera . . . that brought into living rooms the apparent mercilessness of Griffith's final barrage with Paret imprisoned helplessly on the rope. Suddenly it became a horror movie."[22] New York Assemblyman Francis Souhan, a former member of the state athletic commission, blamed television for turning boxing from the "art of self-defense" into a spectacle where boxers "brutalized and walloped each other" merely to "make a good (television) program."[23] Fighters became "TV maulers," in the words of former heavyweight champion Gene Tunney. Fixated on the knockout punch, boxers avoided throwing body punches as if they were illegal.[24] The fact that Benny Paret was killed during the televised broadcast of *Saturday Night Fights* was surely coincidental, not causal. But the fact that the demands of television had changed the face of boxing may well have played an invisible but significant role in his death.

Who killed Benny Paret? On the most obvious level, as well as the most deeply hidden, Emile Griffith killed him. His lightning-quick fists bruised Paret's brain; his unyielding onslaught drove Paret to the canvas. Paret's blood was on Griffith's gloves. No observer, then or now, contends that Griffith intended to kill Paret that night, but many historians and journalists believe that Griffith had extra motivation when he and Paret toed the line for the third time in less than a year.

Paret and Griffith shared a common history long before March 1962. Eleven months earlier in Miami Beach, Griffith had taken Paret's welterweight title by a thirteenth-round knockout. A return match in September 1961 delivered the crown back to Paret, this time by a split decision. "I thought I beat him," Griffith proclaimed, "[It was] disappointing to lose it, knowing I beat the guy, knowing I was robbed, I was determined to win it back."[25] That alone might have helped Griffith to remain tightly focused during the third fight at Madison Square Garden. "Perhaps he was remembering the split decision he lost to Paret here last Sept. 30," speculated Robert Teague at ringside. "Whatever it was that Griffith was thinking about last night," wrote Teague, "it certainly was translated into something akin to savagery."[26] A rubber match between fighters typically generated heat, but not this type of explosive rage. As Teague intimated, the history between the fighters extended well beyond their clashes in the ring.

The fighters' feud, based on suspicions about Griffith's sexuality, started to simmer at the weigh-in before the rematch in September 1961. Most fighters at the time, according to former lightweight champ Jose Torres, knew that Griffith was gay, even if none talked about it in public. Paret had heard the rumors and taunted Griffith by floating a limp wrist in the air and whispering *maricón* within earshot of Griffith. To Paret, who grew up surrounded by machismo culture in Cuba, the epithet represented the cruelest word directed at any self-respecting man. Paret's actions "stung me more, I guess," remembered Griffith, "because no one ever made anything about it or said anything to me—except my brother Franklin. I had my girl friend Esther and I had my boy friends. That's the way it was and that's the way I liked it and this was the first time anyone made fun of me like that."[27] In defining his complex sexuality, Griffith's attitude anticipated many of the central ideas that would later inform queer theory. According to theorist Noreen Giffney, queer "signifies the messiness of identity, the fact that desire and thus desiring objects cannot be placed into discrete identity categories, which remain static for the duration of people's lives."[28] Griffith's attitude and behavior defied categorization and he refused throughout his life to identify himself as gay or bisexual.

Griffith lost the rematch and the title in the September fight. In the days following his defeat, writes boxing historian Troy Rondinone, Griffith "began to fixate on the Cuban" and even told a reporter that he would like to kill Paret.[29] Six months later, Griffith was ready to respond should Paret run his mouth at the weigh-in. Griffith's manager Gil Clancy cautioned his fighter to hold back until the bout began. Paret's manager Ruben Alfaro, on the other hand, pressed Paret to renew his taunt, to get inside Griffith's head again. While Griffith stood at the scales, Paret sidled up to him, patted his backside, and slurred, "Hey maricón . . . I'm going to get you and your husband."[30]

An enraged Griffith kept his fists back and stored his fury. The fighter later "admitted being angered by Paret at the weigh-in." Paret "made insulting remarks questioning [my] manliness," Griffith testified to a legislative committee, but the fighter "denied being angry in the ring. . . . 'You cannot be angry at a guy and go in the ring and fight with a cool head.'"[31] Other versions of that evening's events, however, do not quite match the description of a levelheaded Griffith simply going about his business. Several months after the deadly fight, Griffith confided in reporter Jimmy Breslin that his anger had not cooled between the weigh-in and the opening bell. After the fight, Griffith "sat in his dressing room and sobbed, 'I wanted to kill him. I hated him so much for what he said, I wanted to kill him.'" Griffith's anger had been compounded by sharp

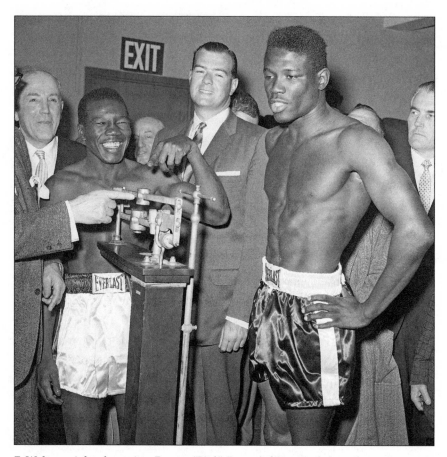

7. Welterweight champion Benny "Kid" Paret (white trunks) smiles as he reads the weight of challenger and former champion Emile Griffith during weigh-in in New York City, March 24, 1962. Their title fight that evening in Madison Square Garden was televised on ABC's *Saturday Night Fights*. (AP Photo/John Lindsay)

instructions from his corner man before the decisive twelfth round. "He goes in this round," Gil Clancy ordered. "And I want you to do it like a real professional. Start with the left hand. Then I want you to be a cold, cruel, calculating killer. Understand? A killer. I don't want you to lose your head and do it sloppy. I want you to be a killer. I want to see him go down. And I want him to stay down." The intense pep talk redoubled the tensions from the weigh-in and a long night in the ring. Clancy did not want Paret dead, just defeated. But his words, and his anger, provided

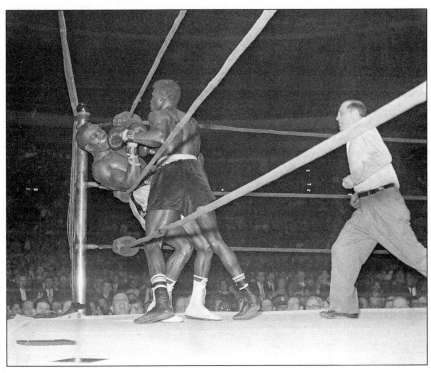

8. Emile Griffith, right, sends welterweight champion Benny "Kid" Paret into the ropes with a left to his face just before the referee stopped the fight in the twelfth round. Referee Ruby Goldstein, right, moves in to stop the fight. (AP Photo)

more fuel for Griffith's raging fire. And Benny Paret unfortunately got caught in the conflagration.[32]

For weeks after the bout, kids on the streets of New York called out to Griffith, asking him why he killed Paret. A protector and patron of young men in his neighborhood, Griffith patiently pulled the boys aside to "explain it was a terrible accident and how [he] didn't want such a thing ever to happen. And then the kids—they would understand and say, 'I'm sorry.'"[33] Griffith characteristically referred to the event as "my accident with the late Benny."[34] Undoubtedly, Paret's untimely death was accidental, but even accidents emerge out of historical contexts. The circumstances surrounding this bout ranged from questionable refereeing to the demands of broadcast television, but overshadowing Griffith, Paret,

Goldstein, and Clancy was the hypermasculinity imperative in combative sports like boxing. The "manly art" brooks no femininity. Even the hint of suspicion about a boxer's masculinity prompts an immediate, and often savage, response. Sticks and stones, like jabs and hooks, can break bones, but words like *maricón* can destroy a boxer's career.

A "Most Unusual Champion"

Perhaps fighters overreact to masculine slights because the sport combines violence with physical intimacy: half-naked men punching, clenching, hugging, sharing sweat, and swapping blood in the public arena. In the words of novelist and fight fan Joyce Carol Oates,

> No sport is more physical, more direct, than boxing. No sport appears more powerfully homoerotic: the confrontation in the ring—the disrobing—the sweaty heated combat that is part dance, courtship, coupling—the frequent urgent pursuit by one boxer of the other in the fight's natural and violent movement toward the 'knockout': surely boxing derives much of its appeal from this mimicry of a species of erotic love in which one man overcomes the other in an exhibition of superior strength and will. The heralded celibacy of the fighter-in-training is very much a part of boxing lore: instead of focusing his energies and fantasies upon a woman the boxer focuses them upon an opponent. Where Woman has been, Opponent must be.[35]

The bulging, exaggerated muscles adorning the boxer's physique attract not only female interest, but have become an enduring standard of beauty for gay men as well. The ring, then, becomes more than a sacred "squared circle" where masculinity is on display; the ring also expresses an ambiguous sexual message as a space where hetero- and homosexual exist in tandem. Because boxers necessarily walk a fine gender line when they toe the scratch, male fighters fear that any connection to the feminine might irrevocably destroy a reputation made in the ring.

Paret's emasculating accusation regarding Griffith's sexuality was more than simple prefight posturing. The slur was particularly potent because it drew its venom from a central aspect of Latin American machismo culture that was familiar to both Paret and Griffith. More than mocking Griffith's sexual interests, the insult cast doubt on his masculinity in ways that Griffith could not misinterpret. Queer theorist Roger N. Lancaster argues that the machismo element of many Latin American cultures imbues boys with a deep-seated fear of homosexuality. Lancaster writes, "Boys are constantly disciplined by their elders—by parents and siblings alike—with the humiliating phrase, *'No sea cocbón!'* ('Don't be a queer!') when their demeanor falls short of the assertive, aggressive, masculine ideal. Any show of sensitivity, weakness, reticence—or whatever else is judged to be a feminine characteristic—is swiftly identified and ridiculed. By adolescence, boys enter a competitive arena, where the signs of masculinity are actively struggled for, and can only be won by wresting them away from other boys around them."[36] Paret's attempt to gain an edge in the ring was, at least in part, an outgrowth of his cultural background. Griffith's forceful response to the attempted embarrassment may have been inscribed on his psyche while growing up in the machismo-based culture of the Virgin Islands. Paret fully understood the implications of his accusation and so did Emile Griffith.

Griffith's sexual proclivities were an open secret in the boxing world. Fighter Jose Torres knew. Reporter Jimmy Breslin knew. The rumors circulating in Griffith's neighborhood had even reached Benny Paret. People talked, but that was it. No reporter broke the story in the newspaper; no exposé appeared on television. Although the public would have been shocked to learn that the welterweight champion of the world was bisexual, the press sat on the story. The same discretion that kept Franklin D. Roosevelt's wheelchair off the front page and John F. Kennedy's sexual peccadilloes off the nightly news also left Griffith's private life alone. No reporter would have dared to write about Griffith's sexuality.[37]

Although no reporter in the 1960s "outed" Griffith, a close reading of press coverage reveals that stories about Griffith contained subtexts and word choices that hinted at Griffith's sexuality. If Jimmy Breslin did not dare to write the whole story, he dared to come pretty close. In an article published in the *Saturday Evening Post* in December 1962, Breslin offered a detailed portrait of Griffith in the months following Paret's death. The story is sad, filled with tortured memories and ghostly visitations from the dead fighter. Beneath the narrative, however, Breslin provides the savvy reader with clues about Griffith's "secret" life. "The big trouble is," wrote Breslin, "that Griffith is unusually sensitive for a professional prize-fighter." Charismatic and likeable, the fighter "snaps his fingers and does a little dance step" whenever music plays. Breslin repeated the story of how Griffith was discovered working in the shipping department of a hat factory owned by Howard Albert (who later became Griffith's co-manager). Griffith "brought with him a calypso approach to the daily rush-rush of New York's garment center." Particularly notable was the "light-footed way he walked around."[38]

Griffith's employment at the hat factory became a staple used by journalists to draw attention to Griffith's complex sexuality without revealing too much. Though the boxer never actually designed hats, as he occasionally claimed, he played up the image throughout his career. In fact, Griffith had initially entered the ring to prove his masculinity and toughness. Griffith had never wanted to be a fighter, but Howard Albert noticed how his employee's forty-four-inch shoulders tapered to a twenty-six-inch waist and knew that he had a diamond in the rough, even if Griffith took some convincing. Albert "had the girls in the shop tell [Griffith that he] was scared to fight, that [he] was chicken." Griffith answered those questions by stepping into the ring. It would not be the last time that such accusations spurred him to fight.[39]

Griffith was not like other fighters—he seemed thoughtful, caring, and kind. More like an artist or dancer than a fighter. How could the persona of this sensitive young immigrant from the Virgin Islands be reconciled with his cold-blooded assault on Paret? In Chandler Brossard's assessment, Griffith was "a most unusual champion." Brossard profiled Griffith for *Look* magazine in 1967 and loaded his article about the boxer with coded language that was not difficult to decipher. The uncertainties facing a gay boxer emerge in the article's lead paragraph and set the tone for the piece. "[Griffith] is the middleweight boxing champion of the world, and he is an exuberant garden of surprises and contradictions. Can you imagine a bloodstained lyric? A violent orchid? Consider an applause-soaked hero whose companion is loneliness. A self-confessed party boy whose morality is tense and Puritanical. . . . All of this is Emile Griffith. He carries with him that indispensable requirement of the artist:

surprise." A flower? A lyric? An exuberant garden? Few boxers fit that description—just imagine Smokin' Joe Frazier as an orchid. According to Brossard, when Howie Albert asked Griffith if he had considered becoming a fighter, the young man "could have collapsed down to the floor. 'Me a fighter!'" Griffith then "giggled with the absurdity of it all." His "almost frivolous" demeanor, however, belied an interior aggression that was "deadly serious."[40]

Even Griffith's intensity had a softer, more introspective side. Brossard observed that a "sensitive, hurt look came over [Griffith's] face" when the fighter contemplated his obligations to his large family. To relax, Griffith attended Broadway plays (usually by himself) and took long drives in the country. Griffith craved respect for his ring accomplishments and his complex personality. In a "voice high and strong," Griffith criticized the simplistic expectations of fight fans. "You know what gets me," he told Brossard, "is what people think fighters ought to be. Tough and mean like hoods and dumb. What a silly, stupid idea. If you don't act like that, they think something is the matter with you. . . . I tell you, my friend, the tough boys, they are not so tough. I assure you." Brossard and the "poet" then stepped into the car to take a long ride to "assuage [Griffith] in his apartness."[41] Tough boys were not what they appeared to be, and neither was Griffith. Different, apart, and unusual described Griffith's lifestyle without actually explaining it.

Death Comes to the Living Room

Television beamed Paret's death into millions of homes and created indelible memories for many fight followers, especially younger viewers. During the pioneering years of the 1950s, television had presented escapist programming with little conflict and inevitable happy endings. For many American viewers, the Paret–Griffith fight ushered in a new age of on-screen violence that would eventually define television in the 1960s.

Few viewers of any age were prepared when the Paret–Griffith match transformed the set in the front room into a killing field. No TV private eye or smooth-talking attorney rushed in at the last moment to rescue the faltering Paret. A real life-and-death drama unfolded before millions of Americans that night. TV was not supposed to be real but, in the blink of an eye, the *Saturday Night Fights* became a televised execution. In ways that cannot be measured, watching Paret die changed how viewers saw the world, not to mention the place of boxing and television in it. Gerald Early, noted literary critic and commentator on boxing and other sports, recalled the fallout from Paret's death as a transformative moment in his life. "I remember very well that I could not sleep the night that Benny Kid Paret was knocked into a coma by Emile Griffith. . . . I had watched that fight on television and when Paret was carried from the ring, unconscious, and, for all intents and purposes, lifeless, I felt myself quivering on the inside." Later, Early "prayed to God to save Paret's life. Indeed, I remember being on my knees and praying very hard, having learned in church that God answers those who truly believe. I thought I truly believed but Benny Kid Paret died anyway." Ten-year-old Early had thoughts that ventured well beyond sports that night. "Not only did I learn something about the inscrutable whimsicalness of God but also about the precariousness of the life of a fighter," wrote Early. "It was then that I felt that professional prizefighting should be banned, not because it was brutal . . . and not even because it was absurd . . . but because it was so uncaring."[42] To Early and others, watching Paret's death in its immediacy, magnitude, and finality became a watershed moment of disillusionment, a prelude to the televised assassination of John F. Kennedy Jr. a year later.

The Paret–Griffith fight likewise ushered in television's use of slow-motion replay, a videotape-based system recently perfected by ABC engineers.[43] Fight announcer Don Dunphy insisted that the new technology exacerbated the tragedy in the ring. "The replays went on the air and showed the beating Paret was taking," wrote Dunphy. "Again and again they were repeated." Dunphy later learned that the postfight show earned a higher rating than the fight itself. "Apparently people were calling friends and telling them to tune in, that a guy was getting beaten to death on the TV."[44] Again and again. In slow motion.

Paret's death in front of fourteen million viewers heralded a decade of violence in the public square, on American streets, and on nightly news programs. Daily footage from the battlefields of Vietnam brought home the ravages of war in greater detail and faster than ever before. Televised assassinations defined the era—John and Robert Kennedy, Lee Harvey

Oswald, and Martin Luther King Jr. all had their murders broadcast into living rooms throughout the world. Benny Paret's death was simply the decade's first.

KO for Boxing?

The cries to "stop the fight" began at ringside, when onlookers implored Ruby Goldstein to end Paret's punishment before he was "battered into insensitivity."[45] In the weeks and months following, the calls to prohibit prizefighting emanated from rural Mississippi to the Vatican, and most places in between. Talk about boxing reform was cheap, and all manners of commentators chipped in their two cents; meaningful regulation, however, came much more slowly as entrenched interests squared off in the aftermath of Paret's death. As *Time* magazine recorded, "for the moment, the ritual of the Saturday night bloodbath was clearly on trial."[46]

The decade preceding Paret's televised tragedy had not been kind to the business of boxing, despite its newfound popularity on television. As Troy Rondinone describes, boxing was besieged by cultural critics on one side and legislators investigating the relationship between organized crime and professional fighters on the other. From the cultural side, movies like *On the Waterfront* (1954), *The Harder They Fall* (1956), and *Requiem for a Heavyweight* (1962) revealed the seamier side of the sport and called attention to the "way boxing chewed these poor souls up and then spat them out when their usefulness as entertainers had evaporated."[47]

Far from the silver screen, boxing's most damaging drama played out in the legislative halls of Washington, DC, where Senator Estes Kefauver turned the nation's attention to the criminal underworld and its behind-the-scenes control of prizefighting. Champion boxers including Jake LaMotta, Ike Williams, and Carmen Basilio testified concerning their inability to stage an honest fight due to the influence of gangsters like Frankie Carbo and Frank "Blinky" Palermo. The mob controlled access to title fights and retained the lion's share of a boxer's winnings. Boxers refusing to submit to the mob's management found themselves on the outside, with no hope of return. By shining a light on the backroom deals at the heart of the sport, Kefauver spun political gold out of the hearings and triumphantly called for federal regulation of boxing. The call went unheeded.[48] As Steven A.

Riess details, the link between mobsters and fighters was never completely severed: "underworld influence did not disappear from the prize ring, though becoming less pervasive, less obvious, and less centralized. Fighters continued to turn to gangsters with important connections to help them in their careers, often because they knew no one else to turn to."[49]

In the aftermath of the Paret–Griffith fight, New York politicians reacted with an "irrational outburst of moralism" while Paret still clung to life in Roosevelt Hospital.[50] Governor Nelson Rockefeller ordered Melvin L. Krulewitch, chairman of the New York State Athletic Commission, to investigate the circumstances surrounding the bout and to ensure that all proper precautions had been taken to ensure the safety of the fighters.[51] Two days later, the commission granted the match "a clean bill of health" and absolved Goldstein and the attending medical officers of any responsibility for Paret's condition.[52] Not to be outdone by the governor, the New York state legislature empaneled a joint legislative committee to investigate all aspects of boxing in the state, including the future of the sport, the safety of boxers, and the effects of radio and television broadcasts on the sport.[53]

Other American politicians pressed the case further, calling for strict reforms and even the abolition of prizefighting. California Governor Edmund G. Brown lashed out at the "dirty, rotten, brutalizing" sport, though he fell short of asking the busy California legislature to enact a ban.[54] The governor promised to approach the legislature about the issue should he be reelected in the fall. Brown's primary opponent in the race, former Vice President Richard M. Nixon, insisted that the corrupt elements in the fight game should be "cleaned up or kicked out."[55] Legislators in Illinois condemned boxing on moral grounds as the only sport that "has one purpose, to knock a man senseless." Animals received more protection from the state than boxers did. "We outlaw cockfights and bullfighting," argued State Representative Paul Simon, "and yet let two human beings knock each other senseless." Simon promised to sponsor legislation to ban professional prizefighting, but gave few details.[56] Boxing became a ready-made political punching bag used by candidates to make popular moralistic pronouncements and win points in the short term without spending any political capital to enact real change.

Calls for reform sounded from all corners of the globe. In Canada, one member of Parliament referred to Paret's death as "organized murder" and urged that regulations be tightened in Ontario. Danish Parliament member Berner Sinnbeck, a former fighter, proposed that his nation outlaw boxing.[57] Three major daily newspapers in Tokyo denounced the Paret–Griffith match as "brutal television fare."[58] The British House of Lords debated a bill to ban boxing, which had been proposed by Lady Edith Summerskill. A physician and longtime opponent of prizefighting, Summerskill railed against the sport's "unsavory traffic in young bodies" before watching her bill go down in defeat. Across the channel, *Paris Match* published a series of "savage boxing photographs" that piqued the interests of French reformers and "helped to stir this international revulsion toward boxing."[59]

The Vatican City newspaper, *Osservatore Romano*, took to the moral high ground in denouncing boxing. Responding to "the crude end of a poor Negro fighter" who was "massacred on the ropes," an editorial argued that any sport where physical injuries are part of the expected course of competition must contradict the teachings of the church. "Deaths in the ring of 400 fighters in the last sixty years," claimed the paper, "offer irrefutable argument about the morality or immorality of this sport."[60] Boxers and promoters would do well to remember the fifth commandment, "thou shalt not kill," before organizing matches or stepping into the ring.[61] Catholic journalists in the United States followed the Vatican's lead by welcoming "the day when the American people finally reject professional boxing for good, and inter it by the side of cockfighting, bearbaiting, and the public execution of criminals."[62]

Isvestia, a leading newspaper in the Soviet Union, reported that Paret had fallen victim to "businessmen who deal in human blood." Metaphorically, the paper certainly had a point—boxers, managers, and promoters all profited from the violent, even bloody, business in the ring. But the accusation smacked more of propaganda than legitimate news reporting. By April 1962, relations between the United States and the Soviet Union were even colder than usual. Not long after the fiasco at the Bay of Pigs and just months before the Cuban Missile Crisis, the nations were locked in an ideological battle in which each side angled for any advantage. Paret's imminent death allowed *Isvestia* to sensationalize the tragedy and condemn American capitalism. In New York, according to the Soviet newspaper, there were businessmen for "whom the sale of human blood—not their own but somebody else's—has become ordinary business permitted by corresponding laws."[63]

The *New York Times* echoed *Isvestia* in demanding a "KO for prizefighting" in the wake of numerous serious injuries and deaths in the ring, including Paret, Sonny Nunez, Sammy Romero, and a battered Floyd Patterson. Pulling no punches, the paper whaled away: "Grand old sport, this manly art. Stimulating to watch, although lethal to take part in." It was time for the state to "outlaw this brutal professional spectacle of prizefighting. If it doesn't, its social conscience—awakened to belated indignation by the Benny Paret death last March—has gone punch-drunk."[64] A later editorial claimed that a prizefighting ban would ensure safety in the ring and promote social order. The "unsavory characters" associated with boxing required more public policing than the sport was worth. Boxing "brutalize[d] boxers and watchers alike." It had to go.

An editorial in the *Christian Century* excoriated professional prizefights and nearly everyone associated with them—legislatures, commissions, medical associations, promoters, participants, television networks, advertisers, and viewers. The "millions of Americans [who] prepared for the Sabbath by watching the brutality on their television screens" were "accessories to murder." In this blood sport, "the attempt to bring about injury is [the] only goal. Death is therefore not an accidental by-product. The men who entered the ring at Madison Square Garden that Saturday evening had made clear their hatreds and intentions to injure. . . . And we are not proud."[65] *Ebony* magazine reached a similar conclusion. "With the moans of the mother mingled the indignant outcries of thousands," wrote Hans J. Massaquoi, "who decreed that because Paret had died, professional boxing, too, had forfeited its right to live."[66]

The drive to outlaw boxing was far from universal, however. Charles Larson, president of the National Boxing Association (certainly not the most objective observer), warned against the "emotional annihilation" of prizefighting while the memories of the Paret tragedy hung thick in the air. "Boxing is sick, to be sure," Larson admitted, "but to kill because the patient is sick is certainly wrong. A major airplane crash does not call for condemnation of the entire industry." Recent events justified the calls for change, but reformers needed to be careful not to destroy the "only true international sport."[67] Other supporters of the sport feared that an abolition of prizefighting would close down opportunities for poor and minority fighters. Called before a joint legislative committee investigating boxing in February 1963, state officials and several former and current fighters, including Carmen Basilio and Cassius Clay, testified against any move to forbid professional boxing. Notably, James Hicks, editor of the *Amsterdam News* in Harlem, argued that boxing was "one area of the sports world where equal opportunity is granted to members of my race. Negroes may not be accepted on the tennis courts at Forest Hills or other sports areas, but they are accepted as equals in the boxing ring."[68] As might have been expected, members of the Boxing Writers Association defended prizefighting in a statement delivered to the legislative committee. Boxing was relatively safe compared to sports like hunting, argued the writers, and provided physical exercise for sedentary kids. "We have over the years divined a goodness in boxing," concluded the report.[69]

Journalists joined in the call to save boxing, too. An editorial in *Sports Illustrated* praised the boxer who "runs a considerable risk but . . . stands to win a great deal, too, and not merely money." "Boxing is a hard sport," the editorial concluded, "but it is a sport and a valid one."[70] Red Smith, sports columnist for the *New York Herald-Tribune*, provided a full-throated defense of boxing against the "part-time bleeding hearts, the professional sob sisters of press and politics and radio, who seize these opportunities to parade their own nobility, demonstrate their eloquence, and incidentally stir the emotions of a few readers, voters or listeners."[71]

Boxing survived the onslaught that followed Paret's death. But the popularity of the sport, and its ubiquity on television, could not stem the tide of popular outrage. Concerned about the backlash against ring violence as well as the relationship of prizefighting to organized crime, ABC cancelled its weekly coverage of boxing in 1964.[72]

Cultural Echoes

Paret's death continues to resonate decades later in part because his story was memorialized almost immediately by inspired writers, poets, and singers. Norman Mailer, the iconoclastic novelist and inveterate blowhard, sat ringside at Madison Square Garden and wrote an extraordinary essay for *Esquire* magazine in December 1962. "I had never seen a fight like it," wrote Mailer. In the final seconds of the bout, "Paret got trapped in a corner. Trying to duck away, his left arm and his head became tangled on the wrong side of the top rope. Griffith was in like a cat ready to rip the life out of a huge boxed rat. He hit him eighteen right hands in a row, an act which took perhaps three or four seconds, Griffith making a pent-up whimpering sound all the while he attacked, the right hand whipping like a piston rod which has broken through the crankcase, or like a baseball bat demolishing a pumpkin. . . . I had never seen one man hit another so hard and so many times." Though hypnotized by the mayhem in the ring, Mailer remained alert enough to feel that "some part of [Paret's] death reached out to us. One felt it hover in the air." A chilling scene, marvelously rendered. Mailer's description of Paret's final fall ranks with the best of the novelist's work. "He went down more slowly than any fighter had ever gone down, he went down like a large ship which turns on end and slides second by second into its grave. As he went down, the sound of Griffith's punches echoed in the mind like a heavy ax in the distance chopping into a wet log."[73]

The echo of Griffith's punches landed in other ears as well, provoking a variety of artistic tributes, commentaries, and explanations. Folk singer Gil Turner borrowed from the events in the ring to craft the folk ballad, "Benny 'Kid' Paret," released in 1963. Echoing the style of labor songs from the early twentieth century, Turner's ballad begins with the image of a young Paret chopping sugar cane amid the tropical idylls of prerevolutionary Cuba and moves to Paret's American workplace, the modern sporting arena. Critical of a society that could host such barbaric entertainments, Turner condemned modern boxers and their deadly gloves as no more civilized than Roman gladiators. "There's danger in the boxing ring," intoned Turner. The singer plaintively cried out for reforms to ensure that Benny would be the "last to die on the canvas floor, while the crowd called for more." Far from the cane fields of his youth, Paret was chopped down to lifelessness alone in a crowded corner at Madison Square Garden. Americans "hanged a Cuban boy that night upon a cross of rope." Perhaps by remembering Paret's death, Turner suggested, American society might find redemption in his memory, if not in his blood.[74]

More than a decade later, poet Paul "Red" Shuttleworth composed a series of "Poems to the Memory of Benny Kid Paret," which circle around some of the themes introduced by Turner, but also contain an emotional connection to Paret's death that eluded the folk singer. The poet moved beyond sympathy by conflating himself and the fallen fighter. In "You're Dead When They Pull the Boxing Gloves Off," Shuttleworth could not quiet the echoes of Paret's pounding:

> Around the time Bobby Gleason first nailed
> a portrait of Ike on his gym wall,
> Saturday night meant T.V. boxing.
> Even when he lost and died,
> I loved the puncher with the iron will.
> Benny Kid Paret, this poem
> about velvet shark fin eyes
> snapping into the deep skull
> of our roadwork dreams
> is for you gladiator prince.
> But it's also for me
> as I look for the fine deed
> battered onward without whiskey or salvation.
> I'm trying to hear the last right hook.[75]

Love, lust, attraction, emulation, nostalgia, and fear of the future contoured Shuttleworth's memories of Paret. Another poem, titled "Watching the Bout on TV, Benny Kid Paret's Two-Year-Old Son Screamed: Papa Papa Papa," illustrates how deeply the poet had imagined himself into the boxer's world.

Dry leaves skitter against the door.
That's what I hear, but if I step
into the float-away night to look,
white bone chips from a skull
will snow-drift about my shoes.

It is the absence of echo
the buzz of a surgeon drilling
for blood clots as if they were
tiny fists swinging against jelly.[76]

In addition to using Paret as a subject, Shuttleworth turned to him as a muse. Social change was not the call emanating from these poems, but personal reconciliation with, and even redemption from, the past.

For Emile Griffith, redemption was never in the cards. Although he fought professionally for fifteen years after Paret's death and won three more world titles, Griffith never escaped the specter of that deadly night in Madison Square Garden. According to his biographer, Griffith's "haunting continues. He knows that it is not a ghost following him, but, rather, a slight, a taunt, an accusation made decades ago that refuses to be put to rest. It is what people remember of that long-ago March night—a championship prizefight in which one man mocked the other's manhood and was beaten to death because of it. It is a memory that distorts reality and alters truth. This is the ghost that follows Emile Griffith his every waking day."[77]

Griffith's story continues to transfix Americans. Now, though, less attention is paid to the Paret tragedy than to the complex relationship of sexuality and athletic masculinity embodied by Griffith. Looking back on his life and career, Griffith recognized the impossibility of being an omnisexual athlete in twentieth-century America: "I kill a man and most people understand and forgive me. However, I love a man, and to so many people this is an unforgivable sin; this makes me an evil person. So even though I never went to jail, I have been in a prison almost all my life. I am a prizefighter. I won six world championships. My life could have been and should have been like a wonderful dream. Some of it was but a good part of it was more like a nightmare."[78] Although Griffith rightly deserves recognition as a trailblazing LGBTQ athlete, the sports world continues to force gay men into the prison of the closet. The situation for lesbian athletes has improved dramatically, but more than fifty years after Benny Paret's death, too many Americans still view homosexuality and masculinity in oppositional terms.

When Dan Klores, director of the documentary *Ring of Fire: The Emile Griffith Story*, visited the Virgin Islands after the film's release, he set out to learn about Griffith's influence in his former home. He found a Griffith Gym, Griffith Park, and Griffith Stadium—clearly the fighter had become a beloved hero. But when Klores spoke with local residents, their memories of Griffith took him aback. Asked about the former world champion, people responded, "'Oh, yeah, the faggot?' That's what they say. 'Oh, he was a fag.'"[79] Seemingly, little had changed in fifty years except the language of the slur.

"Princess Diana with a Pushbroom Mustache"

Dale Earnhardt and the Narratives of a NASCAR Death

D ale Earnhardt's death was likely the most shocking and consequential death in American sports history. Never before had a sport's most popular athlete been killed participating in the sport's premier event in front of 150,000 people in the stands and thirty million more watching on television. When the incomparable NASCAR driver struck the wall on the final lap of the Daytona 500 on February 18, 2001, the nation took a collective gasp. Almost immediately, Earnhardt's death joined the handful of public memories that begin with "I remember where I was when I heard about the death of" and end with names like John F. Kennedy, Princess Diana, and John Lennon. By leaving mortality so abruptly, Earnhardt joined the revered list of celebrities struck down in the prime of life.

To be sure, other American athletes have died in the public eye—New York Yankee legend Lou Gehrig, Princeton's gridiron and hockey star Hobey Baker, and champion distance runner Steve Prefontaine come to mind. In the cases of Gehrig and Baker, circumstances caused Americans to expect the bad news. Gehrig's physical decline began several years before his death and Baker died at the helm of an aircraft in France at the close of the First World War.[1] Although Prefontaine dominated on the track at the University of Oregon and in national trials, he had failed to win Olympic gold in 1972 and was still chasing a paramount achievement to define his career.[2] A handful of prominent players died during actual games, including Cleveland Indians' shortstop Ray Chapman, who died in August 1920 after being hit in the head by a pitch from Carl Mays of the New York Yankees.[3] Even incidents when nearly every member of

9. NASCAR driver Dale Earnhardt looks out of the garage at the Daytona International Speedway on February 9, 2001. (AP Photo/Chris O'Meara)

a team was killed—like when plane crashes decimated Marshall University's football team in 1970 or the U.S. women's figure skating team a decade before—such tragedies cannot match the impact of Earnhardt's death.[4] Whereas other examples from the realm of global sports, including the death of Brazilian three-time Formula One World Champion Ayrton Senna while leading the 1994 San Marino Grand Prix, or the plane crash in 1958 that killed eight Manchester United soccer players, may have had supreme importance in Brazil and England, the influence of Earnhardt's death has few American rivals.[5] Most recently, the death of Pat Tillman, the NFL star turned Army Ranger, in a firefight in Afghanistan received outsized attention, but just imagine if he had died playing in the Super

Bowl.[6] Earnhardt, according to one observer, "was American stock car racing. He drove a Chevy, he was a homemade hero, and surely he invented apple pie."[7]

In the immediate aftermath of the crash at Daytona, NASCAR drivers, fans, and journalists struggled to explain the significance of Earnhardt's death. Journalist Ken Willis admitted that the tragic news was "absolutely, without question, the most unbelievable thing [he had] ever heard."[8] H. A. "Humpy" Wheeler, president of Lowe's Motor Speedway and one of NASCAR's leading promoters, ranked the loss of Earnhardt "right up with the death of JFK."[9] Erstwhile gonzo journalist Hunter S. Thompson agreed that the "violent death of Dale Earnhardt hit the sport of professional auto racing harder than anything in memory since the assassination of John F. Kennedy."[10] Writing for the *Orlando Sentinel*, columnist Mike Bianchi turned over every imaginable stone to find an apt comparison. First, he looked at the sports world. Earnhardt's death was not like the retirement of Michael Jordan from the NBA; it was more akin to Jordan "expiring in Game 7 of the NBA Finals" or Tiger Woods "suffering a heart attack as he charge[d] up the 18th on Sunday at Augusta National." Even then, the comparisons fell flat. Undeterred, Bianchi looked for an analog in popular culture. Earnhardt was "John Wayne on a 3,000 pound steel horse, spurs sparkling, guns blazing, kicking up grass and taking names." Or maybe "Elvis before the fried banana sandwiches" or Bruce Springsteen before "he went commercial." Ultimately, to Bianchi, "no other sports figure, no other entertainment figure, no other political figure [came] close to Earnhardt's cult appeal"—only the historical figure of Confederate General Thomas Jonathan "Stonewall" Jackson deserved equal billing with Earnhardt. Jackson, a southern icon central to the cult of the Lost Cause following the Civil War, died as the result of an accident (he was shot by his own troops at the Battle of Chancellorsville, which led to his death from pneumonia) and lost his life doing what he loved. "And the death of both cast a foreboding pall over their people," wrote Bianchi. "The Confederacy never recovered from Jackson's death, and you wonder whether the NASCAR nation ever will be the same now that Earnhardt is gone." Much more than just the nation's "greatest sportsman," Earnhardt was America's "most compelling figure."[11] Overblown and emotional, Bianchi's struggle to contextualize the death of NAS-CAR's greatest champion appears excessive, but it clearly illustrates the human desire to comprehend unexpected tragedy.

Just after Dale Earnhardt fatally struck the wall, journalists, race fans, and Americans of all stripes began to devise narrative story lines about the accident and Earnhardt's life that helped them to understand the NASCAR legend's untimely death. The narratives—and there are hundreds written in poetic form alone—portray the deep grief of mourners (most of whom had never met Earnhardt) who unexpectedly lost their icon. Shocked and in disbelief, fans constructed a narrative arc about Earnhardt's last days that transformed him from the bristly "Intimidator" in the black Chevy into a kind, Christlike figure who sacrificed himself to help others gain the victory in his final race. Brian Williams, then host of the NBC *Nightly News* and a friend of Earnhardt's, perfectly described the postmortem metamorphosis. In an essay for *Time* magazine, Williams wrote that the news media turned Earnhardt into "America's Diana with a pushbroom mustache."[12]

In laying out what became the standard model for understanding narrative in the Western world, the ancient Greek philosopher Aristotle argued that a tragic plot inevitably "gives rise to a change from good fortune to bad fortune, or from bad fortune to good fortune."[13] The stories that emerged after Earnhardt's death did the ancient Greek one better and contained both elements. The driver's death proved tragic, according to one version of the narrative, because he fell so precipitously from the heights of American celebrity and left behind a beautiful wife and family—a clear case of fortunes turning from good to bad. A parallel narrative suggested that Dale's final race exemplified the quality of his character and offered a shining illustration of his redemption. Racing's bad boy was transformed into the Good Shepherd. He became his sport's martyr, the patron saint of NASCAR nation. As Aristotle knew, both plot styles provide catharsis, the emotional purging that helps audience members reconcile the hero's demise.

Southern novelist Ann Patchett, adapting Aristotle to fit the modern South, describes how Dale Earnhardt embodied the "fundamental elements of Southern heroism." From her home in Tennessee, Patchett observes that "it takes a certain amount of storytelling to make a person into a myth, and that's something we've specialized in down here since Davy Crockett first cut his name into a tree. But as any good storyteller knows, the heroes we are most likely to root for are the ones who look like us." The "collective regional affection" for Earnhardt stemmed from the belief that, despite his accomplishment and acclaim, the NASCAR superstar never left the South behind. His roots were there and so were his branches. Southerners, who felt "separate, apart from the country [they] live in," loved Earnhardt because he was "different the way [they] were] different."[14]

Having come of age in the rustic locales of North Carolina and Virginia, NASCAR itself basked in "southern-ness" and became a cultural touchstone for white southern men. By the 1930s, automobiles had spread across the South and reshaped the region's notion of masculinity. "On farms and in the mill towns of the Piedmont," argues Daniel S. Pierce in his insightful history of NASCAR, "the ability to drive became an important step into manhood, much like the ability to shoot a gun, ride a horse, or fight had been in an earlier era." A knack for fixing cars fit comfortably in the tradition, and the "'shade-tree' mechanic developed into an enduring regional icon." Pierce asserts that "the automobile meshed perfectly with the cultural values Piedmont men had retained from their rural Southern roots. Not only could one experience the type of freedom and self-confidence valued in the southern male world through driving around in a car, but one could tap into the wildness, the need for excess, competition, and even violence by driving that car to its very limits, often racing head to head with another 'hell of a fellow.'"[15] White men in the "new South" of steel mills and factory towns tapped into new technologies to perpetuate essential cultural values.

The Good Shepherd

Even before the official announcement of Dale Earnhardt's death, his transformation from Intimidator to selfless shepherd had begun. Coming into the last turn of the 500, Earnhardt stood in third place behind Michael Waltrip and Dale Earnhardt Jr., both of whom raced in cars owned by Dale Earnhardt Industries. Earnhardt Sr., driving for Richard

Childress Racing, uncharacteristically turned his attention from taking the checkered flag to protecting the positions of the leaders by blocking the trailing cars. Earnhardt Sr. held the chasing throng at bay while his protégés sprinted to the finish line. Miraculously, Waltrip won the race, his first trip to victory lane in 462 NASCAR starts. Waltrip's brother Darrell, television commentator and former NASCAR champion, started Earnhardt's transformation by applying a religious gloss to the Intimidator's last act. Taking the heat for his teammates, Earnhardt "shepherd[ed] his flock into victory lane." Beginning with Waltrip's television commentary, Earnhardt stepped aboard the "beatification express"—a trip that defined Earnhardt's legacy and catapulted NASCAR racing into the national consciousness. Moreover, the story provided fans with a ready-made framework to understand Earnhardt's tragic death.[16]

Jeff Alan's treatment of the tragedy, which appeared in the online racing journal *Catchfence*, provides a good sense of what thousands of others believed at the time. "Dale died a Martyr," wrote Alan. "He heroically blocked cars behind him in the last few laps, which allowed his son, Dale, Jr, and Michael Waltrip to battle it out for the win without interference from a pack of angry wolves that were closing in. Dale sacrificed himself so that two, younger drivers piloting cars he himself owned, would have a chance at winning the race that had eluded him until 1998."[17] Michael Waltrip agreed that "a different Dale was racing his car that day. The Intimidator was being the Defender. He was fighting people off for Dale Junior and me. . . . Ultimately, being the Defender was why Dale crashed."[18]

For many journalists and NASCAR fans, the image of Earnhardt-as-shepherd proved irresistible. The biblical metaphor deflected attention from Earnhardt's typically aggressive racing style and elevated his death from an accident to martyrdom. Leaning heavily on the shepherd metaphor, CBS reporter Mark Swanson detected a nearly instantaneous change in Earnhardt, a man who "would have run his mama into the wall on Mother's Day if it meant getting a victory." The once "tough son of a bitch" became "the shepherd. . . . [A] father watching over his son's second-place standing, an owner protecting his driver and longtime peer who had seen victory elude him in every possible way." Earnhardt stood watch until "the hunt for his sheep was over." Turn four at Daytona, in

Swanson's estimation, provided a conclusion "befitting a god."[19] On the pages of *Sporting News*, Lee Spencer told much the same story about Earnhardt blocking "the oncoming assault" to "open the door for Waltrip and Junior to battle for the victory." She, too, witnessed the birth of a new Dale Earnhardt that day. "This wasn't the Dale Earnhardt who said he probably would bump Junior's No. 8 out of the way if the black No. 3 had a chance to win," Spencer noted. "This was the ultimate act of selflessness from a driver who began the season with the deep-seated belief he would win his eighth Winston Cup championship." As it turned out, "that act of selflessness might have cost him his life."[20] Brian Schmitz, a reporter for the *Orlando Sentinel*, likewise witnessed a new Dale Earnhardt who "wanted to make everybody else happy—his wife, his kids and his friends."[21] Even Earnhardt's former crew chief Larry McReynolds commented that "those last 10 laps, I saw such a different Dale Earnhardt. . . . I can't imagine how proud he was to look out his windshield to see his son and his good friend up there" leading the race.[22] For the first time in his career, maybe his life, Dale Earnhardt beamed as he was beaten. Of course, no one could see the look on his face or know his thoughts. By framing his actions within the shepherd metaphor, though, Earnhardt emerged from his fatal pileup like a reformed Grinch whose heart had grown three sizes that day.

Rev. Pat Evans, founder of Racing with Jesus Ministries, which sponsored prerace prayer meetings for NASCAR drivers, put his own spin on the shepherd metaphor and positioned Earnhardt as a contemporary Christ figure. In Evans's telling, Earnhardt controlled the events on the track that afternoon and willingly gave up the victory and his life. Had he wanted to win the race, Earnhardt "would have worked his way around his son and Michael Waltrip using his years of experience. Instead, he gave up the chance to win this coveted event in favor of seeing his boy and his driver get the glory. He thought he was doing a giving thing because of his love for them both." Giving the glory to others, Earnhardt "offered the ultimate expression of love as Jesus said, 'Greater love hath no man than this, that a man lay down his life for his friends.'"[23]

The use of biblical analogues to explain Earnhardt's actions brought attention to the growing relationship between big-time sports and evangelical Christianity. A similar movement had occurred in American politics with the election of born-again Christian conservative George W. Bush in the 2000 election. Bush's call for "compassionate conservatism" had reinvigorated the national conversation about religion and politics. According to *New York Times* columnist Robert Lipsyte, "The current beatification of Dale Earnhardt as a man's man who sacrificed himself to shepherd his flock to the finish line, a hero who in death evoked both John Wayne and Jesus, has presented America with its biggest jolt of sports and evangelical Christianity since Billy Sunday left the Chicago outfield a century ago to become a superstar preacher." Some varieties of Christian theology, especially the "born-again" beliefs popular in the American South, maintain that it is never too late to find redemption through Christ, a lesson emphasized in the Earnhardt-as-shepherd narrative. William J. Baker, author of *Playing with God*, a history of American sports and religion, told Lipsyte that "when good old boys say Dale's in a better place now, they mean it. . . . You go to Heaven because you believe in Jesus, not by your good works. You can live your life like a dog, but be saved at the end. And that's like sport, too. You can win on the last lap."[24] In Earnhardt's case, he won eternal glory by losing on the last lap, but losing for the right reasons. Earnhardt's widow Teresa amplified her husband's affinity for Jesus in "An Open Letter to Fans," which appeared in *USA Today* one week after Dale's death. Allowing fans a glimpse into her feelings about her husband, she vowed to ask "what would Dale do?" when she faced future decisions. Surely, Teresa (and most other American Christians) knew that her husband's name replaced the name of Jesus in that popular evangelical aphorism.[25]

Race fans propagated the shepherd myth as well. On countless websites devoted to Earnhardt's memory, fans like Greg Engle found comfort in the Intimidator's selfless sacrifice down the stretch at Daytona and exhibited a determined "will to believe" in the shepherd imagery. Engle's online letter to a posthumous Earnhardt related his "last memory" of Earnhardt "holding off the compitition [sic] so Michael Waltrip and your son could finish one and two in the Daytona 500. Maybe you could have set yourself up to win, I know you had the talent to, but instead you unselfishly put yourself in a position to allow someone who'd never known it, the thrill of standing in a victory lane."[26] Others memorialized their fallen hero in verse. A month after Earnhardt's death, Timothy Jon Barrett wrote "Seagull Flying Low" with "love and admiration" for his favorite driver. Written from the perspective of Earnhardt behind the wheel, Barrett reminds grieving fans of the driver's inevitable immortality: "I'll surely miss you every one. About that I will not lie./But as long as you remember me—I really didn't die."[27] For Earnhardt fans, the shepherd imagery placed God's imprimatur on the driver's untimely death. Their idol had proven his worth on the racetrack throughout his long career but his final act, protecting his little flock, proved his fealty to God. In giving his life, he had saved his soul. Much like ancient Achilles, Earnhardt's place in the afterlife was ensured by his heroic death.

While the image of Earnhardt as the Good Shepherd filled news columns and comforted grieving fans, some journalists cried foul at the thought of the hard-driving Earnhardt giving quarter to any driver on the track, even his own son. The first reporter to question the developing narrative surrounding Earnhardt's last lap was Monte Dutton, of the *Gaston (Florida) Gazette*. A seasoned journalist who knew his way around a racetrack, Dutton wondered about the sanctification of St. Dale. Irritated by the testimonials elevating Earnhardt toward heaven, Dutton contended that Earnhardt's "greatness does not require us to romanticize his memory." He then took aim at "every glib TV stooge in Florida" who repeated the narrative about Earnhardt clearing a path to victory for his teammates. "That was a lie," Dutton asserted. "A pleasant lie, perhaps, but a lie told to raise Nielsen Ratings, not accurately portray a man. The point at which Earnhardt kept other cars at bay was the point at which Earnhardt figured out he had no chance to win, and that was probably somewhere on the last lap. Earnhardt made a career out of looking out for himself, and that was why he won 34 races at Daytona. A split-second before he left this earth, he was running hard for third place, and that was because third place was the best he could do when he arrived in the turn four of his life."[28] Earnhardt left the world the same way that he lived—charging hard to finish at the top. No last-minute transformations changed his approach.

Earnhardt's son, Dale Jr., supposedly one object of his father's protection at Daytona, was already on the record about his father's utter determination to win. Asked at a press conference if his father would use one of his legendary tricks to knock Dale Jr. out of the lead so that he could claim a victory, Jr. responded without hesitation: "He would do what it took to win."[29] Jr.'s comments echo something that his father had said a couple of years earlier when asked about his desire to keep winning as he got older. "You be leading the race on the last lap and let me be behind you and see," Earnhardt replied. "When drivers get older, they get smarter. They don't forget anything they've ever done. I don't. So I would hate to have me behind me on the last lap and I hadn't won a race all year and his bumper could get to me."[30]

About a month after Earnhardt's death, Robert Lipsyte questioned the "legend of the man in black" as a benevolent figure (which Lipsyte had mentioned in his column the previous month) and wondered why "no one suggest[ed] that Dale Sr. stood to make more money in prizes and eventual sponsorship deals with cars he owned coming in first and second, than in coming in first himself in someone else's car."[31] More befitting a business titan than father figure, Earnhardt's last lap strategy may have stemmed from pecuniary rather than paternal interest. In the long run, the reality of what happened that afternoon in Daytona is much less powerful than the emergence of the image of Earnhardt as the Good Shepherd, Lipsyte concluded. The Intimidator "may be even more compelling as a ghost than he was as a fading, although still competitive, superstar with a racing team of his own."[32] With Earnhardt no longer around to put up an argument, racing fans could shape their icon into whatever image they preferred. What would Dale do? No one could say for sure because there were as many versions of Dale floating around as there were fans with fond memories. From the Intimidator to the Good Shepherd, Earnhardt assumed myriad shapes as he ascended into the Great Beyond.

Before the sun set on the summer of 2001, St. Dale performed one more Daytona miracle. In July, NASCAR returned to Daytona for the Pepsi 400, the first major race on the oval since Earnhardt's death five months earlier. This time, Dale Sr.'s magic propelled his son to victory, a conclusion that provided fans with fresh evidence of the Good Shepherd's power and a fitting final chapter to close the book on Earnhardt's tragic ending. Michael Waltrip saw the hand of Dale at work in the finish at Daytona that day. "Just as I drafted up on Junior's bumper and went to make the pass" on the final lap, "something happened that I can't explain," wrote Waltrip. "Instead of whipping out and going around, I just held the wheel straight and rolled right in behind [Dale Junior]." Waltrip could not understand what he was doing. "What happened? . . . Why didn't I pass him? . . . Who's driving my car here?" Once again, Big E had taken control of the racetrack. Waltrip eventually understood: "I was pushing Dale Junior to the checkered flag, just like he had done for me back in February. Dale told Junior to push me then. Did he just tell me to push Junior?" Despite finishing as the runner-up, Waltrip had never "felt more like a winner."[33] Dale Sr. might not have been on the track, but he was hovering nearby, close enough to make a difference. Some fans reported seeing a cloud shaped like a celestial number three floating above the speedway. And Dale Sr. was not the only one looking in. About six million viewers watched on NBC as Junior won the race, and the network dominated prime time that Saturday night. The hole that had torn through NASCAR's heart began to heal when Junior rolled into Daytona's victory lane, this time with Michael Waltrip in his rearview mirror, all beneath a curiously shaped cloud.[34]

NASCAR to the Promised Land

Earnhardt's death spawned the creation of another NASCAR narrative—this time emphasizing the ascent of stock car racing toward mainstream national popularity. To explain how much NASCAR had changed, Earnhardt was invoked as the last of the originals, a remnant of the old school of racin' (the missing "g" harks back to the good ol' boy drivers who grew up in the red clay of rural Dixie) when competitors swapped paint down the backstretch and settled scores with their fists. Twenty-first-century drivers, on the other hand, appeared corporate and urbane in comparison—"cookie-cutter" drivers who needed "to have as much talent in front of a camera as [they did] behind the wheel."[35] They did not talk or act like southerners and had not grown up tinkering with carburetors and racing down dirt roads for entertainment. Typified by Jeff Gordon, the new generation spread the sport's popularity throughout the country but represented a new NASCAR that was miles away from the world built by the founding fathers of stock car racing in the 1940s and 1950s. One strand of this narrative depicted Earnhardt as a modern-day Moses, able to glimpse but not allowed to enter the Promised Land of the new NASCAR. Earnhardt's death tolled the final bell of the old school and opened the way for the sport's booming popularity. Other features of the narrative wrapped Earnhardt in the Confederate flag and lamented the passage of a unique southern way of life, a twenty-first-century echo of the Lost Cause.

Rick Bragg, a Pulitzer Prize–winning journalist and native of Alabama, portrayed Earnhardt as the link connecting the generations. "He was the bridge between that slick neon world of modern-day drivers who race in exhibitions in Japan and tune their engines with computers, and the men who learned to drive by running whiskey on dirt roads in a time when a man tested his car's electrical system by grabbing a wire to see if it shocked him," wrote Bragg in a front-page story for the *New York Times*. Off the racetrack, Earnhardt stood as a masculine pillar of the old South— rural, independent, resourceful, and competitive. Southerners "loved him because he sounded like them when he talked, because he hunted deer and didn't care who approved, who owned chicken houses and a bass boat, who crawled into that race car on Sundays and ran as if he had stolen something. And when the cameras found him in victory lane, he was just Dale, grinning like the devil."[36] In the week between races, lucky fans might run into Earnhardt at the local Walmart, standing in line like everybody else. It was hard to imagine running into Jeff Gordon or Tony Stewart at the neighborhood grocery. Earnhardt represented "the last of a breed dating back 60 years."[37]

Although he was worth millions of dollars and sat on numerous corporate boards when he died, Dale Earnhardt epitomized democratic America, where success rewarded the ambitious, hardworking, and determined. Down-home and humble, he "was nothing but a working stiff like everybody else, no better and no worse." Ironically, Earnhardt took the lens of sporting success and turned it around. Where Muhammad Ali, Michael Jordan, and others had taken their sports to new levels of global prominence, Earnhardt "brought racin' back to the simple days, when the money was nothin', and the crowds were nothin', and you drove cars fast for the thrill and the checkered flag." This nostalgic connection to the good old days, as noted by Joe Posnanski, ran on the emotion created by generational change: "NASCAR drivers today are, technically, as good and courageous as any of those drivers in the past. They drive their cars to the limit, and they react with superhuman reflexes, and death hovers over them just as it has always hovered over the men who race cars. And always will." But something was different now. Whatever connected Earnhardt to his father's generation (Ralph Earnhardt had been an early stock car champion) and separated him from his son's proved difficult to nail down. After explanation failed, the sportswriter turned to comparison. "Faith Hill sings pretty," wrote Posnanski. "That doesn't make her Patsy Cline." "Jeff Gordon drives fast. That doesn't make him A.J. Foyt." Earnhardt was the "last of the dangerous men" less because the nature of racing had changed than because times had changed.[38] At some point, racin' became racing, a tectonic shift in the sport's landscape that widened the gap between the generations of NASCAR heroes.

NASCAR's popularity had been growing since 1979, when a wild Daytona 500, brimming with fistfights and simmering bad blood, had thrust the sport into national prominence. Tuned in to CBS for the first nationwide broadcast of a 500-mile stock car race, viewers watched Donnie Allison and Cale Yarborough slug each other in the infield while Richard Petty whipped past to win his sixth Daytona 500 title. Historians look back on the 1979 race as the watershed event in NASCAR history. Earnhardt burst onto the race scene that same year, carrying away NASCAR's Rookie of the Year award. Two decades later, at the time of Earnhardt's death, NASCAR stood poised to join the traditional Big Three—baseball, basketball, and football—at the center of American sports television. In fact, the 2001 Daytona 500 was the first event broadcast under a new six-year, $2.4-billion contract among NASCAR, FOX, and NBC. Television executives believed that the sport's most popular driver, Dale Earnhardt, would lure sponsors and viewers to the three dozen broadcasts scheduled that season (twenty-six split between FOX and NBC and ten races on cable-only Turner Sports).[39] The maiden race on FOX proved to be one for the ages and catapulted stock car racing into the forefront of American spectator sports—just not in the way NASCAR (or anyone else) had imagined.

From the moment of impact, Earnhardt's crash moved NASCAR from the sports page to the front page of newspapers across the country, not to mention the covers of *Sports Illustrated, Time,* and *Newsweek.* Coverage of Earnhardt's death certified that NASCAR had outgrown its regional roots and become a national phenomenon, "sanctified by a hero's death."[40] For the sport's "true believers," according to Robert Thompson, professor of media and cultural studies at Syracuse University, "there [was] almost a feeling of the death of Elvis . . . and it will probably bring Nascar into the consciousness of everyone who may have been lagging behind in paying attention." Thompson surmised that Earnhardt became "a martyr for the sport of auto racing" and, moreover, his death proved that auto racing was "a dangerous sport and every now and then really bad things can happen." The inherent danger of racing a car traveling 200 miles per hour made NASCAR a popular topic of conversation and strengthened its claim as an extreme sport.[41]

On the pages of *Time,* Frank Pellegrini posited that Earnhardt's crash could be NASCAR's ticket into the American mainstream, a "blessing draped in black" delivered just at the moment when stock car racing most craved legitimacy. For Americans who had never before considered the sport, the "Earnhardt obituary [made] a sad-but-perfect introduction" to NASCAR. Central casting could not have done it any better: "For Earnhardt, at 49, to die at the top of his sport and the height of his popularity, on NASCAR's biggest stage . . . may be as good, and as poignant, as sport gets, even if sports fans generally like their life-and-death struggles a little more on the metaphorical side." Earnhardt bequeathed his sport "the promo of a lifetime . . . when he hit that wall between the third and fourth turn."[42] No less a voice than Frank Deford, the erudite dean of American literary sportswriters, accorded NASCAR a place at the table in his weekly commentary on National Public Radio. "Although NASCAR may be too loud and tacky, too fast and garish for many of us," he intoned, "it is a perfectly honorable slice of American life and death." In the wake of Earnhardt's death, even "old-line sports fans" who may have harbored a "visceral deep-seated antipathy toward NASCAR" should rightfully place stock car racing within the confines of civilized American sports.[43]

Iconoclastic journalist Hunter S. Thompson, who applied his over-the-top approach to everything from presidential politics to striptease joints to psychedelic drugs, detected in Earnhardt's death the portents of future calamity not just for NASCAR but for American life generally. The day after the accident, Thompson wrote that "people who'd never even watched a NASCAR race were deeply disturbed by [Earnhardt's death], for reasons they couldn't quite explain." Witnessed live in millions of homes, the crash sent "a message, an urgent warning signal that something with a meaning beyond the sums of its parts had gone Wrong & would go Wrong again if something big wasn't cured—not just in racing, but in the machinery of the American nation." Thompson had long railed against the excesses and absurdities of politics and the power-hungry and now he envisioned a public mesmerized by blood lust. The American consumer demanded "blood & guts, bread & Circuses, human brains all over the asphalt." "The people of Rome demanded more & more Death & Cruelty on their Sunday afternoons at the Coliseum," warned Thompson, "until Nobody was left to Sacrifice. They ran out of Victims." Clanging his fire bell in the night, Thompson foretold that the NBA, NFL, and NASCAR would soon run out of victims, too. That fear, he concluded, "is what makes people nervous about the meaning of Dale Earnhardt's death. It is the American Dream run amok. Watch it & weep."[44] The unlikely author of a Monday-morning jeremiad, Hunter Thompson predictably cut against the grain in assessing the death of Dale Earnhardt. His was nearly a lone voice crying in the wilderness.

Fans may have wanted bread and circuses, but they also wanted everything else that was remotely connected to their favorite driver. Earnhardt's death propelled interest in stock car memorabilia to new heights. Earnhardt was recognized as the king of NASCAR merchandising, and sales of items bearing his likeness, name, or signature reached sixty million dollars in the year following his death. Sales skyrocketed in the hours and days after his crash at Daytona and, despite predictions from industry experts, the value of the memorabilia continued to increase. *Antiques & Collecting* magazine compared the craze for Earnhardt collectibles to the flush-faced frenzy that had once surrounded Cabbage Patch dolls, Tickle Me Elmo, Mighty Morphin Power Rangers, Holiday Barbie, Beanie Babies, and Pokémon trading cards—unusual company for a man whose nicknames included "Ironhead" and "The Man in Black."[45] Action

Performance, the company that produced and licensed official Earnhardt products, struggled to meet the demand for t-shirts, photographs, caps, mementoes, car hoods, flags, and just about anything else that could be imprinted with the number three, be painted black, or carry the Intimidator's signature. Three semitruck trailers packed with Action's merchandise traveled to every NASCAR race in 2001. "I look at it like a James Dean or Elvis Presley phenomenon in that it could go on for a long time," predicted Fred Wagenhals, president of Action Performance. J. W. Klassnik, a longtime follower of the memorabilia business, sounded just as rosy about the future: "The fact that [Earnhardt] got killed at the Daytona 500 just increased the myth and legend. As more and more people come into the sport as fans, the legend of Earnhardt will grow."[46] And so would sales. In 2003, Earnhardt memorabilia sold more merchandise than all other NASCAR teams combined.[47]

Mourning Together

To NASCAR fans like Terry Higgins, a bar owner from Hixson, Tennessee, losing Dale Earnhardt was as painful as losing a family member. "You know how sad [Earnhardt's death] made me?" Hixson asked journalist Leigh Montville. Hixson then pointed to a motor home parked outside the Talladega race track. "See those boys on the roof? I love 'em all. One of 'em's my son. If one of those boys fell off right now, broke his neck and died, I wouldn't feel any worse than I do about Dale Earnhardt. And that's the honest-to-God truth." On the night of Earnhardt's death, back home in Hixson, friends and customers poured into Higgins's tavern— dozens of distraught men "howling like hound dogs." The bar became a makeshift memorial when cards and flowers arrived to pay tribute to the fallen driver. Higgins parked his black Chevy Lumina (detailed to mirror Earnhardt's racing car) outside underneath a sign reading, "Honk Three Times for Dale." The three-note salutes rang out all night.[48]

Other memorials sprung up across the country—in Chevy dealerships, on dirt race tracks, in backyards and bedrooms. Just about any place that had a connection to auto racing or the number three soon had a pile of flowers or a handwritten note attached. Daytona Speedway resembled

Kensington Palace after the death of Princess Di, surrounded by flowers and pilgrims, both cast down at the feet of the fallen idol. Mourners flocked to the headquarters of Dale Earnhardt, Inc., in Mooresville, North Carolina, to support the Earnhardt family and share their emotional burdens with like-minded souls. Hardly spontaneous, such impromptu memorials represent "highly orchestrated and self-conscious acts of mourning aimed at expressing, codifying, and ultimately managing grief."[49]

Since ancient times, people have gathered at birth and death sites to pay their respects to loved ones. Technological developments, however, have created new spaces for mourners to gather and commiserate. In 2001, for the first time, more than half (51 percent) of American homes had access to the Internet and nearly every public library of any size provided Web access to patrons.[50] Countless fans created and visited Internet sites dedicated to the memory of Dale Earnhardt. Online communities of mourning emerged in the hours after Earnhardt's death, and fans posted their stories, memories, and condolences. Far-flung race fans did not have to travel to North Carolina or Daytona to gather together. With just a few clicks, mourners could find a shoulder to cry on, read a funny story about Earnhardt, or bask in the accomplishments of number three. Perhaps most importantly, the anonymity of the Internet freed fans from their inhibitions. People too timid to speak in public opened up online, expressing personal feelings for Earnhardt and connecting with others who felt the same way. In addition to notes, letters, and photos, fans dedicated hundreds of poems to the Intimidator.

Few NASCAR fans will be mistaken for Tennyson, but their heartfelt tributes to Earnhardt reveal more than simple admiration for number three. Many of the poems portray Earnhardt as the Good Shepherd and most picture him happily in heaven, pursuing the pole against the immortal souls of other dead racers like Adam Petty, Neil Bonnett, and even Ralph Earnhardt. Dale Earnhardt simply traveled ahead of his fans, showing them the way to eternal happiness in Christian heaven. His celestial repose would someday be theirs. One example, titled "One Quarter-Mile from Heaven," resonated with Earnhardt fans who posted the poem countless times on the Internet:

But forever in our hearts, and in the scheme of things,

We'll picture him circling heaven with black and red wings.

Grinning; telling angels, and even the Creator,

"Look out over there . . . here comes the 'INTIMIDATOR.'"[51]

Even in the afterlife, Earnhardt was not afraid to swap a little paint with the Creator. Fan-poet Timothy Jon Barrett describes how the "Heaven 500" was postponed awaiting Earnhardt's arrival. Barrett nearly equates Earnhardt with the Jesus of born-again Christianity, who just happens to be the Intimidator's number-one fan. In the poem's closing stanza, Jesus reminds Earnhardt and his fans, "There are no losers, on this Heavenly track, this was a welcome home party, for The Man In Black!"[52] Unlike the player in Grantland Rice's famous paean to perseverance, "Alumnus Football," the "One Great Scorer" who came to mark Earnhardt's name did seem concerned with whether he won or lost, not how he played the game.[53]

The poetic narratives go on and on, multiplying in the ether of the Internet. Seemingly every Dale Earnhardt fan has a story about his life or his afterlife that helped them to carry on in the wake of his tragic death. For thousands of years, stories, traditions, and legends have helped humans to understand the vagaries of life and death by turning events into stories. At the turn of the twenty-first century, journalists, NASCAR fans, and Americans of all stripes transformed the events of Dale Earnhardt's death into narratives that both preserved and refashioned the Intimidator. Aristotle could not have imagined how right he was. Whether you grew up in the shadow of the Acropolis or the red clay of Kannapolis, North Carolina, stories of tragic heroes were the fast track to catharsis—and immortality.

To an Athlete Dying Old

Joe DiMaggio, Mickey Mantle, and Ted Williams

Theirs was the trio of odd numbers—five, seven, and nine—that defined baseball in the middle decades of the twentieth century. Number five, Joe DiMaggio of the New York Yankees, inherited center stage from Babe Ruth and patrolled center field at Yankee Stadium from 1936 to 1951. Mickey Mantle, number seven for the Yankees, played one year beside DiMaggio before taking over as the brightest star in the constellation that was New York baseball during the 1950s, a decade in which the Yankees won six World Series titles. Mantle's career outlasted that Yankees dynasty and he retired in 1968, just before the tectonic shift of free agency rearranged the landscape of professional baseball. Number nine in the triumvirate of midcentury stars belonged to Ted Williams, the cranky, confident, larger-than-life left fielder for the Boston Red Sox. Williams's team played in the shadow of the juggernaut Yankees, but his individual accomplishments more than matched up to his pin-striped contemporaries. In the decades after their retirements, five, seven, and nine—DiMaggio, Mantle, and Williams—not only defined athletic excellence but became cultural touchstones, symbols of a bygone era when baseball ruled the sports world and America dominated the globe.

Connected in life by circumstance and accomplishment—on the playing field, at old-timer's games, or as the leading attractions driving the memorabilia craze during the 1980s and 1990s—the three baseball legends remained linked until their deaths at the turn of the twenty-first century (Mantle died in 1995, DiMaggio in 1999, and Williams in 2002). Taken together, their deaths provide a new perspective on how death itself shapes the memories of athletic heroes. Unlike most of the other athletes in this book, DiMaggio, Mantle, and Williams lived for decades after they retired from baseball. During those years, each man stood in the shadow of his former self and perpetually failed to measure up. The inescapable effects of aging widened their waistlines, slowed their gaits, and stooped their shoulders. By the end of the century, DiMaggio, Mantle, and Williams could no longer fit into their uniforms or meet the expectations associated with their famous numbers. Though at one time each had won Housman's proverbial race, each also lived well beyond his laurel crown. Each failed to heed Housman's warning and lived long beyond the erosion of their beauty, skill, and popularity. By granting longevity, the gods had played a nasty trick on the former players. Erstwhile immortals, the players and their reputations shriveled until they became "white-hair'd shadow[s]" of themselves.[1]

DiMaggio, Mantle, and Williams gained their reputations in newspaper columns and newsreels, neither of which delved too deeply into an athlete's personal life. The business of reporters at that time, according to journalist and biographer Richard Ben Cramer, was to "make heroes, to make Larger-Than-Life, to make the Great National Game a drama to hold readers in thrall."[2] And few were better at the job than Grantland Rice who epitomized the "gee-whiz" school of sports journalism during the golden age of sports in the 1920s. Rice consistently praised athletes without acknowledging the darker side of sports. "When a sportswriter stops making heroes out of athletes," he advised, "it's time to get out of the business."[3] Red Smith, who wrote for the *New York Herald Tribune* and later the *New York Times*, upheld the "gee-whiz" tradition through the middle of the century but occasionally tempered his coverage of the athletes with a touch of reality. Smith tried to "preserve a sense of proportion" in his columns without unduly exaggerating "the glory of athletes." He admitted, however, that the "heavy majority of sportswriters, [himself] included, have been and still are guilty of puffing up the people" they wrote about—"Godding up those ballplayers," in the phrase of Stanley Woodward, sports editor at the *Herald Tribune*. Though not every sportswriter portrayed players in the best possible light (Westbrook Pegler was a well-regarded exception), the "godding up" of athletes remained a common feature of sport sections in newspapers throughout the country for the first half of the twentieth century.[4] The sports page reported the action on the field. Postgame exploits in barrooms and bedrooms rarely merited coverage—not because they were unknown, just unwritten. That modus vivendi between athlete and scribe lasted until the 1960s, when an emerging form of reporting, often referred to as "New Journalism," focused on the athlete-as-human-being and tore down the wall of privacy that had shielded an athlete's private life from the public. Rejecting the style of their forebears, a generation of journalists "de-godded" athletic heroes like DiMaggio, Mantle, and Williams, knocking them off the pedestals created by the prior generation of "gee-whiz" practitioners. By the close of the twentieth century, biographers had examined the heroic lives of midcentury baseball stars, assessed their shortcomings, and could not resist, in the cases of DiMaggio and Mantle, placing them back on the pedestal—in effect, "re-godding" the Yankee greats. Williams's story followed a different trajectory. Initially despised by the Boston press and then lionized by John Updike, Williams's final "de-godding" occurred during his dying days and provided a pathetic conclusion to his life story.

5

Reporters like Walter Winchell and *New York Post* columnist Jimmy Cannon certainly knew about DiMaggio's nocturnal ramblings because they often spent the early morning hours together. Many nights, the unlikely trio whiled away the time listening to Winchell's police radio and driving to crime scenes. Hungry for the ballplayer's friendship, Winchell and Cannon kept most of the details in their vest pockets when writing about DiMaggio.[5] Cannon's columns notably helped to construct the nearly impenetrable public persona of the Yankee center fielder. According to historian David Halberstam, Cannon "wrote often and well about DiMaggio and in the process he helped create not just the legend of DiMaggio as the great athlete but, even more significant, DiMaggio as the Hemingway hero, as elegant off the field as on it. Cannon was in awe of his friend, and he lovingly passed that on to his readers. . . . Only the better qualities were worth mentioning, of course—those allowed near the star knew what to write and what not to write."[6] Cannon fell head over heels for the center fielder and, according to Roger Kahn, "courted DiMaggio as if he were a broad."[7] Of course, DiMaggio did shape the template of the Hemingway hero. In *The Old Man and the Sea*, DiMaggio becomes an idol worthy of devotion, if not worship. In one of the book's classic passages, Hemingway's protagonist Santiago reminds his apprentice Manolin to "have faith in the Yankees my son. Think of the great DiMaggio."[8] By the time of the book's publication in 1952, there was virtually no other way to think about the center fielder.

The newspaper coverage at the bookends of DiMaggio's public life illustrates the importance of the press in building the reputation of the Yankee Clipper. In DiMaggio's rookie year of 1936, *New York Telegram* columnist Dan Daniel succinctly placed an Everest of expectations on DiMaggio's shoulders: "Here is the replacement for Babe Ruth."[9] Nearly fifty years after DiMaggio's debut, in the last line of the last column that Red Smith wrote, the columnist channeled Hemingway's Santiago: "I told myself not to worry. Someday there would be another Joe DiMaggio."[10] Reflecting on the relationship between DiMaggio and journalists, Roger Kahn wrote, "the columnists loved [the] big-shouldered character from San Francisco, who played ball with a special, stately grace. DiMaggio's New York press was a long love letter."[11]

But love letters and playing careers have to end. Following his retirement in 1951, DiMaggio, as Halberstam explains, was singularly "devoted to being Joe DiMaggio. He puts himself on exhibit, carefully rationing the number of exposures. He guards his special status carefully, wary of doing anything that might tarnish his special reputation. He tends to avoid all those who might define him in a way other than as he defined himself on the field."[12] Eventually, though, a new generation of reporters revisited DiMaggio's reputation and reported with much less deference than Cannon and his contemporaries. By 1966, fifteen years after his retirement, the cracks in DiMaggio's character widened into fissures when journalist Gay Talese detailed the center fielder's postretirement life in "The Silent Season of a Hero," published in *Esquire* magazine in July 1966. Having worked at the *New York Times*, Talese knew the tradition of "godding up" athletes but he represented a new breed of journalists aiming to dispel myths and expose the feet of clay inside an athlete's cleats.

Talese studied DiMaggio and, ever so gently, pulled back the curtain on the hero and on the process that had sustained his legendary status. The former Yankee, Talese reported, "tries hard to remain as he was—he diets, he takes steam baths, he is careful; and flabby men in the locker rooms of golf clubs sometimes steal peeks at him when he steps out of the shower, observing the tight muscles across his chest, the flat stomach, the long sinewy legs. He has a young man's body, very pale and little hair; his face is dark and lined, however, parched by the sun of several seasons." Although aging, DiMaggio remained "an impressive figure . . . an immortal sports writers called him, and that is how they have written about him and others like him, rarely suggesting that such heroes might ever be prone to the ills of mortal men, carousing, drinking, scheming; to suggest this would destroy the myth, would disillusion small boys, would infuriate rich men who own ball clubs and to whom baseball is a business dedicated to profit. . . . And so the baseball hero must always act the part, must preserve the myth, and none does it better than DiMaggio."[13] Once upon a time, DiMaggio's style and grace had been effortless, even according to sportswriters who presumably knew better.

Merely by describing how hard DiMaggio worked to protect his image, Talese nimbly turned the tables on the aging superstar. When Talese (appearing in the article as an anonymous "man from New York") approached DiMaggio, the journalist was initially rebuffed and then forcefully rebuked. Using, in Robert Lipsyte's phrase, "the grand sweep of fiction to string little facts to tell true stories," Talese included as much detail as possible.[14] "You are invading my rights," DiMaggio told Talese. "I have my privacy; I do not want it violated." Then DiMaggio, "erect and beautifully dressed in his dark suit and white shirt with the gray silk tie and the gleaming silver cuff links," told Talese: "I do not interfere with other people's lives. And I do not expect them to interfere with mine. There are things about my life, personal things, that I refuse to talk about. And even if you asked my brothers, they would be unable to tell you about them because they do not know." At the end of his rope, his voice subdued, DiMaggio made one final appeal. "I'm not great . . . I'm just a man trying to get along."[15] That was Talese's point, too. DiMaggio, desperate to maintain his privacy, had never looked so earthbound as when Talese showed him struggling to protect his public persona. According to one biographer, DiMaggio "came along just as we found the means to peer into our heroes' lives," and we did not always like what we saw. Even though DiMaggio's downfall may have been "an accident of timing," biographer Richard Ben Cramer concluded, "you could say the same about a train wreck."[16] Like Superman without his cape, DiMaggio without his pinstripes could not prevent the disaster. Talese's "Silent Season of a Hero" inspired a generation of journalists to take a fresh look at American heroes, including once-sacrosanct athletes like Joltin' Joe.

More interested in the spade work of reporting than in pushing the boundaries of language or literature, New Journalists believed in immersion reporting, a technique wherein a reporter often spends copious amounts of time with subjects, finding truth in day-to-day activities— "drilling down into the bedrock of ordinary experience." Cultural historian Kasia Brody portrays this new generation as "reporters who, in another era, had worked on a piece for a day or two, now spent up to two months honing them for up-market men's magazines such as *Esquire* or *Playboy*."[17] Talese, for example, used the immersion approach to discover "the fictional current that flows beneath the stream of reality." Whereas New Journalists like Tom Wolfe used extensive dialogue to get inside a character's head, Talese and others pored over the everyday realities of a character's environment to give a full portrait of a subject's life.[18] When Talese wrote about the daily lives of extraordinary characters, he often turned to aging athletes who were struggling with life outside of the spotlight. Joe Louis, Floyd Patterson, and DiMaggio all received the full Talese treatment. In the process of detailing their daily lives, Talese influenced the writing of narrative nonfiction and reshaped the contours of sportswriting. Talese and his journalistic cohort demystified athletic heroes, drawing them down from Mt. Olympus and placing them in the earthly confines of living rooms, kitchens, and neighborhood bars. New Journalists went beyond exposing peccadilloes and personal quirks to contemplate the space between ordinary and extraordinary and the limits of fame.[19]

Talese's innovative style, tagged by protégé David Halberstam as "journalism vérité," meant "staying with his subjects until he caught them in moments of candor, and not as they and their public relations people wanted them defined." Halberstam, speaking from personal experience, noted that "a generation of young reporters, restless with what they were doing and wanting to make their names and expand their horizons, had sat around in America's city rooms dreaming of writing the great American novel. Now they sat around and dreamed about the nonfiction books they would one day write."[20] By the 1980s, biographers trained in the techniques of New Journalism took aim at DiMaggio.

Richard Ben Cramer, a Pulitzer Prize–winning reporter, applied his talents in long-form journalism to the task of setting the record straight about Joe DiMaggio. It took him five years. Proudly sporting a revisionist mindset, Cramer wanted to dig deeper than previous DiMaggio biographers whose work bore a "well-trodden sameness along a few practiced paths" of familiar stories that "Joe approved." This "vast and mostly shallow cover" created a "character who was at once gigantic and flat—there was so little about him that felt human and alive." Cramer longed to get below the surface silence of DiMaggio to unearth the hidden history of the man, not repeat the biographical chestnuts that had been perpetuated for decades.[21]

From the first paragraph of the prologue, Cramer dug in. The book opens on the "last public day" of the great slugger's life, "Joe DiMaggio Day," held at Yankee Stadium on September 27, 1998. DiMaggio was dying of lung cancer, but that news remained private as he returned to New York. The Yankees planned to honor DiMaggio with replicas of nine World Series rings to replace the originals that had been stolen from a hotel room in the 1960s (at least that was the story that DiMaggio had told for years). In characteristic fashion, DiMaggio presented only a façade to Yankee fans. Until the very end, DiMaggio "cultivated the distance that set him apart from every other person of fame. He was revered for his mystery. We cheered him for never giving himself entirely to us." Cramer wanted DiMaggio in his totality, and the closer he got to his subject the smaller DiMaggio appeared. From Cramer's perspective on DiMaggio Day, the hero had become "a sad figure. It wasn't just the effects of age— the way he'd shrunk—that bent old man who took his rings behind home plate and tottered off the field. . . . More to the point, it was his cloak of myth that had shrunk."[22] And for the next five hundred pages of Cramer's book, the cloak kept shrinking.

Joe DiMaggio: The Hero's Life portrays Joe DiMaggio as anything but heroic. The book's most memorable images are not of World Series victories or the high life in Manhattan, but of DiMaggio as the violently possessive husband of Hollywood starlet Marilyn Monroe or as a stooped figure carrying a plastic garbage bag from his Marina home in the hours after the San Francisco earthquake in 1989. The bag—a makeshift tax shelter—held $600,000 in cash. Cramer's DiMaggio was cheap, greedy, and psychotically protective of his fortune.[23] A solitary figure, DiMaggio restricted his inner circle to men who were singularly committed to gratifying every need of the aging hero. DiMaggio never hesitated to end a relationship if he suspected that the former friend had benefitted from Joe's proximity. His judgments were swift, final, and merciless. Because of his unwillingness to participate in the give-and-take of friendship, DiMaggio was not just solitary, but lonely. Even Joe's brother Dominic (who played center field for the Red Sox from 1940 to 1953) avoided attending All-Star games or old-timer's gatherings because Joe would fume and complain that Dominic was trying to steal his limelight. The two brothers, who shared so much, did not speak to each other for years. Cramer concluded that Joe's solitude atop his imaginary Olympus was "his bargain with the hero's life. Day to day, that was surely his doing. Or you could conclude it was just part of the package, from the start—Joe was sufficient to Joe. And no matter what else was going on—for one night, one vote of sportswriters, or through decades, twenty thousand days and nights—or in an earthquake . . . it was his destiny to stand alone."[24] This was not a hero's life that anyone would recognize or envy. In Cramer's hands, according to one reviewer, DiMaggio came off as "a scowling, calculating and sometimes cruel phantom lurking behind the splendid image created more by collective need than by reality."[25]

Despite the public "de-godding" that transformed the "avuncular Mr. Coffee into an avaricious icon" in his final years, sportswriters and biographers returned to the more comfortable terrain of Joltin' Joe's immortality after his death in 1999.[26] Even Richard Ben Cramer, DiMaggio's literary bête noire, could not resist a little "re-godding" in *Joe DiMaggio:*

10. Joe DiMaggio, left, and rookie Mickey Mantle shoulder bats at Ebbets Field in Brooklyn, April 14, 1951, before an exhibition game with the Brooklyn Dodgers. (AP Photo)

The Hero's Life. Although he resented DiMaggio's duplicity in constructing his public persona, Cramer found something genuinely remarkable in DiMaggio's demeanor. At the very moment when Cramer unveiled the cupidity behind the curtain of DiMaggio's last trip to Yankee Stadium, the author simultaneously portrayed DiMaggio's quasi-spiritual power to connect with the cheering throngs. Perched in a luxury suite, "He'd part his hands, throw them open toward the crowd, both at once, so his thanks, his acknowledgment—and more, a whiff of his chrism, some glint of his godhood—would fly from him back to the crowd, to all those thousands standing on the steep tiers, in their shorts, with their beer cups, cheering his name in the midday glare. Joe would say that he was touched by their welcome. But they were the ones who'd feel touched by the hero."[27] Cramer did not record whether virtue fell from the hem of DiMaggio's finely tailored suit, but the biographer deciphered something otherworldly in DiMaggio's performance.

DiMaggio did not just play to the masses, either. In private settings, Joe's presence was just as intoxicating and invited thoughts of immortality: "There was something special about being with DiMag . . . [t]he old DiMag, especially. Because nothing stopped him—not even time. In the army of steamrollers, he was in the lead car. And always would be. And while you were with him it was possible to think all the rules could be cheated—age, frailty, and the flight of fame . . . to hell with death and taxes—he even faced them without a flinch."[28] Stephen Jay Gould, evolutionary biologist and baseball fan extraordinaire, cast aside his hardheaded objectivity when it came to his reverence for DiMaggio and his fifty-six-game hitting streak, "the most extraordinary thing that ever happened in American sports." Gould believed that "DiMaggio activated the greatest and most unattainable dream of all humanity, the hope and chimera of all sages and shamans: he cheated death, at least for a while."[29]

7

When Mickey Mantle reached the Bronx as a nineteen-year-old rookie in 1951, DiMaggio still reigned over center field at the stadium, and his elegant, sophisticated style lit up New York's nightlife. Initially, Mantle, resembling a "refugee from a Ma and Pa Kettle movie," played the towheaded rube, fresh from Oklahoma, waiting in the wings for DiMaggio's graceful departure. Mantle may have been a hayseed but he was flush with potential.[30]

By the mid-1950s, sportswriters determined to "god up" athletes like Mickey Mantle turned to new outlets like *Sports Illustrated* to spread the good word. For example, in a 1957 article titled "All Hail the Hero Mighty Mickey," writer Gerald Holland described how "the Hero was 25 years old and already a legend. By his deeds and by his courageous triumph over his physical handicaps [a series of leg injuries dating back to high school], he was Everybody's dream miraculously come to life. He was being hailed as baseball's alltime superstar. He could do everything: he could run with the speed of a jack rabbit, he could throw strikes to home plate from deep in the outfield: a switch-hitter, he could blast a ball farther than any man who ever lived. He was Elmer the Great, Frank Merriwell and a blond Li'l Abner rolled into one." With television beaming his exploits into homes across the country, Mantle had been seen by more fans in his first few years in the majors than had watched Babe Ruth during his entire career. Mantle's stature—and his accessibility on the small screen—transformed him into a national role model expected to "live every public and private moment in a manner that would dismay a saint." Americans needed Mickey Mantle to be otherworldly, on the field and off. Men approached Mantle at banquets or other gatherings and implored him to live up to their exalted expectations. "We fathers can do only so much, Mickey," said one fellow. "It is up to you to set the example for our kids."[31] Newspapermen were not the only ones who could god up an athlete.

Jimmy Cannon, a nationally syndicated columnist by the 1960s, placed Mantle beside his old pal DiMaggio in the club of transcendent sports stars. Mantle must "be the greatest athlete of these times," Cannon asserted. "He performs on a plateau above ability, on the peaks of mountains no other athlete can scale. In him are the virtues on which competition in sports are founded. The code goes back to antiquity, and the good men have cherished it eternally. It may be insignificant because Mantle lavishes it on a game. But it is rare no matter where it happens, and it exalts the human race."[32] Mantle not only occupied an elevated station with Joe DiMaggio but he also belonged on the mountaintop with Zeus and the other immortals who spawned eternal virtues. Although he probably was not thinking about it at the time, Yankee second baseman Jerry Coleman linked the fleet-footed and often injured Mantle with another ancient, Achilles. Mantle has "the body of a god," Coleman observed. "Only [his] legs are mortal."[33]

On the day his number seven was retired in June 1969, Mantle approached the apotheosis promised to sports immortals. Reporter Maury Allen described how, "for the first time in his life, Mantle seemed to recognize his impact on perfect strangers. He knew his teammates loved, admired, and even worshipped him. He knew fans always cheered his homers. On this day, after eighteen Yankee seasons, he finally accepted and came to understand his stature in their eyes. They saw him as a sort of god among men."[34] That may well have been the case. But Mantle knew better. More than any other modern superstar athlete, Mantle was painfully aware of his own mortality. Mantle's fears of an early grave drove him to succeed on the baseball diamond and pushed him to excess in barrooms and bedrooms throughout his playing career and beyond.

As a child standing beside his grandfather's casket, young Mickey scarcely comprehended mortality but he did realize that his male relatives seemed to be dying at an alarming rate and at early ages. The "Mantle curse" took his uncles and then his father Mutt, who was diagnosed with Hodgkin's disease while Mickey recuperated in the hospital after an outfield collision with DiMaggio in the 1951 World Series. The nineteen-year-old Mantle could read the writing on the wall. He later recalled that those deaths "[molded] my belief that I would die young. I lost my grandfather, my father and two uncles, all to Hodgkin's disease. None of them lived beyond the age of forty-one. I took it for granted that this would be my fate; it took all the Mantle men. Once I mentioned it for the first time in an interview, it became a part of my permanent record. I'm surprised that it didn't turn up on my bubble gum cards."[35] Never able to shake his fear of death, Mantle was determined to wring every drop from the years that he had. No night was too late, no drink was too many, no woman off limits. Once, after Mickey arrived late at the ballpark following a drinking spree, Yankee right fielder Hank Bauer lectured his hungover teammate on the need to take care of his body and modify his lifestyle. Mantle responded, "My father died young. . . . I'm not going to be cheated."[36] With the shadow of mortality never far away, Mantle mastered the lush life.

If Joe DiMaggio lost favor due to his staunch unwillingness to loosen up, Mickey Mantle's reputation fell prey to his long years of carousing—plus a former teammate who broke baseball's primary commandment, "what happens in the locker room, stays in the locker room." Jim Bouton, a Yankee pitcher in the mid-1960s, assumed the garb of a New Journalist when he depicted the gritty details of life in the major leagues in *Ball Four*, his first-person account of the 1969 season. Bouton stripped away the myths and mysteries that separated the locker room from the world outside. The book portrayed professional baseball players as puerile postadolescent boys addicted to amphetamines, sex, and practical jokes. Mantle, Bouton's teammate for seven seasons, garnered more than his share of attention from the author, the press, and readers. Bouton's descriptions of Mantle's behavior would hardly raise an eyebrow today but in 1970 fans were shocked by the book's revelations. It was one thing to show Mantle commanding a late-night expedition to the roof of the Shoreham Hotel to peer at stewardesses through open windows, but quite another when Bouton questioned Mantle's character and his dedication to base-ball. Mantle "pushed little kids aside when they wanted his autograph," humiliated reporters, and "refused to sign baseballs in the clubhouse before the games." Bouton blamed Mantle's nightlife for the long string of injuries that dogged him throughout his career. "I often wondered," Bouton wrote, "if [Mantle] might have healed quicker if he'd been sleeping more and loosening up with the boys at the bar less." Mantle appeared out of control, unable to keep his drinking from affecting his performance on the field. Bouton recounted one game in which Mantle ("hung over out of his mind") was called to pinch hit. After staggering to the plate, Mantle smashed a tape-measure home run to left field. Squinting through blood-shot eyes, Mantle gazed at the grandstand and muttered, "Those people don't know how tough that really was." If anything heroic still clung to Mantle, it was not Bouton's fault.[37] *Ball Four* ended up on the best-seller list and the book marked the end of the "uncritically adoring view the public had of" Mantle. Driven from Mt. Olympus, Mantle became "someone who surfaced for a few weeks each spring to stand around for several hours in his old uniform and then to carouse at night."[38]

Immediately following the book's release, Mantle's supporters flocked to his defense. Yankee Joe Pepitone responded: "I've seen Mickey break down and cry because he thought he wasn't doing enough for the team. He gives eight hundred percent. He had an image and I don't think Jim [Bouton] should have torn it down like that. It wasn't necessary to say those things. The kids will read all that about the guy they looked up to. What will they think?"[39] Sportswriters, led by Dick Young of the *New York Daily News*, circled the wagons to preserve the myth of Mickey Mantle by launching a blistering ad hominem attack on Bouton. Bouton was a social outcast, embittered by his own experience in baseball. Holding to the adage that one cheap shot deserves another, Young even accused Bou-ton of being a bad tipper.

Condemnation of Bouton was far from universal, however. David Halberstam, reviewing *Ball Four* in *Harper's* magazine, called the myth-makers on the carpet and singled out Young as the self-appointed "arbiter of what is right to tell . . . what's good for you to hear . . . [and] what should remain at the press-club bar." After all, sportswriters had created the myths, washing out an athlete's "darker side" and accentuating the positive. Young feared that Bouton's ballplayers would "become what they are, not larger than life, but perhaps, if anything, a little smaller."[40]

Mickey Mantle had less to lose from critical biographers because he had been much less assiduous in shaping his legacy than the enigmatic DiMaggio. Tony Castro's well-crafted and insightful biography of Mantle explained that "unlike cultural icons such as Elvis, Marilyn, and JFK, Mickey had the hero's 'misfortune' of not dying young—although he always thought he would—and had to be examined in middle age and as an older man. Although his myth aged well, Mickey did not." Mantle's alcoholism left him a "broken-down drunk," incapable of maintaining relationships even with his children.[41] To earn a living and find a good time, Mantle became the stereotypical ex-jock willing to trade on his name for a few dollars and some attention. In one instance, Mantle and former teammate Whitey Ford visited trotting tracks where the aging athletes signed autographs and raced sulkies. Mickey (not to mention Whitey) had become, in the words of biographer David Falkner, "yesterday's hero willing to make a spectacle of himself for some needed extra cash."[42]

The New Journalists did not reorient the reputations of DiMaggio and Mantle without help. Father Time got his digs in as well. American heroes, as a class, are young, strong, virile, and fearless. Aging populations like the baby boomers who cut their teeth watching Mickey Mantle on television turned to new heroes or tried to entomb past heroes in the fossilized amber of memory. But Mantle never receded completely from the public eye, and the reality of a middle-aged "immortal" proved difficult for sports fans to accept. Simply by growing old, he destroyed the myth of immortality he had once symbolized. Mantle's later life turned out even more disastrous. Living in Dallas after his retirement, Mantle was relatively isolated from his fame, and not by choice. "It was like Mickey Mantle was dead," said the former slugger. "It was weird. I'm thinking, 'Geeze, what did I do?' It seemed nobody cared what I was doing." Without question, many who met Mantle during this period may well have wished that he *had* died. When Jickey Harwell, a golf professional in Dallas, encountered Mantle in the early 1970s, the former demigod was mostly clay feet. "I was excited beyond belief because Mickey Mantle had been my hero growing up. . . . So can you imagine my disappointment when Mickey arrived drunk and not very friendly either. We were all taken aback. *This* was Mickey Mantle? *This* was the guy who had been our hero?" Mantle recognized the magnitude of his fall from grace and felt humbled, if not chastened. On one occasion during the 1980s, Mantle tripped into a gutter outside the St. Moritz Hotel in New York. "A helluva place for America's hero, ain't it?" Mantle remarked to no one in particular.[43]

But Mickey did not stay in the gutter forever. The rehabilitation of Mantle's reputation began in 1994 when he publicly admitted his alcoholism, checked into the Betty Ford Center, and detailed the personal and family problems caused by his unconscionable behavior. Mantle chose the pages of *Sports Illustrated* to tell his version of the story. Beset with memory loss and anxiety attacks, Mantle confessed that "it got to the point where I was worrying so much about everything—what was happening to my memory, how awful my body felt, how I hadn't been a good husband or a good father—that I was even afraid to be alone in the house. I'd ask my youngest son, Danny, to please stay at home with me. And there were times when I locked myself in my bedroom to feel safe." Mantle hesitated to enter a therapy program because he did not want to open up about his feelings and feared that he "was going to cry in front of strangers" and that people would lose respect for him. He believed that "Mickey Mantle shouldn't cry."[44] Humbled by the recognition of his weaknesses, Mantle sought forgiveness and understanding from the American public. This time the aging superstar was not caught with his pants down by a New Journalist; he chose to tell his story as part of his personal therapy and managed simultaneously to resuscitate his reputation.

In the months before his death in 1995, Mantle once again became a media sensation as he struggled against end-stage liver disease and received a controversial liver transplant. The press rushed to the Baylor University Medical Center in Dallas shortly after doctors announced that

Mantle needed a transplant. Jennifer Coleman, vice president of public affairs for the hospital system, had never seen anything like it. "I have been here 15 years, and have handled stories ranging from the exhumation of Lee Harvey Oswald, to celebrity patients," she said. "This case has probably generated the biggest press crush."[45] Doctors, ethicists, and journalists questioned whether an alcoholic like Mantle deserved a transplant at all. Dr. Mark Siegler, the director of the University of Chicago's clinical ethics program, argued that Mantle was "a real American hero" and that "we have to give deference to the rare heroes in American life. . . . We don't have enough of these people in America, and when one comes along, we have got to take them with all their warts and failures and treat them differently."[46] The doctors at Baylor and the United Network for Organ Sharing had followed their selection protocol in choosing Mantle, but controversy surrounded his transplant in June 1995. For many who had loved ones waiting for similar transplants, Mantle had stolen a liver from a worthier recipient. One letter to the editor in *The Dallas Morning News* decried Mantle's vault to the top of the transplant list: "As a volunteer at Children's Medical Center, I am aware of the agonizing wait the children with diseased livers experience seeking a transplant donor. That Mickey Mantle's deteriorating liver should propel him to the top of the list for a liver transplant is deplorable. My sympathy and compassion are for those with diseased livers due to hepatitis, viral infections, etc., not substance abuse, i.e. alcohol, who are moved down on the list while celebrities such as a Mickey Mantle . . . are given priority. Perhaps one should not be surprised. After all, the name is what counts! Meanwhile, the 'real' heroes keep waiting."[47] Mantle's death from cancer just two months after the transplant brought little consolation to either side in the debate. Following Mantle's death, the task of returning Mantle to the ranks of the immortals commenced in earnest.

At Mantle's funeral, broadcaster Bob Costas introduced a theme that was repeated continuously in the following weeks: Mantle was the supernal athlete who symbolized an era of ascendency for baseball that would never be repeated. The "re-godding" of Mantle found its urtext in Costas's eulogy. Mickey, he recalled, was "always too honest to regard himself as some kind of deity" (apparently the question came up) but he was the "baseball hero" for whom Costas's generation built a shrine and kept a candle glowing. Simply stated, Mantle was "the most compelling baseball hero of our lifetime." Even more than that, he was "our symbol of baseball at a time when the game meant something that it perhaps no longer does." Costas's reverence for Mantle transcended "objective fact." As a young man Costas thought Mantle was so gifted that even God would want his autograph. Costas imagined that God would reserve a special corner of heaven where Mantle "can run again. Where he can play practical jokes on his teammates and smile that boyish smile, 'cause God knows no one's perfect. And God knows there something special about heroes."[48] Mickey was not gone forever; he had merely relocated to an eternal spring training where he could flex his muscles and regain the glory of his youth, back when he *was* immortal. Heaven was not a cornfield in Iowa, it was center field at Yankee Stadium in the 1950s.

In the days following Mantle's death, *Sports Illustrated* writer Richard Hoffer struggled to explain the viselike grip that Mantle had on the generation of boys that came of age in the 1950s and 1960s. For these baby boomers, Mantle was "the guy, has been the guy, will be the guy." Defining just what it meant to be "the guy," Hoffer related an example that bordered on biblical. "A woman beseeches Mantle," wrote Hoffer, "to surprise her husband. Mantle materializes at some cocktail party, introductions are made, and the husband weeps in the presence of such fantasy made flesh." In this case, "the guy" possessed unique powers to invoke heartfelt adoration and transport middle-aged men back to their boyhoods. Mantle's midlife problems may have scarred family and friends but they could not sully Hoffer's memories of the Mick: "Still, looking at the slightly uplifted square jaw [on the cover of that week's magazine], all we see is America's romance with boldness, its celebration of muscle, a continent's comfort in power during a time when might did make right." Lest anyone should discount Mantle's place in the cosmos, Hoffer ramped up the dewy-eyed nostalgia: "Mantle was the last great player on the last great team in the last great century."[49] Of course, Hoffer mourned for more than Mantle—Mantle's demise marked the end of an era and sent shivers of mortality down the spines of aging baby boomers. Staring at Mantle on the cover of *Sports Illustrated*, Hoffer saw his own reflection.

Mantle's biographers likewise used the events and epiphanies of his final weeks to revive his immortality. Maury Allen suggested that as Mantle struggled to die with some measure of dignity, the former slugger ironically caught sight of his own immortality. As his life ebbed away, Mantle "finally knew, finally recognized and appreciated, his own stature in American life. It didn't change him one whit. He wouldn't tolerate frauds or phonies in his life. It just wasn't his style. As he came to recognize the scope of his fame, his significance to the American scene, his own immortality, he was more tolerant of the hero-worshipping attitude of fans."[50] Seeking the proper context to understand Mantle's life and death, biographer Tony Castro placed Mickey in the company of Elvis Presley and Marilyn Monroe: "a cultural symbol whose life can now be made into anything with impunity . . . a reflection of the public's mass fears and aspirations. . . . Mantle, Elvis, and Marilyn alike have evolved into a collection of cultural deities—modern-day equivalents of the Greek gods, who were immortal but shared the characteristics of the human beings who worshipped them."[51] Biographer David Falkner characterized Mantle's final days in biblical terms. Mantle proved "as heroic in the manner of his dying as he ever was in his greatest seasons on the field." Mantle's power only grew with his demise, eventually redeeming his reputation and more. When Mantle "left the game," Falkner wrote, "he left it more like a prodigal son than like an old ballplayer put out to pasture. He came back to us larger than ever, a memory we needed to heal *our* wounds. Then we learned just how deep his own wounds went, and like the prodigal son who returned or the blinded king who had finally seen, he became a wholly different kind of hero at the end."[52] Wholly different, perhaps, but not unrecognizable—one who returned to his people with the power to heal their wounds in spite of his own. Now that is immortality.

Bill Liederman, one of the owners of Mickey Mantle's namesake restaurant in Manhattan, claimed that after Mickey's death, his spirit continued to haunt his old stomping grounds. Despite personal irreligion, Liederman believed in the spirit of Mickey Mantle if nothing else. "The presence of Mickey just hangs over [the restaurant]. You can feel it. You can see it. . . . [I]n some strange way I think people understand all this when they come in here—about Mickey's presence and all, about the fact that nothing really has changed [since his death]. Mickey will always be a part of this place." To Liederman, Mickey Mantle was "like Elvis and John Lennon, bigger in death than he ever was in life."[53] Lumping Mantle in with the Beatle who once claimed to have been more popular than Jesus may have seemed apropos to the restaurateur. If given the choice, though, Mantle might have preferred to spend eternity alongside fellow immortal Marilyn Monroe.

9

Perhaps the last word on the immortality of American athletes in the twentieth century rightfully belongs to Ted Williams. Although "the Boston press waged a twenty-year war" with the antagonistic Williams, he was rewarded with an unparalleled "godding up" in an elegiac essay by novelist John Updike in 1960.[54] By the time of his death in 2002, however, Williams had been "de-godded" in the most vicious and public manner possible—by his son John Henry's deranged quest to have his father's remains preserved cryogenically.

In 1960, on the pages of the *New Yorker*, John Updike captured the surly sublimity of Ted Williams as the Red Sox left fielder retired from baseball. Updike's essay more than made up for any praise that had been withheld by reporters during Williams's career in Boston. After attending Williams's last game at Fenway Park, the twenty-eight-year-old Updike wrote what many consider to be the finest essay ever written about baseball, "Hub Fans Bid Kid Adieu." The essay is best remembered for Updike's eloquent account of Williams's refusal to tip his cap to the fans after hitting a home run in the last at-bat of his career. Throughout the essay, Updike situated the slugger among characters from mythology and world literature. In keeping such company, Williams transcended the bounds of time and entered the never-ending "present tense" accorded to the literary characters who fill the pages of Updike's novels and short stories.[55]

Right off the bat, Updike established the context of Williams's career. He wrote that the relationship between the longtime Red Sox star and the residents of Boston ("no mere summer romance . . . [but] a marriage") comprised three stages: "Youth, Maturity, and Age; or Thesis, Antithesis, and Synthesis; or Jason, Achilles, and Nestor." The use of capital letters effectively plucked Williams from his daily surroundings (the grass, leather gloves, and wooden bats) and turned him into a timeless expression of the human condition ("Youth, Maturity, and Age"). Updike's hero belongs in the dialectical process preached by Hegel and Marx. Hits, runs, and errors merely hinted at Williams's greatness, so the diamond got left behind and Updike wrote Williams into the primary metaphor describing the history of the modern world. Not bad for a skinny kid from San Diego.[56]

But there is more. Updike, a "Williams partisan," compared the outfielder to the legends of the ancient world, rather than his pedestrian contemporaries like Mickey Mantle, Rocky Colavito, and Al Kaline, whose "inconsistency . . . served to make Williams appear all the more singular." Williams resided more comfortably in the mythologies of ancient Greece with Jason, Nestor, and Achilles at his side. Sometimes even the ancients did not measure up. Achilles, "the hero of incomparable prowess and beauty who nevertheless was to be found sulking in his tent while the Trojans (mostly Yankees) fought through to the ships," gained as much fame for his vulnerability as his beauty. Unprotected at the heel, Achilles fell prey to mortality. The knock against Ted Williams had been his lackluster performance in important games (he hit only .200 in the 1946 World Series against the St. Louis Cardinals). Updike dismissed Williams's "Achilles's heel" in scientific fashion, noting that "a mass of statistics can be set showing that day in and day out [Williams] was no slouch in the clutch." Achilles may have been good in his day, but he was no Ted Williams.[57]

Updike next turned to ancient Christianity to find a worthy equivalent to the retiring slugger. As a freshly minted major leaguer at age twenty ("the young bridegroom [who] came out of the West"), Williams was the "child who spake as a God." Williams's unexpected wisdom sparked his rocky relationship with the Boston press; those "dowagers of local journalism" who found themselves "rebuked" simply did not understand who it was that walked in their midst. It does not take a biblical scholar to see the allusions to Christ in Updike's language—both Williams and Christ were misunderstood by their contemporaries but overcame the challenges of scribes and Pharisees to reign triumphant. The only thing missing was Ted Williams casting the money changers out of Fenway Park.[58] The

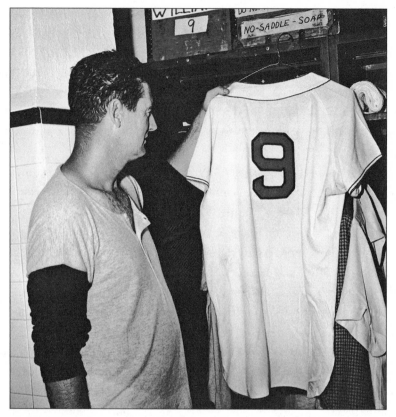

11. Ted Williams hangs up his shirt with number nine on it for the last time in the dressing room at Fenway Park in Boston, September 28, 1960. (AP Photo)

beatification reached its pinnacle in Updike's unparalleled rendering of Williams's final trip around the bases. The scene is an American classic: the up-and-coming superstar writer describing the swan-song swing of his childhood hero. And the prose proved worthy of the moment:

> Like a feather caught in a vortex, Williams ran around the square of bases at the center of our beseeching screaming. He ran as he always ran out home runs—hurriedly, unsmiling, head down, as if our praise were a storm of rain to get out of. He didn't tip his cap. Though we thumped, wept, and chanted "We want Ted" for minutes after he hid in the dugout,

he did not come back. Our noise for some seconds passed beyond excitement into a kind of immense open anguish, a wailing, a cry to be saved.
But immortality is nontransferable. The papers said that the other players, and even the umpires on the field, begged him to come out and
acknowledge us in some way, but he never had and did not now. Gods
do not answer letters.[59]

The Good Ted giveth and the Good Ted taketh away. Now immortal—and
unreachable in his corner of the universe and the dugout—Ted Williams
was a god, and John Updike wrote the scripture that verified it.

Williams lived for more than forty years after Updike immortalized
him. In the winding-up scenes of his life, Williams was once again caught
like a feather in a vortex, but this storm of events proved calamitous.
Guided by his son John Henry, the elderly Ted Williams limped across
the public stage in his final years and became a national laughingstock
when John Henry turned to the sham of cryogenic science to preserve
his father's remains. The body of the "Splendid Splinter" may have been
preserved but his reputation and legacy took a posthumous pummeling.

In 2002, an aged, cadaverous Williams made his final public appearance at the induction ceremony for the Hitters Hall of Fame, an auxil-
iary of the Ted Williams Museum in Hernando, Florida.[60] The event felt
more funereal than celebratory, however, as everyone in attendance recognized that Williams was at death's door. At one point, former teammate Elden Auker bent down and gently kissed Williams's forehead in a
touching farewell. Writer Leigh Montville described the scene: "The face
of the man in the wheelchair hardly resembled the face on the lids from
the Dixie Cups, the covers of the *Life* magazines, the special edition litho-
graphs all the collectors owned. The drawn skin was almost transparent.
The gray hair was a lifeless winter grass. The eyes were unfocused. A
tracheotomy tube was stuck in Ted Williams's throat." Older ballplayers
who had known Williams in his prime broke down, tearfully cursing the
agony of aging. Those seeing Williams for the first time "simply stared at
the sadness as if it were a traffic accident."[61] The years had defeated the
muscles, the brawn, and the incomparable vision of this paragon of manliness; the hitter, hunter, and fisherman could no longer stand, holler, or

see. For a man obsessed with maintaining his privacy, this public display of frailty must have stung bitterly. This was not Ted Williams. The man in the wheelchair was Williams's specter—sent from the gods to torment his final days and to force others to confront the reality of death. The man was no longer "The Kid." Williams's once dark, vibrant curls had turned to lifeless winter grass, crowned not by a laurel wreath, but a cheap hat to shade him from the Florida sun.

While Ted Williams's life ebbed away, John Henry searched desperately for a way to ensure that his father would live forever. The much-maligned John Henry deserved most of the scorn directed at him, but his quest to deny his father's mortality was understandable, if misguided. John Henry decided to have his father frozen—in space, if not in time. Using the techniques of cryonics pioneered by the Alcor Life Extension Foundation in Scottsdale, Arizona, the body of "the greatest hitter who ever lived" would be "drained of fluids, refilled with antifreeze solution, frozen, placed in a refrigerated cylinder in Scottsdale, and left there in the long-shot hope that generations from now science would be able to fix and replace the organ and body parts that had failed. Life after death. John Henry actually was taking a shot at it with his father."[62] John Henry envisioned that, one day soon, there would be any number of "little Ted Williams's running around."[63] Not only did John Henry hope to make some money selling his father's DNA, he wanted to ensure that a revivified form of Ted Williams would be around forever—always the Splendid Splinter, the picture of health and vitality.

After Ted Williams died on July 5, 2002, John Henry put his scheme into action despite the protests of his half-sister, Bobby-Jo. John Henry secured his father's remains and shipped them to Scottsdale where a team from Alcor prepared Williams's body for long-term suspension in containers of liquid nitrogen. Doctors decapitated Williams (euphemistically referred to as "neuroseparation" by Alcor) and placed his body and head in separate containers. By the end of the process, as Tom Verducci of *Sports Illustrated* reported, "[Williams's] head ha[d] been shaved, drilled with holes, accidentally cracked as many as 10 times and moved among three receptacles."[64] News of this gruesome process sparked a national discussion that generally condemned John Henry's behavior and turned

Ted Williams's final resting place into the punch line of countless dreadful jokes.

Rick Reilly, back-page columnist for *Sports Illustrated*, got some easy chuckles at Williams's expense. In an article titled "Chillin' with the Splinter," Reilly savaged Alcor Life Extension and took a few jabs at Williams. Noting that the freezing process lowered body temperature to nearly –200°C, Reilly recalled Williams's frosty relationship with the press in quipping that "some old sportswriters will tell you that is just a little warmer than Williams was with them." The liquid nitrogen solution turned Williams into an eternal member of the "Boston Blue Sox." Reilly then considered the ironic position of Williams's repose: "Williams, one of the greatest big-game fishermen ever, is hanging upside down until his next life cycle begins. Somewhere a whole lot of marlin are giggling."[65] The marlin were not laughing alone. In Bisbee, Arizona, about two hundred miles southeast of Scottsdale, the minor league Copper Kings baseball team celebrated "Ted Williams Night" by giving popsicles to the first five hundred fans through the gates.[66]

Williams's experiment with cryonics tarnished the reputation he had built as a baseball star, sportsman, and public figure. "Ted was a man of enormous self-respect," Williams's longtime friend Arthur Hamon remarked. "His legacy is being compromised."[67] The image of his head floating in a bubbling solution somewhere in Arizona reminded everyone that Ted Williams was as mortal as the rest of humanity. Yet many refused to believe, including his biographer Leigh Montville. Williams's head may have been "frozen in some . . . steel can, but his life is frozen in memory and daydream, recollection and tall tale. He did not hesitate often on his walk across this American landscape. He was Ted Williams." And Montville was determined to keep him that way: "His face has never changed. He is in the finish of a swing, his eyes looking upward at the certain home run he has just hit. (To rightfield.) He is still young and perfect and indomitable, able to do any damn thing he wants to do. And I am still ten years old."[68]

The cryogenic version of immortality was never what fans wanted. They long for the Ted Williams of 1941 because fans want to recapture the 1941 version of themselves. Williams's frozen head is a bizarre and macabre reminder of his mortality and ensures that his final years will not be framed in heroic glory. Athletic heroes are allowed to fight against that dying light, just not in front of their fans. When it comes to posthumous integrity, maybe it is better to roll over into an early grave than be rolled out on a stage as a shadow of your former self. Just ask Ted Williams. Or Mickey Mantle. Or Joe DiMaggio.[69]

In many ways, the athletes analyzed in this book followed Achilles's ancient path toward immortality. Although Benny Paret and Lane Frost did not choose to die young, they did consciously choose to play dangerous games where glory and fame share the field with injury and death. The unfulfilled potential and unanswerable questions that accompany the deaths of young athletes ensure that their legends, like Achilles's, will never die. Or as Philadelphia Eagles linebacker Tim Rossovich described his quest for glory on the football field: "Many times when I'm walking on the beach, I think that I'd like to be in the Super Bowl and be playing middle linebacker and make every tackle in the game. But my final tackle would be a game-saving tackle. And making it I would die and go to heaven and live in happiness for eternity."[70]

.   .   .

Not all immortalities are created equal. Although Achilles won eternal glory and muse-inspired poetry, one of his contemporary Greeks, Tithonos, did not have nearly the same luck after being dipped in the waters of eternal life. Tithonos, described in the *Iliad* as the son of Laomedon and brother of Priam, often spent the night with Eos until the goddess of the dawn rose "up from bed by her lordly mate Tithonus" and brought "light to immortal gods and mortal men."[71]

Smitten with the mortal Tithonos, Eos hastily appealed to Zeus to make her lover "be immortal and live forever." Zeus acceded to her wish; however, as the *Homeric Hymn to Aphrodite* records, "Foolish mistress Eos did not think in her mind to ask for youth and to scrape painful old age from him." Tithonos would live forever, but not in youthful beauty and vigor. Unlike Ganymede, who remained eternally young, Tithonos was destined to age forever. While he remained young and virile, Tithonos and Eos delighted in each other. But as the years piled on Tithonos, Eos saw him in a much different light. "When the first grey hairs flowed down from his beautiful head and noble chin," the hymn reveals, "then indeed did queenly Eos keep away from his bed." When Tithonos entered middle age, Eos faithfully cared for her aging, erstwhile lover by plying him with ambrosia and "keeping him in her great halls." As middle age became "hateful old age" and Tithonos lost control of his limbs, Eos could take no more. Unwilling to serve her eternally aging lover, the goddess "put him away in a chamber and shut the gleaming doors. There his voice flows on unceasingly and there is no strength at all as there once was in his flexible limbs." Eos's dream had become Tithonos's nightmare. Later, the immortal Aphrodite recognized the implications for her own mortal lover Anchises:

> But I would not choose such a fate for you [Anchises] among the immor-
> tals, to be immortal and to live forever. But if, remaining, as you are now
> in form and figure, you could live on and be called my husband, then
> grief would not enfold my wise heart. But soon now pitiless old age will
> enfold you, the leveller which, in the end, stands beside men, deadly,
> wearying, hated even by the gods.

In short, do not be like Tithonos.[72]

Tithonos has not been completely forgotten, however. In the middle of the nineteenth century, Tennyson poetically captured the plight of Tithonus (using the Roman variant) and the curse of eternal aging. All too familiar with the aging process, Tithonus laments his long life and envies the mortal death that had once seemed so cruel:

> The woods decay, the woods decay and fall,
> The vapours weep their burthen to the ground,
> Man comes and tills the field and lies beneath,
> And after many a summer dies the swan.
> Me only cruel immortality
> Consumes; I wither slowly in thine arms,
> Here at the quiet limit of the world,
> A white-hair'd shadow roaming like a dream
> The ever-silent spaces of the East,
> Far-folded mists, and gleaming halls of morn.
> . . . .

To dwell in presence of immortal youth,
Immortal age beside immortal youth,

. . . .

Coldly thy rosy shadows bathe me, cold
Are all thy lights, and cold my wrinkled feet
Upon thy glimmering thresholds, when the steam
Floats up from those dim fields about the homes
Of happy men that have the power to die,
And grassy barrows of the happier dead.
Release me, and restore me to the ground.[73]

Tithonus's pleadings prove useless—he knows that "the Gods themselves cannot recall their gifts." Perhaps the lesson is to be careful what you ask for, or at least be precise.

To be sure, all immortalities are not created equal—even in the mythic realms of ancient Greece. In choosing heroic death, Achilles acquires a transcendent glory that ensures the immortality of his story, if not his physical body. Tithonos, on the other hand, agrees to physical immortality but is left alone to age, decay, and crumble. Although it would be unwise to draw too strong a parallel between these ancient Greek myths and our contemporary athletic culture, the paradoxical fates of Achilles and Tithonus reverberate throughout the book, linking life, death, and heroism across the millennia. If the quest is athletic immortality, then maybe Lou Gehrig *was* the luckiest of all.

Notes | Selected Bibliography | Index

Notes

Introduction

1. Gregory Nagy, *The Ancient Greek Hero in 24 Hours* (Cambridge, MA: Belknap Press, 2013), 9–10, italics in original. For more on the cult of the hero and its relationship to immortality in ancient Greece, consult David Lunt, "Athletes, Heroes, and the Quest for Immortality in Ancient Greece" (PhD diss., Pennsylvania State Univ., 2010), especially chapters 1 and 2. A fascinating modern retelling of the *Iliad* is Madeline Miller, *The Song of Achilles: A Novel* (New York: Ecco, 2012).

2. This translation by Gregory Nagy appears in Nagy, *Ancient Greek Hero*, 23.

3. A. E. Housman, "To an Athlete Dying Young," in *A Shropshire Lad* (Portland, ME: Thomas B. Mosher, 1906), 26–27.

4. Norman Page, *A. E. Housman: A Critical Biography* (London: Macmillan Press, 1983), 42, 87, quote appears on 192.

5. Simon Barnes, *The Meaning of Sport* (London: Short Books, 2006), 305–6.

6. Garry Wills, *Reagan's America* (Garden City, NY: Doubleday, 1987), 129.

7. Quoted in Ian Marquand, "Covering America's Heroes," *Quill* 89, no. 7 (2001): 13.

8. Margaret Atwood, *In Search of Alias Grace* (Ottawa: Univ. of Ottawa Press, 1997), 39.

9. Erika Doss, *Memorial Mania: Public Feeling in America* (Chicago: Univ. of Chicago Press, 2010), 98.

10. Drew Gilpin Faust, *This Republic of Suffering: Death and the American Civil War* (New York: Alfred A. Knopf, 2008), 269.

11. Pierre Nora, "Between Memory and History: *Les Lieux de Mémoire*," *Representations* 26 (Spring 1989): 12, 19. For further analysis of Nora's ideas, consult Aleida Assmann, "Transformations between History and Memory," *Social Research* 75, no. 1 (Spring 2008): 49–72; John Bodnar, "Pierre Nora, National Memory, and Democracy: A Review," *Journal of American History* 87, no. 3 (2000): 951–63.

12. Wulf Kansteiner, "Finding Meaning in Memory: A Methodological Critique of Collective Memory Studies," *History and Theory* 41, no. 2 (2002): 188, 180. The work of Erika Doss proved especially useful; see *Elvis Culture: Fans, Faith, and Image* (Lawrence: Univ. Press of Kansas, 1999) and *Memorial Mania*.

13. Joseph L. Price writes intelligently about how Americans reconcile themselves to the deaths of athletes. See Price, "Dying to Win: America's Grieving for Athletes," *Journal of American and Comparative Cultures* 25, no. 3–4 (2002): 405–11; quote appears on 409.

14. Price, "Dying to Win."

15. Tony Castro, *Mickey Mantle: America's Prodigal Son* (Washington, DC: Brassey's, 2002), xiii.

16. Faust, *This Republic of Suffering*, xii, 193.

17. For more on Roberto Clemente, see David Maraniss, *Clemente: The Passion and Grace of Baseball's Last Hero* (New York: Simon & Schuster, 2006). Recent work on Hobey Baker includes Emil R. Salvini, *Hobey Baker, American Legend* (Minneapolis: Hobey Baker Foundation, 2005). The death of Ray Chapman is well covered in Mike Sowell, *The Pitch That Killed: The Story of Carl Mays, Ray Chapman, and the Pennant Race of 1920* (Chicago: Ivan R. Dee, 1989). Although there is no full-length biography of Jack Trice, much of his story has been told in Jaime Schultz, "The Legend of Jack Trice and the Campaign for Jack Trice Stadium, 1973–1984," *Journal of Social History* 41, no. 4 (2008): 997–1029.

18. Vin Scully tells the story of the quotation—which has been appropriated by sports broadcasters including Dan Patrick and Charley Steiner—in an interview with the *Los Angeles Daily News*; see Tom Hoffarth, "Dodgers Hall of Fame Broadcaster Scully Remains the Voice of Choice," *Los Angeles Daily News*, April 4, 2010, http://www.dailynews.com /sports/ci_14816948.

1. Why Lou Gehrig Was Lucky

1. John Drebinger, "61,808 Fans Roar Tribute to Gehrig," *New York Times*, July 5, 1939, 1, 21. For more on the life and career of Lou Gehrig, consult Jonathan Eig, *Luckiest Man: The Life and Death of Lou Gehrig* (New York: Simon & Schuster, 2005).

2. *The Pride of the Yankees*, directed by Sam Wood, 1942 (New York: HBO Home Video, 1988).

3. Quotation found in Jane Leavy, *The Last Boy: Mickey Mantle and the End of America's Childhood* (New York: HarperCollins, 2010), 292.

4. For an introduction to *ars moriendi*, see Philippe Ariès, *The Hour of Our Death*, trans. Helen Weaver (New York: Barnes & Noble, 1981).

5. Drebinger, "61,808 Fans Roar Tribute," 1, 21. According to Drebinger, only the thirty-nine-year-old Waite Hoyt maintained any semblance of "his boyish countenance."

6. Neil Young and Crazy Horse, "My My, Hey Hey (Out of the Blue)," *Rust Never Sleeps* (Burbank, CA: Reprise Records, 1979).

7. Saul Bellow, *Humboldt's Gift* (New York: Viking Press, 1975), 262.

8. Sigmund Freud, "Thoughts for the Times on War and Death," in *Civilisation, War and Death*, ed. John Rickman (London: Hogarth Press and the Institute of Psycho-Analysis, 1915), 15. Essayist David Shields offers a humorous insight into his own recognition of

mortality. Thinking about the approaching death of his father, Shields connected baldness and death. "Several years ago," he writes, "I stumbled upon the shaved-head-and-goatee approach, which I must say I like. It's an acknowledgment of death rather than a denial of death (as, to take the extreme example, the comb-over is). Your head becomes an early *memento mori*." See David Shields, *The Thing about Life Is That One Day You'll Be Dead* (New York: Alfred A. Knopf, 2008), 110.

9. Ernest Becker, *The Denial of Death* (New York: Free Press, 1973), 55.

10. Michel de Montaigne, *The Essays of Michel de Montaigne*, trans. M. A. Screech (London: Penguin, 1991), 92.

11. Michael Oriard, *Dreaming of Heroes: American Sports Fiction, 1868–1980* (Chicago: Nelson-Hall, 1982), 219, 27, 221.

12. Howard Slusher used the phrase "deathless spirits" in *Man, Sport, and Existence: A Critical Analysis* (Philadelphia: Lea & Febiger, 1967), 210. Writing in the 1930s, social critic Lewis Mumford argued that sports existed to satisfy the "blood lust" generated by the dulling repetition of life in modern, machine-oriented societies. Mass sports—those in which the spectator was more important than the participants—supported the state apparatus by providing an outlet for pent-up frustrations. "Unlike play, mass sport usually requires an element of mortal chance or hazard as one of its main ingredients: but instead of the chance's occurring spontaneously, as in mountain climbing, it must take place in accordance with the rules of the game and must be increased when the spectacle begins to bore the spectators. . . . The dangerous symptoms of that ultimate decay one finds everywhere today in machine civilization under the guise of mass sport." The heart of sports contained a "conflict between the desire for a skilled exhibition and the desire for a brutal outcome: the maceration or death of one or more of the contestants." See Lewis Mumford, *Technics and Civilization* (New York: Harcourt, Brace, 1934), 303, 305.

13. This coping mechanism is described in Irvin D. Yalom, *Existential Psychotherapy* (New York: Basic Books, 1980), 152.

14. Martin Luther King Jr., *Why We Can't Wait* (New York: Harper & Row, 1964), 119. For Margolick's explanation of the story, see David Margolick, *Beyond Glory: Joe Louis vs. Max Schmeling, and a World on the Brink* (New York: Vintage Books, 2005), 126.

15. A. Bartlett Giamatti, *Take Time for Paradise: Americans and Their Games* (New York: Summit Books, 1989), 15, 22.

16. Slusher, *Man, Sport, and Existence*, 208, emphasis in original.

17. Allen Guttmann, *From Ritual to Record: The Nature of Modern Sports* (New York: Columbia Univ. Press, 1978), 55.

18. For more on the agony Maris endured while chasing Babe Ruth's home run record, see Tom Clavin and Danny Peary, *Roger Maris: Baseball's Reluctant Hero* (New York: Touchstone, 2010).

19. Shelly McKenzie, *Getting Physical: The Rise of Fitness Culture in America* (Lawrence: Univ. Press of Kansas, 2013), 86–89, 99.

20. Randy Roberts and James Olson, *Winning Is the Only Thing: Sports in America since 1945* (Baltimore: Johns Hopkins Univ. Press, 1989), 213.

21. Ernest Hemingway, *Death in the Afternoon* (New York: Charles Scribner's Sons, 1932), 213. For more on the cultural importance of bullfighting in Hispanic cultures, consult Carlos Fuentes, *The Buried Mirror: Reflections on Spain and the New World* (Boston: Houghton Mifflin, 1992).

22. Roger Rosenblatt, "Baseball: The Light of Winter Coming," *Time*, August 19, 1996, 76.

23. Simon Barnes, *The Meaning of Sport* (London: Short Books, 2006), 303.

24. Quotes are found on the Alabama Sports Hall of Fame website, accessed May 4, 2006, http://www.ashof.org.

25. Becker, *Denial of Death*, 5.

26. See http://baseballhall.org/hof/lasorda-tommy for Lasorda's comments, accessed December 9, 2016.

27. Roberta Newman, "The American Church of Baseball and the National Baseball Hall of Fame," *Nine: A Journal of Baseball History and Culture* 10, no. 1 (2001): 56, 46–47, 52. For more on baseball as a civil religion, consult Christopher H. Evans, "Baseball as Civil Religion: The Genesis of an American Creation Story," in *The Faith of 50 Million: Baseball, Religion, and American Culture*, ed. Christopher H. Evans and William R. Herzog II (Louisville, KY: Westminster John Knox Press, 2002), 13–33.

28. *Baseball: Bottom of the Seventh Inning*, directed by Ken Burns (Walpole, NH: Florentine Films, 1999).

29. Richard Ben Cramer, *Joe DiMaggio: The Hero's Life* (New York: Simon & Schuster, 2000), 184. Note, of course, the capital letters that redefine DiMaggio's shoes into "The Spikes." The "Sacred Streak" refers to DiMaggio's record-setting fifty-six-game hitting streak in 1941.

30. William Freedman, *More Than a Pastime: An Oral History of Baseball Fans* (Jefferson, NC: McFarland, 1998), 160, 159.

31. Freud, "Thoughts for the Times," 16.

32. Gerard Manley Hopkins, "Spring and Fall," in *Poems of Gerard Manley Hopkins*, ed. Robert Bridges (London: Humphrey Milford, 1918), 51.

33. Christopher Lehmann-Haupt, *Me and DiMaggio: A Baseball Fan Goes in Search of His Gods* (New York: Simon & Schuster, 1986), 157.

34. Katherine Verdery, *The Political Lives of Dead Bodies: Reburial and Postsocialist Change* (New York: Columbia Univ. Press, 1999), 127. Peter Brown discusses the roles that dead bodies played in Latin American Christianity in *The Cult of the Saints* (Chicago: Univ. of Chicago Press, 1981).

35. Cited by Jonathan Israel, *Enlightenment Contested: Philosophy, Modernity, and the Emancipation of Man, 1670–1752* (Oxford: Oxford Univ. Press, 2006), 364.

36. Tony Castro, *Mickey Mantle: America's Prodigal Son* (Washington, DC: Brassey's, 2002), ix.

2. The Gipper Wins One for the Gipper

1. Some have claimed that the speech was actually delivered before the game. See Ray Robinson, *Rockne of Notre Dame* (New York: Oxford Univ. Press, 1999), 214; additionally, consult the incomparable Murray Sperber, *Shake Down the Thunder: The Creation of Notre Dame Football* (Bloomington: Indiana Univ. Press, 1993), 281–88.

2. For convenience, when discussing the historical figure, I will use Gipp or George Gipp. When referring to the legend, created by Rockne and sustained by Reagan, I will use "the Gipper" or Gipper.

3. Russell Baker, "The Road to Superhood," *New York Times*, January 17, 1971, E15.

4. Histories started to appear in the decades following Gipp's death in 1920. See Knute Rockne, *The Autobiography of Knute M. Rockne* (Indianapolis: Bobbs-Merrill, 1931). Arch Ward, longtime Notre Dame public relations man, included the Gipp story in *Frank Leahy and the Fighting Irish* (New York: G. P. Putnam's Sons, 1947); another biographer of Leahy, Wells Twombly, gives his version of Gipp's story in *Shake Down the Thunder! The Official Biography of Frank Leahy* (Radnor, PA: Chilton Books, 1974). The revisionist work of Murray Sperber deserves special mention. Two of his major works masterfully unravel the Gipp story in its historical context. See especially *Shake Down the Thunder* and *Onward to Victory: The Crises That Shaped College Sports* (New York: Henry Holt, 1999). Historians who have tried to salvage Gipp's reputation from the revisionists include George Gekas, *The Life and Times of George Gipp* (South Bend, IN: And Books, 1987). Emil Klosinski's flawed but heartfelt history is *Gipp at Notre Dame: The Truth about "The Gipper"* (Baltimore: PublishAmerica, 2003). Klosinski's father had known Gipp during his playing days and the author never fails to focus on the bright side, even when he has to speculate. A recent children's book, *Win One for the Gipper: America's Football Hero* (Chelsea, MI: Sleeping Bear Press, 2004), written by Kathy-Jo Wargin and illustrated by Bruce Langton, nods to the historical realities of Gipp's life while burnishing his status as an athletic hero.

5. Useful biographies of Gipp include: Jack Cavanaugh, *The Gipper: George Gipp, Knute Rockne, and the Dramatic Rise of Notre Dame Football* (New York: Skyhorse, 2010); and Patrick Chelland, *One for the Gipper: George Gipp, Knute Rockne, and Notre Dame* (Chicago: Henry Regnery, 1973).

6. Gekas, *Life and Times*, 25.

7. Sperber, *Shake Down the Thunder*, 110. This is Sperber's version but the story has been repeated and rewritten countless times since that halftime confrontation.

8. Robinson, *Rockne*, 73.

9. Gekas, *Life and Times*, vii, 74. Paul Hornung wrote the book's introduction. His quote appears on vii.

10. Robinson, *Rockne*, 69, 73.

11. Ibid., 73.

12. Red Smith, "Hunk Anderson, Nicest Tough Guy," *New York Times*, May 26, 1978, A18.

13. John Hall, "One for the Gipper," *Los Angeles Times*, October 29, 1966, A3.

14. *The Man Who Shot Liberty Valance*, directed by John Ford (Los Angeles: Paramount Pictures, 1962).

15. "The Ghost of Washington Hall," *Notre Dame Alumnus* 10, no. 4 (January 1932): 114. The most complete treatment of Gipp's ghost is found in Mark C. Pilkinton, *Washington Hall at Notre Dame: Crossroads of the University, 1864–2004* (Notre Dame, IN: Univ. of Notre Dame Press, 2011), 205–21. For additional brief treatments of the story, see Gary Andrew Poole, "Classic Stadiums, Classic Memories," *New York Times*, October 21, 2005, F4; and Edrick Thay, *Ghost Stories of Indiana* (Edmonton: Ghost House Books, 2001), 78–82. A fictional approach connecting Notre Dame and the spirit of Gipp is Robert Quakenbush, *The Gipper's Ghost* (Chicago: O'Connor Publishing, 1985). The story centers on the spirits of Gipp and Rockne returning to South Bend to save the school's faltering football program. Gipp assumes the name "Dutch Reagan" and teaches the players how to win. Eventually, Gipp remains on earth and plays center field for the Chicago Cubs. Of course, he hits five home runs in a World Series–clinching game for the Cubs. Fiction, indeed.

16. Thomas Lawrence Doorley, "I Was the Second Gipper Fifty Years Ago—September 1929," typescript, Univ. of Notre Dame Athletic Records, 3/7, Univ. of Notre Dame Archives, Notre Dame, IN.

17. Ibid.

18. Ibid.

19. Sperber briefly mentions this episode in *Shake Down the Thunder*, 282.

20. Joseph P. O'Rourke to Knute Rockne, November 12, 1928, Univ. of Notre Dame Athletic Director's Records, 17/93, Univ. of Notre Dame Archives, Notre Dame, IN.

21. Knute Rockne to Joseph P. O'Rourke, November 22, 1928, Univ. of Notre Dame Athletic Director's Records, 17/93, Univ. of Notre Dame Archives, Notre Dame, IN.

22. James J. Whalen, "Purging College Athletics," *New York Times*, June 15, 1987, A17. Frank Merriwell, the consummate fictional sporting hero, was the creation of Gilbert Patten (using the pen name Burt L. Standish). Along with his brother Dick, Frank made all of the right decisions on and off the field during his college career at Yale and beyond. The best treatment of Merriwell remains Michael Oriard, *King Football: Sport and Spectacle in the Golden Age of Radio and Newsreels, Movies and Magazines, the Weekly and the Daily Press* (Chapel Hill: Univ. of North Carolina Press, 2001). Oriard's *Dreaming of Heroes: American Sports Fiction, 1868–1980* (Chicago: Nelson-Hall, 1982) analyzes sports fiction in the broadest time frame and scope. The character of John Humperdink "Dink" Stover, the brainchild of Owen Johnson, resembled Merriwell (he even attended Yale) in providing a fit example for young men at the turn of the twentieth century. First serialized in *McClure's* during 1911, Johnson's novel *Stover at Yale* (Boston: Little, Brown, 1912) appeared a year later. For an interesting look at fictional Yale students like Merriwell and Stover, see Mark Alden Branch, "The Ten Great Yalies Who Never Were," *Yale Alumni Magazine*, February 2003.

23. James A. Cox, "Was 'the Gipper' Really for Real? You Can Bet He Was," *Smithsonian* 16, no. 9 (1985): 132. The sixty-two-yard dropkick field goal, a remarkable athletic achievement, has become analogous to the first miracle performed by a saint. This was, more or less, Gipp's coming-out party, and it offered an intimation of what might happen when he moved to the varsity football squad.

24. Murray Sperber notes that Rockne's ghostwriter at *Collier's*, John B. Kennedy, likely wrote this version of the speech, which has become the most famous. See Sperber, *Shake Down the Thunder*, 284.

25. Scott Ostler crowned the Gipper speech "the most famous speech in U.S. history," beating out the Gettysburg Address and patriots Nathan Hale and Patrick Henry. See Ostler, "Forget about Points; Take the Gipper," *Los Angeles Times*, November 14, 1988, 1. For a contemporary perspective on halftime speeches, see Heywood Broun, "Dying for 'Dear Old—': A Study in Sportsmanship," *Harper's*, June 1925, 60–66.

26. The Univ. of Notre Dame has likewise capitalized on the mystique created by Rockne and the Gipper. "Win one for the Gipper" has become a tag line for the university, and Notre Dame continues to cash in on sports-related merchandise. See Gerald Eskenazi, "Mystique Plus Business Sense Equals Success," *New York Times*, March 18, 1990, S1. For more on Nile Kinnick, see Thomas Lidd, *Nile* (Bloomington, IN: AuthorHouse, 2008) and Paul Baender, ed., *A Hero Perished: The Diary and Selected Letters of Nile Kinnick* (Iowa City: Univ. of Iowa Press, 1992). A useful recent biography of Hobey Baker is Emil R. Salvini, *Hobey Baker, American Legend* (Minneapolis: Hobey Baker Foundation, 2005).

27. Knute Rockne, *Coaching: The Way of the Winner* (New York: Devin Adair, 1929), 159–60.

28. Robert Lipsyte, who worked with Daley at the *Times*, referred to the "faux Homeric mythmaking of rosy-fingered Arthur Daley." See Lipsyte, *An Accidental Sportswriter: A Memoir* (New York: HarperCollins, 2011), 4.

29. Arthur Daley, "Sports of the Times—The Gipper Steals the Show Again," *New York Times*, January 17, 1945, 25.

30. Arthur Daley, "Sports of the Times—One for the Gipper," *New York Times*, June 3, 1945, S2. For more on Chevigny's life, see Jeff Walker, *The Last Chalkline: The Life and Times of Jack Chevigny* (Shelbyville, KY: Wasteland Press, 2012).

31. Arthur Daley, "Sports of the Times—Waiting for Army-Notre Dame," *New York Times*, November 7, 1946, 44.

32. Arthur Daley, "Sports of the Times—Waiting for Army and Notre Dame," *New York Times*, November 6, 1947, 39.

33. Arthur Daley, "Sports of the Times—End of a Great Series," *New York Times*, November 9, 1947, S2.

34. Arthur Daley, "Sports of the Times—After Fifteen Years," *New York Times*, April 10, 1946, 40.

35. Arthur Daley, "Sports of the Times—Twenty Years After," *New York Times*, March 30, 1951, 38.

36. Rockne, *Autobiography*, 247, 248, 292–93.

37. Jimmy Breslin, "The Man Who Died for Notre Dame," *Real*, December 1955, 59, 60.

38. Al Stump, "The Gipper Didn't Die," *Esquire*, October 1952, 103. Stump went on to become Ty Cobb's confidant and biographer. See Stump, *Cobb: A Biography* (Chapel Hill, NC: Algonquin Books, 1996).

39. Robert F. Kelley, "Rockne a Pioneer on Football Field," *New York Times*, April 1, 1931, 33.

40. Twombly, quoted in Sperber, *Shake Down the Thunder*, 119, 120.

41. Sperber, *Onward to Victory*, 4.

42. Sperber, *Onward to Victory*, 17. For more on the political power of Reagan-as-Gipper, see Lou Cannon, *President Reagan: The Role of a Lifetime* (New York: Simon & Schuster, 1991), 41.

43. Ronald Reagan *Where's the Rest of Me?*, with Richard G. Hubler, (New York: Karz Publishers, 1981), 90. This was Reagan's first attempt at autobiography and covered the years before he was elected president. He later wrote an updated version, titled *Ronald Reagan: An American Life* (New York: Pocket Books, 1990).

44. Reagan, *Where's the Rest of Me?*, 93, 95.

45. Reagan, *An American Life*, 92.

46. Reagan, *Where's the Rest of Me?*, 98.

47. Red Smith, "No Tickets for Honeymooners," *New York Times*, April 26, 1976, 49.

48. Steven V. Roberts, "Return to the Land of the Gipper," *New York Times*, March 9, 1988, A28.

49. Michael Paul Rogin, *Ronald Reagan, the Movie* (Berkeley: Univ. of California Press, 1987), 3.

50. Leo E. Litwak, "The Ronald Reagan Story; or, Tom Sawyer Enters Politics," *New York Times*, November 14, 1965, SM46.

51. George Skelton, "'New Majority' Backs Him, Reagan Says," *Los Angeles Times*, May 4, 1976, 24.

52. Howell Raines, "Reagan Is Welcomed on Notre Dame Trip, First Since Shooting," *New York Times*, May 18, 1981, A1. For more on Reagan's commencement address, see "Excerpts from the President's Address," *New York Times*, May 18, 1981, B7.

53. Roberts, "Return to the Land of the Gipper."

54. Steven V. Roberts, "Reagan Invokes Rockne to Encourage Optimism," *New York Times*, March 10, 1988, A29.

55. Ronald Reagan, "Remarks Congratulating the Championship University of Notre Dame Football Team," January 18, 1989, online by Gerhard Peters and John T. Woolley, *The American Presidency Project*, http://www.presidency.ucsb.edu/ws/?pid=35396.

56. Ken Duberstein, "There Is Enough Presidential Interaction with Athletes for a White House Trivia Game," *New York Times*, April 9, 1989, S10. Interestingly, John N. Cackley,

who had donated the sweater to Notre Dame, was aghast at the gift to Reagan. The seventy-year-old Cackley criticized the presentation: "I never dreamed that someone at Notre Dame would go to the extreme of satisfying egos in the White House and at the university just to create an atmosphere of good old-fashioned 'show biz.'" See "Thrown for a Loss by Gift," *New York Times*, January 29, 1989, 18. For more on Cackley's reaction, see Dave Johnson, "He Lost One for the Gipper," *Los Angeles Times*, January 29, 1989, 2.

57. Steven R. Weisman, "The Politics of Popularity," *New York Times*, November 8, 1984, A1.

58. John Sayle Watterson, *The Games Presidents Play* (Baltimore: Johns Hopkins Univ. Press, 2006), 292.

59. Garry Wills, *Reagan's America* (Garden City, NY: Doubleday, 1987), 123.

60. Red Smith, "Too Much Notre Dame," *New York Times*, November 3, 1980, C7.

61. Dave Anderson, "49ers' Super Day," *New York Times*, January 25, 1982, A1.

62. Francis X. Clines, "President Says Social Security Faces a Freeze," *New York Times*, July 7, 1984, O1.

63. Robert Lindsey, "Olympics Are Ushered in by Pageantry," *New York Times*, July 29, 1984, 22.

64. Francis X. Clines, "Crowds Applaud Reagan's Message," *New York Times*, November 3, 1984, 11.

65. Robert Brustein, "Can Bush as Bush Steal the Show?" *New York Times*, August 21, 1988, E25. Jack Kemp was a former professional quarterback and served as a Republican member of Congress from 1971 to 1989. He went on to serve as the secretary of urban development in the George H. W. Bush administration and then was selected as Robert Dole's vice-presidential running mate in 1996. For more on Reagan's convention speech, see E. J. Dionne Jr., "Emotional Address," *New York Times*, August 16, 1988, A1. The "win one for the Gipper" line was suggested by Nancy Reagan according to James Gerstenzang, "Reagan Is Hailed as He Tells Bush to Win for Gipper," *Los Angeles Times*, August 16, 1988, 1.

66. Roberts, "Return to the Land of the Gipper."

67. Reagan, *Where's the Rest of Me?*, 94.

68. The tributes appear in Congress, Joint Committee on Printing, *Memorial Services in the Congress of the United States and Tributes in Eulogy of Ronald Reagan, Late a President of the United States* (Washington, DC: United States Government Printing Office, 2005), 70 (Millender-McDonald), 72 (Larson), xxxvi (Bush), 39 (Hayes).

69. Watterson, *Games Presidents Play*, 291.

70. John M. Broder, "In Search of Reagan," *New York Times*, January 20, 2008, WK1.

71. Maureen Dowd, "Epitaph and Epigone," *New York Times*, June 10, 2004, A27.

72. Broder, "In Search of Reagan."

73. Edmund Morris, "Too Big a Man for the Small Screen," *New York Times*, November 9, 2003, WK11.

74. Klosinski, *Gipp at Notre Dame*, 239.

3. Only Cowgirls Get the Blues

1. Joan Wallach Scott, "Gender as a Useful Category of Historical Analysis," in *Conceiving Sexuality: Approaches to Sex Research in a Postmodern World,* ed. John H. Gagnon and Richard G. Parker (New York: Routledge, 1995), 67. Scott additionally advises that historians "treat the opposition between male and female as problematic rather than known, as something contextually defined, repeatedly constructed, then we must constantly ask not only what is at stake in proclamations or debates that invoke gender to explain or justify their positions but also how implicit understandings of gender are being invoked and reinscribed" (70).

2. See Susan Cahn, *Coming on Strong: Gender and Sexuality in Twentieth-Century Women's Sports* (Cambridge, MA: Harvard Univ. Press, 1994).

3. Heather Raftery, "The Bronc Busters Wore Lipstick," *RANGE* magazine, Winter 2010, 28.

4. Mary Lou LeCompte, *Cowgirls of the Rodeo: Pioneer Professional Athletes* (Urbana: Univ. of Illinois Press, 1993), 9, 8.

5. Renee M. Laegreid, "Rodeo Queens at the Pendleton Round-Up: The First Go-Round, 1910–1917," *Oregon Historical Quarterly* 104, no. 1 (2003): 7–8.

6. "Champion Woman Rider Prefers Broncs to Planes," *Idaho-Free Press* (Nampa), September 23, 1928; copy of newspaper clipping in Bonnie McCarroll scrapbook, found in Bruce McCarroll Collection of the Bonnie and Frank McCarroll Rodeo Archives, 1900–1940, Donald C. and Elizabeth M. Dickinson Research Center, National Cowboy and Western Heritage Museum, Oklahoma City, Oklahoma (hereafter McCarroll scrapbook); copy in author's possession.

7. Introduction, "Guide to the Bruce McCarroll Collection of the Bonnie and Frank McCarroll Rodeo Archives," accessed December 16, 2016, http://drc.nationalcowboymuseum .org/findingaids/collections/mccarroll.aspx.

8. Ibid. One account claims that Bonnie broke her leg during her first bronc ride. See "Money Winners at Stadium's Rodeo"; copy in McCarroll scrapbook.

9. "M'Carrolls Home from Big Season and London Rodeo," *Boise Evening Capital News,* November 10, 1924; copy in McCarroll scrapbook.

10. "Taming the Critter"; copy in McCarroll scrapbook.

11. "M'Carrolls Go to Ride at Roundups"; copy in McCarroll scrapbook.

12. For more about Buffalo Bill, see Louis S. Warren, *Buffalo Bill's America: William Cody and the Wild West Show* (New York: Vintage Books, 2006).

13. "Champion Riders Here to Take Part in Rodeo," *Colorado Springs Gazette,* August 7, 1924; copy in McCarroll scrapbook.

14. "Little Lunnon Makes These Two Happy as Does England"; copy in McCarroll scrapbook.

15. Advertisement, "Elks Roundup"; copy in McCarroll scrapbook.

16. "Gay Throngs in Festive Array Steadily Arriving"; copy in McCarroll scrapbook. Other noted attractions included the "tribesmen" of the Umatilla Indians giving "exhibitions of native dances of the Redman."

17. "Leonard Stroud and Company of Famous Wild West Showmen to Give Rodeo for Orphanage," and "Boise Couple Will Ride in New York"; copies in McCarroll scrapbook.

18. "The McCarrolls, Noted Rodeo Characters, to Contest Here"; copy in McCarroll scrapbook.

19. "Bonnie M'Carroll Officially Champ"; copy in McCarroll scrapbook.

20. "M'Carrolls Enjoying Good Year; No Bones Broken, Frank Says"; copy in McCarroll scrapbook.

21. "East May Be East, But It Took to Western Stuff with a Bang"; copy in McCarroll scrapbook.

22. "World Champs Now"; copy in McCarroll scrapbook.

23. "Girls Retain Titles"; copy in McCarroll scrapbook.

24. "Money Winners at Stadium's Rodeo," September 7, 1923; copy in McCarroll scrapbook.

25. "Thousands Packed New York 'Gardens' See Western Rodeo," copy in McCarroll scrapbook. On another occasion, Rogers watched the action at Madison Square Garden "but efforts to induce him to mount a bronco were fruitless, because, he said, he had on his Sunday clothes." See "Bonnie M'Carroll Hurt in New York during Exhibition," *New York Times*, October 20, 1924. A self-effacing Rogers admitted that there were cowboys in the 1922 version of the Madison Square Garden rodeo "that I ain't fit to carry a rope to." See "Cowboys Do Tricks in Rodeo at Garden," *New York Times*, November 5, 1922.

26. "Cowboys 'All Dressed Up,'" *Daily Mail* (London), June 3, 1924; the information on the cowboy's dining habits appears in "Cowboys at Sea"; copies in McCarroll scrapbook.

27. Vera McGinnis, *Rodeo Road: My Life as a Pioneer Cowgirl* (New York: Hastings House, 1974), 184.

28. "Man v. Bullock," *Daily Mirror* (London), June 16, 1924; copy in McCarroll scrapbook.

29. "Wild West Thrills at Wembley," *Daily Chronicle* (London), June 16, 1924; copy in McCarroll scrapbook.

30. "A Rodeo Romance"; copy in McCarroll scrapbook.

31. Bonnie McCarroll, "Whoopee! Ride 'Im, Cowboy!" *Illustrated Sunday Herald* (London), June 8, 1924, 4; copy in McCarroll scrapbook.

32. "Champ Rider," *Daily Mirror*, October 2, 1924; copy in McCarroll scrapbook.

33. "Rodeo Not Guilty of Sabbath Law Violation Charge," *The World* (New York), October 27, 1924; copy in McCarroll scrapbook.

34. "Woman Rodeo Rider Is Hurt by Steer"; copy in McCarroll scrapbook. I have surmised from contextual evidence in the article that the location was Fort Worth.

35. "Bonnie McCarroll's Escape"; copy in McCarroll scrapbook.

36. For more on the different riding styles, see Raftery, "Bronc Busters Wore Lipstick," 30.

37. "Boise Rodeo Performers Entertain Coolidge," *Idaho Statesman*, August 28, 1927; copy in McCarroll scrapbook.

38. Marjorie Wilson, "Want to Escape Housework?"; copy in McCarroll scrapbook.

39. LeCompte, *Cowgirls of the Rodeo*, 26, 78.

40. "The Corral," *Billboard*, October 5, 1929, 61. For more on the history of rodeo queens, see Laegreid, "Rodeo Queens at the Pendleton Round-Up," 6–23. For the experience of rodeo royalty in the second half of the twentieth century, see Joan Burbick, *Rodeo Queens and the American Dream* (New York: Public Affairs, 2002). For more on the Round-Up, see "Pendleton Round-Up Keeps Rabid Throngs Thrilling and Gasping," *Idaho Statesman*, September 23, 1929, 2.

41. "The Corral," *Billboard*, October 5, 1929, 61. In all likelihood, this article had gone to press before news of Bonnie McCarroll's death had reached the magazine.

42. "Guide to the Bruce McCarroll Collection."

43. Quoted in Michael Allen, "The Rise and Decline of the Early Rodeo Cowgirl," *Pacific Northwest Quarterly* 83, no. 4 (1992): 126. According to one newspaper account, Black Cat had been knocked down by the horse of the "pick-up" man who was attempting to retrieve Bonnie. See "Injured in Pendleton at Roundup," *Boise Capital News*, September 30, 1929, 1.

44. One report described Bonnie regaining consciousness briefly in the hospital; see "Injured in Pendleton at Roundup," *Boise Capital News*, September 30, 1929, 1.

45. "The Corral," *Billboard*, October 19, 1929, 61.

46. "Injured in Roundup at Pendleton," *Boise Capital News*, September 30, 1929, 1.

47. Andrea Mugnier, "Ridin', Ropin', and Rodeoin': Champion Cowgirls of Professional Rodeo, 1930–1945," *Nevada Historical Society Quarterly* 44, no. 2 (2001): 169.

48. Allen, "Rise and Decline of the Early Rodeo Cowgirl," 126.

49. Burbick, *Rodeo Queens and the American Dream*, 87.

50. Renee M. Laegreid, "'Performers Prove Beauty and Rodeo Can Be Mixed': The Return of the Cowgirl Queen," *Montana: The Magazine of Western History* 54, no. 1 (2004): 46, 48.

51. See "Bonnie McCarroll," National Cowgirl Museum and Hall of Fame, accessed December 16, 2016, http://www.cowgirl.net/?s=bonnie+mccarroll.

52. "The Corral," *Billboard*, February 15, 1930, 59.

53. "The Corral," *Billboard*, March 1, 1930, 59.

54. "The Corral," *Billboard*, March 22, 1930, 59.

55. "The Corral," *Billboard*, May 10, 1930, 55.

56. Kendra Santos, "A World Champion in Life," *ProRodeo Sports News*, August 11, 1999, 28; see also Peter Richmond, "The Death of a Cowboy," *National Sports Daily*, July 22, 1990, 30–33. I wish to thank Sherry Compton of the Professional Rodeo Cowboys Association media department for her help in locating this and other sources about Lane Frost.

57. Kevin Simpson, "Pain and Glory," *Denver Post*, December 7, 2004.

58. Skip Myslenski, "A Rodeo Cowboy's Perfect Ride Ends in Death," *Chicago Tribune*, August 6, 1989, 10.

59. "Quotes," *Remembering Lane Frost*, accessed December 2, 2016, http://www.lane frost.com/quotes.htm.

60. *Cowboy Up: Inside the Extreme World of Bull Riding*, directed by David Wittkower (Calabasas, CA: Lighthouse Productions, 2002). In the days before widespread cable TV access, Michaels's Washington, DC–based program offered a syndicated weekly wrap-up of the week's sports highlights.

61. See *Cheyenne Frontier Days: Daddy of 'Em All*, George Michael's Sports Machine, VHS; copy in author's possession.

62. Janet Williamsen, "A Tribute to Lane Frost World Champion Bull Rider 1963–1989," accessed December 16, 2016, http://www.cowgirls.com/dream/jan/frost.php.

63. *Remembering Lane Frost*, accessed December 16, 2016, http://lanefrost.com. For an in-depth look at Elsie Frost's version of her son's life, see Elsie Frost, *Lane Frost: A Mother's Story* (Durant, OK: Victory Life Church, n.d.).

64. *New Testament: New International Version* (Crete, IL: The Bible League, 1984).

65. *8 Seconds*, directed by Charlie McDade (New York: Harper, 1994), back cover of DVD.

66. Josh Peter, *Fried Twinkies, Buckle Bunnies, and Bull Riders: A Year inside the Professional Bull Riders Tour* (New York: Rodale, 2005).

67. Dan Halpern, "Bull Marketing," *New York Times Magazine*, February 12, 2006, 56. The bulls officially reached the pinnacle of athletic superstardom when the Professional Bull Riders (PBR) began testing the bulls for steroids in 2008. See Gary Mihoces, "Bright Lights, Big Bulls," *New York Times*, January 4, 2008, 7C.

68. Jeffrey Johnstone and Keith Ryan Cartwright, *Professional Bull Riders: The Official Guide to the Toughest Sport on Earth* (Chicago: Triumph Books, 2009), 85, 1, 138, 143.

69. Michael Parfit, "Rodeos: Behind the Chutes," *National Geographic* 196, no. 3 (September 1999), 116.

70. E. M. Swift, "Whoopee Ty Yay!" *Sports Illustrated*, December 24, 1990, 49.

71. Gary Mihoces, "Sport's Risks Lurk in Each Ride; Riders Take Danger in Stride; PBR Hopes to Alter Mind-Set," *New York Times*, January 4, 2008, 9C.

72. Parfit, "Rodeos," 117.

4. Who Killed Benny Paret?

1. Ernest Hemingway in *Death in the Afternoon*, his paean to Spanish bullfighting, defines a *maricón* as a "sodomite, nance, queen, fairy, fag, etc. . . . In bullfighting circles the word is used as a term of opprobrium or ridicule or as an insult." See *Death in the Afternoon* (New York: Charles Scribner's Sons, 1932), glossary entry for *maricón*.

2. Joyce Carol Oates, *On Boxing* (Garden City, NY: Dolphin/Doubleday, 1987), 10.

3. For more on the social turbulence of the 1960s, see Todd Gitlin, *The Sixties: Years of Hope, Days of Rage*, rev. ed. (New York: Bantam, 1993) and Mark Kurlansky, *1968: The Year That Rocked the World* (New York: Vintage Books, 2004).

4. Norman Cousins, "Who Killed Benny Paret?," *Saturday Review*, May 5, 1962, 14.

5. Oates, *On Boxing*, 42, 18.

6. Lewis Mumford, "Sports and the Bitch Goddess," in *Technics and Civilization* (New York: Harcourt, Brace, 1934), 304.

7. Howard A. Rusk, "Paret: A Prognosis," *New York Times*, April 1, 1962, 52.

8. Robert M. Lipsyte, "Paret's Manager Says Goldstein Should Have Halted Bout Sooner," *New York Times*, March 26, 1962, 40. Historian Christina D. Abreu analyzed Paret's death in light of Cuban-American relations in the early 1960s in "The Story of Benny 'Kid' Paret: Cuban Boxers, the Cuban Revolution, and the U.S. Media, 1959–1962," *Journal of Sport History*, 38, no. 1 (2011): 95–113. Donald McRae's *A Man's World: The Double Life of Emile Griffith* (London: Simon & Schuster, 2015) examines new source material and offers a poignant portrait of Griffith's life.

9. Gay Talese, "The Loneliest Guy in Boxing," in *The Silent Season of a Hero: The Sports Writing of Gay Talese*, ed. Michael Rosenwald (New York: Walker, 2010), 41. The essay had originally appeared in *New York Times*, September 15, 1957, SM 115.

10. Robert L. Teague, "Griffith Is Victor," *New York Times*, March 25, 1962, 1.

11. Lipsyte, "Paret's Manager."

12. "Magnified by TV," *Time*, April 6, 1962. Thirty years later, boxing analyst Larry Merchant described the culture of boxing in the 1960s. "The ethic in prize fighting at the time was brutally primitive," he wrote in 1991. "The fight wasn't over until one man crumpled in a heap or battered helpless, or until the final bell sounded." See Merchant, "Boxing's Hardest Call Is Its Most Important," *New York Times*, March 31, 1991, S10.

13. Lipsyte, "Paret's Manager."

14. Ruby Goldstein, "The Middle Man," *The Ring* 79, no. 3 (1999): 84, 87, 89. This article originally appeared in *The Ring* in August 1962 and was republished as a *Ring* "classic" in 1999.

15. "Benny Paret Dies of Fight Injuries," *New York Times*, April 3, 1962, 1. For more on the role of Paret's death in shaping Goldstein's reputation, see Deane McGowen, "Ruby Goldstein Is Appointed State Boxing Judge by Dooley," *New York Times*, November 30, 1968, 56. Goldstein's obituary also highlights his role in the Paret–Griffith fight (Thomas Rogers, "Ruby Goldstein, Ex-Fighter and Controversial Referee," *New York Times*, April 24, 1984, B6). A brief career retrospective appears in Barney Nagler, "Recalling Ruby Goldstein, the Jewel of the Ghetto," *New York Times*, April 29, 1984, S2.

16. Frank M. Blunk, "Referee Testifies on Paret–Griffith Fight as Legislative Hearing Opens," *New York Times*, May 22, 1962, 42.

17. Randy Roberts and James S. Olson, *Winning Is the Only Thing: Sports in America Since 1945* (Baltimore: Johns Hopkins Univ. Press, 1991), 103. Kasia Brody agrees with the

centrality of boxing to television: "Boxing . . . with its well-lit enclosed setting and cast of only two, was ideal for the TV screen, and during the late forties and early fifties, the sport became 'television's darling,' with prime-time fights broadcast almost every evening." See Kasia Brody, *Boxing: A Cultural History* (London: Reaktion Books, 2008), 316.

18. Details on the TV schedule come from Randy Roberts, "The Wide World of Muhammad Ali: The Politics and Economics of Boxing," in *Muhammad Ali, The People's Champ*, ed. Elliott J. Gorn (Urbana: Univ. of Illinois Press, 1995), 28. Additional detail about the centrality of boxing in early television programming appears in Jeff Neal-Lunsford, "Sport in the Land of Television: The Use of Sport in Network Prime-Time Schedules, 1946–50," *Journal of Sport History* 19, no. 1 (1992): 56–76. See also Red Smith, "TV Returns to the Scene of the Crime," *New York Times*, January 31, 1977, 37. Smith wrote that "prize fights had all the ingredients that were then and are today considered ideal TV fare—blood, pain, violence and suspense."

19. Richard O. Davies, *America's Obsession: Sports and Society Since 1945* (Belmont, CA: Wadsworth, 1994), 75.

20. Pete Hamill, "Blood on Their Hands: The Corrupt and Brutal World of Professional Boxing," *Esquire*, June 1, 1996, 94.

21. "Magnified by TV," *Time*, April 6, 1962. The estimate of fourteen million viewers appeared in "Death in the Ring," *New York Times*, April 8, 1962, E2.

22. Arthur Daley, "Is It Worth the Price?" *New York Times*, April 1, 1962, 186.

23. "Boxing Hearings End a Prejudice," *New York Times*, February 6, 1963, 16.

24. James Tuite, "K.O. for Pro Boxing?" *New York Times*, April 7, 1963, E10.

25. Quoted in Peter Heller, *In This Corner . . . !* (New York: Simon & Schuster, 1973), 386.

26. Teague, "Griffith Is Victor," 3.

27. Quoted in Ron Ross, *Nine . . . Ten . . . and Out! The Two Worlds of Emile Griffith* (New York: DiBella Entertainment, 2008), 50.

28. Noreen Giffney, "Introduction: The 'Q' Word," in *The Ashgate Research Companion to Queer Theory*, ed. Noreen Giffney and Michael O'Rourke (Burlington, VT: Ashgate, 2009), 18.

29. Troy Rondinone, *Friday Night Fighter: Gaspar "Indio" Ortega and the Golden Age of Television Boxing* (Urbana: Univ. of Illinois Press, 2013), 189.

30. Gary Smith, "The Shadow Boxer," *Sports Illustrated*, April 18, 2005, 60. For more from Torres, see *Ring of Fire: The Emile Griffith Story*, directed by Dan Klores and Ron Berger (Troy, MI: Anchor Bay Entertainment, 2005). Robert Lipsyte confirms a similar version of events at the weigh-in. He wrote that Paret "could also be thoughtlessly cruel. During the weighing-in ceremonies for Saturday night's fight, he needled Griffith, in Spanish, calling him names that infuriated Griffith." See Lipsyte, "The Story of Benny (Kid) Paret: From $4 a Day to a World Title," *New York Times*, April 3, 1962, 47. Biographer Ron Ross portrays Paret as more playful than cruel at the weigh-in. "Taunting and teasing was a relatively gentle form of gay-baiting in most of the Caribbean cultures," wrote Ross. See *Nine . . . Ten*, 60.

31. Robert L. Teague, "Griffith Testifies He Didn't Realize Paret Was Helpless in Fatal Bout," *New York Times*, May 23, 1962, 57.

32. Jimmy Breslin, "The Champion Who Can't Beat a Memory," *Saturday Evening Post*, December 8, 1962, 64. In 2005, Griffith told *New York Times* columnist Bob Herbert that "He called me a name. So I did what I had to do." See Herbert, "The Haunting of Emile Griffith," *New York Times*, April 14, 2005, A27.

33. Robert M. Lipsyte, "Griffith: The Pied Piper of Chelsea," *New York Times*, June 17, 1962, 154.

34. Dave Anderson, "The Burden of the Haunted Boxers," *New York Times*, December 2, 1979, S4.

35. Oates, *On Boxing*, 30.

36. Roger N. Lancaster, "'That We Should All Turn Queer?' Homosexual Stigma in the Making of Manhood and the Breaking of a Revolution in Nicaragua," in *Conceiving Sexuality: Approaches to Sex Research in a Postmodern World*, ed. John H. Gagnon and Richard G. Parker (New York: Routledge, 1995), 100–101.

37. Breslin's comments appear in *Ring of Fire*.

38. Breslin, "Champion Who Can't Beat a Memory," 62, 64.

39. "Griffith Still Likes to Mix Hats with Gloves," *New York Times*, March 7, 1965, S3.

40. Chandler Brossard, "A Most Unusual Champion," *Look*, April 18, 1967, 54, 56, 58.

41. Ibid., 58, 60.

42. Gerald Early, "Three Notes toward a Cultural Definition of Prizefighting," in *Reading the Fights*, ed. Joyce Carol Oates and Daniel Halpern (New York: Henry Holt, 1988), 31.

43. Roberts, "Wide World of Muhammad Ali," 34.

44. Don Dunphy, *Don Dunphy at Ringside* (New York: Henry Holt, 1988), 146, 163.

45. "Demand Growing for Ban on Boxing," *New York Times*, March 27, 1962, 57.

46. "Magnified by TV," *Time*, April 6, 1962.

47. Rondinone, *Friday Night Fighter*, 181.

48. Rondinone's analysis of the Kefauver Committee appears on pages 169–78 of *Friday Night Fighter*. For an exhaustive account of the Kefauver Committee hearings, see United States Senate Committee on the Judiciary, Professional Boxing. Hearings before the Subcommittee on Antitrust and Monopoly of the Committee on the Judiciary, United States Senate, Eighty-sixth Congress, second session, Parts 1–4 (Washington, DC: United States Government Printing Office, 1960–64).

49. Steven A. Riess, "Only the Ring was Square: Frankie Carbo and the Underworld Control of American Boxing," *The International Journal of the History of Sport* 5, no. 1 (1988): 48.

50. Jack Newfield uses the phrase in *Ring of Fire*.

51. Emanuel Perlmutter, "Investigations Open as Governor Demands Complete Report on Paret Fight," *New York Times*, March 26, 1962, 40.

52. Warren Weaver Jr., "Commission Report to Governor Backs Goldstein's Judgment in Paret Bout," *New York Times*, March 28, 1962, 42.

53. Leyhmond Robinson, "State Legislature Creates Committee for Boxing Inquiry," *New York Times*, March 31, 1962, 19.

54. "Brown Calls Boxing 'Rotten,'" *New York Times*, March 28, 1962, 42.

55. Robert L. Teague, "Ring Inquiry Gets under Way Today," *New York Times*, April 6, 1962, 56.

56. "Illinois Joins Anti-boxing Agitation," *New York Times*, January 23, 1963, 14.

57. Deane McGowen, "Clamor Grows Here and Abroad for End to Professional Boxing," *New York Times*, April 5, 1962, 52.

58. Teague, "Ring Inquiry."

59. Robert Daley, "Paret's Ring Death Shocks Europeans; Boxing Is Assailed," *New York Times*, April 10, 1962, 75; see also "House of Lords Halts Pro Boxing Ban Move," *New York Times*, May 11, 1962, 22.

60. "Injured Boxer, 32, Shows Slight Gain," *New York Times*, April 8, 1962, S7.

61. McGowen, "Clamor Grows."

62. "A Ring Requiem," *America*, April 21, 1962, 73.

63. "Paret's Mother Arrives to Join Vigil at Ex-champion's Bedside," *New York Times*, March 31, 1962, 19.

64. "KO for Prizefighting," *New York Times*, September 29, 1962, 17.

65. "Murder by TV," *Christian Century*, April 18, 1962, 482.

66. Hans J. Massaquoi, "Should Boxing Be Abolished?" *Ebony*, June 1962, 44.

67. "Emotionalism Is Cited," *New York Times*, March 28, 1962, 42.

68. "Boxing Defended at Hearing in N.Y.," *New York Times*, February 5, 1963, 16.

69. "Boxing Writers Ask Better Regulation," *New York Times*, January 3, 1963, 19.

70. "Scorecard," *Sports Illustrated*, April 16, 1962, 4.

71. Quoted in Massaquoi, "Should Boxing Be Abolished?," 45.

72. Boxing did not stay off the air for long. For the next couple of years, ABC broadcast several of Muhammad Ali's fights on "Wide World of Sports." Although the fights were often broadcast weeks after the actual event, they still garnered respectable ratings. By the end of the 1960s, boxing had returned to the small screen, although it would never regain the same prominence it enjoyed in the 1950s. See Roberts, "Wide World of Muhammad Ali," 43–50.

73. Norman Mailer, *The Presidential Papers* (New York: G. P. Putnam's Sons, 1963), 243, 244, 245.

74. Gil Turner, "Benny 'Kid' Paret," *Broadside Ballads No. 1* (New York: Folkway Records, 1963); copy in author's possession.

75. Paul Shuttleworth, *Poems to the Memory of Benny Kid Paret* (West Lafayette, IN: Sparrow Press, 1978), 13. I would like to thank Red for the grace and kindness that he showed me in allowing the publication of his poetry. He is truly an American original.

76. Ibid., 14.

77. Ross, *Nine . . . Ten*, 176–77.

78. Ibid., xiv.

79. Michael Giltz, "Mortal Combat," *Advocate*, April 26, 2005, 66.

5. "Princess Diana with a Pushbroom Mustache"

1. On Gehrig, consult Jonathan Eig, *Luckiest Man: The Life and Death of Lou Gehrig* (New York: Simon & Schuster, 2005), especially chapters 18–26. Baker's story appears in John Davies, *The Legend of Hobey Baker* (New York: Little, Brown, 1966) and, more recently, in Emil R. Salvini, *Hobey Baker, American Legend* (Minneapolis: Hobey Baker Foundation, 2005).

2. For more on Prefontaine, see Tom Jordan, *Pre: The Story of America's Greatest Running Legend*, 2nd ed. (Emmaus, PA: Rodale, 1997) and Kenny Moore, *Bowerman and the Men of Oregon: The Story of Oregon's Legendary Coach and Nike's Cofounder* (Emmaus, PA: Rodale, 2006). On the commercially driven growth of Prefontaine's popularity, see Theresa A. Walton, "Steve Prefontaine: From Rebel with a Cause to Hero with a Swoosh," *Sociology of Sport Journal* 21, no. 1 (2004): 61–83.

3. For more on the Chapman story, see Mike Sowell, *The Pitch That Killed: The Story of Carl Mays, Ray Chapman, and the Pennant Race of 1920* (Chicago: Ivan R. Dee, 1989). Chapman remains the only baseball player killed in a major league game. Historian Bob Gorman has collected the stories of players who died in baseball's minor leagues in "'I Guess I Forgot to Duck': On-Field Player Fatalities in the Minor Leagues," *Nine: A Journal of Baseball History and Culture* 11, no. 2 (2003): 85–96.

4. Nikki Nichols, *Frozen in Time: The Enduring Legacy of the 1961 U.S. Figure Skating Team* (Cincinnati: Clerisy Press, 2006).

5. See Jeff Connor, *The Lost Babes: Manchester United and the Forgotten Victims of Munich* (London: HarperSport, 2006); Senna's life has been chronicled in the documentary film *Senna*, directed by Asif Kapadia (Universal City, CA: Universal Pictures, 2010).

6. Jon Krakauer tells Tillman's story with impressive detail in *Where Men Win Glory: The Odyssey of Pat Tillman* (New York: Anchor Books, 2010).

7. Dave Van Dyck, "Fallen Hero," accessed July 14, 2004, http://www2.foxsports.com /obits/earnhardt/vandy2.sml (site discontinued); copy in author's possession.

8. Ken Willis, "Overwhelming Disbelief," *Motor Racing Network*, February 19, 2001, http://www.mrn.com/Race-Series/NASCAR-Sprint-Cup/News/Articles/2001/02/Over whelming-Disbelief.aspx; copy in author's possession.

9. Quoted in Sandra McKee, "'The Intimidator' Had Soft Side, Too," *Baltimore Sun*, February 19, 2001.

10. Hunter S. Thompson, "Death in the Afternoon," ESPN, last modified February 19, 2001, http://www.espn.go.com/espn/page2/story?id=1095213.

11. Mike Bianchi, "Greatest Driver? Isn't Earnhardt More Than That?" *Orlando Sentinel*, February 20, 2001.

12. Brian Williams, "No. 3 and Me," *Time*, March 5, 2001, 67.

13. Aristotle, *Poetics*, trans. Malcolm Heath (London: Penguin, 1996), sec. 5.2.

14. Ann Patchett, "Southern Comforts," *New York Times Magazine*, December 30, 2001, 40.

15. Daniel S. Pierce, *Real NASCAR: White Lightning, Red Clay, and Big Bill France* (Chapel Hill: Univ. of North Carolina Press, 2010), 25, 26.

16. Robert Lipsyte, "Window into America's Hottest New Reality Show," *New York Times*, February 26, 2001, D10. Darrell Waltrip's autobiography describes his relationship with Earnhardt as well as his reaction to the crash at Daytona; see Darrell Waltrip, *Sundays Will Never Be the Same*, with Nate Larkin (New York: Free Press, 2012).

17. Jeff Alan, "Shock. Disbelief. Sadness," Catchfence, accessed August 12, 2003, http://www.catchfence.com (site discontinued); copy in author's possession.

18. Michael Waltrip, *In the Blink of an Eye: Dale, Daytona, and the Day That Everything Changed*, with Ellis Henican (New York: Hyperion, 2011), 187.

19. Mark Swanson, "Intimidator Goes Out Protecting His Own," CBS Sportsline, February 18, 2001, accessed August 12, 2003, http://www.cbssportsline.com (site discontinued); copy in author's possession.

20. Lee Spencer, "Black Sunday," *Sporting News*, February 26, 2001, 17.

21. Brian Schmitz, "The Making of Dale Earnhardt," *Orlando Sentinel*, February 22, 2001.

22. Robert Sullivan, "Dale Earnhardt, 1951–2001: The Last Lap," *Time*, March 5, 2001, 60–69.

23. Pat Evans, "For the Love of Dale," accessed August 12, 2003, http://www.rwjm.com (site discontinued); copy in author's possession. The biblical quotation is from John 15:13.

24. Robert Lipsyte, "The Crossing of Faith and Big-time Sport," *New York Times*, March 4, 2001, SP10. See William J. Baker, *Playing with God: Religion and Modern Sport* (Cambridge, MA: Harvard Univ. Press, 2007).

25. Teresa Earnhardt, "An Open Letter to Fans from Teresa Earnhardt," *USA Today*, February 23, 2001.

26. Greg Engle, "An Open Letter to Dale Earnhardt," accessed August 25, 2004, http://www.ajnascarracing.com/earnhardt.htm (site discontinued); copy in author's possession.

27. Alan R. Gatrell, "It Only Takes a Tap," in *Cowboy and Cowgirl Poems* (Bloomington, IN: AuthorHouse, 2007), 43. This poem appeared on websites within a month of Earnhardt's death, but without attribution and usually titled "A Seagull Flying Low." That title refers to the disembodied Earnhardt taking the shape of a seagull and flying into victory lane to congratulate Michael Waltrip on his victory.

28. Monte Dutton, "Working-class hero," *Gaston Gazette*'s "Dale Earnhardt: Tribute to a Racing Legend," accessed September 8, 2004, http://www.gastongazette.com/portal/sports/nascar/earnhardt/articles/nascar10.htm (site discontinued); copy in author's possession.

29. Touré, "Kurt Is My Copilot," in *Never Drank the Kool-Aid* (New York: Picador, 2006), 223.

30. Quoted in Leigh Montville, *At the Altar of Speed: The Fast Life and Tragic Death of Dale Earnhardt* (New York: Doubleday, 2001), 139.

31. Robert Lipsyte, "An Empire Built on a Chassis Continues On," *New York Times*, March 18, 2001, SP13.

32. Robert Lipsyte, "Ghost of the Intimidator Stalks the Track," *New York Times*, December 2, 2001, SP13.

33. Waltrip, *In the Blink of an Eye*, 202.

34. For more on the race, see Robert Lipsyte, "'The Call' Is Answered in Earnhardt's Pepsi 400 Victory," *New York Times*, July 9, 2001, D1.

35. Greg Engle, "Where Do We Go From Here?," accessed August 25, 2004, http://www.ajnascarracing.com/earnhardt.htm (site discontinued); copy in author's possession.

36. Rick Bragg, "Racer's Death Leaves Hole in Heart of His Hometown," *New York Times*, February 21, 2001, A1, A2. In 2003, Bragg resigned from the *New York Times* following a dispute over his use of unattributed stringers in a story about oystermen in Florida. See Howard Kurtz, "Rick Bragg Quits at *New York Times*," *Washington Post*, May 29, 2003, C1.

37. Paul Hemphill, "One Last Lap around the Speedway," *New York Times*, February 24, 2001, A13. A southern journalist and novelist, Hemphill had long followed stock car racing and was the author of *Wheels: A Season on NASCAR's Winston Cup Circuit* (New York: Simon & Schuster, 1997).

38. Joe Posnanski, "Earnhardt's Death Severs Last Link to Racin'," *Kansas City Star*, February 20, 2001.

39. Micheline Maynard, "After Earnhardt's Death, a Rebound for NASCAR," *New York Times*, March 25, 2001, BU9.

40. Robert Lipsyte, "Nascar Doesn't Linger, and Keeps Its Nerve," *New York Times*, February 25, 2001, SP5.

41. Quoted in Allen St. John, "Reality TV's Ultimate Death Trip," *New York Times*, February 25, 2001, WK4.

42. Frank Pellegrini, "They're Crying over Dale Earnhardt Now," *Time*, February 23, 2001, http://content.time.com/time/pow/article/0,8599,100437,00.html.

43. Frank Deford, "Tragic Death of Dale Earnhardt and Trying to Understand the Popularity of Automobile Racing," transcript of commentary delivered on National Public Radio, Morning Edition, Washington, DC, February 28, 2001, 1.

44. Thompson, "Death in the Afternoon."

45. Harry L. Rinker, "There Is Nothing Wrong with It, Except It Just Does Not Seem Right," *Antiques & Collecting* magazine, July 2001, 47. In what must have been a heaven-sent commercial crossbreeding, a black beanie baby complete with number three (and trademark shades) was not far behind.

46. Richard Alm, "Earnhardt Legend Drives Strong Memorabilia Market," *Dallas Morning News*, February 15, 2002.

47. Mike Bianchi, "They Still Look Up to Dale, Sr." *Orlando Sentinel*, February 15, 2003.

48. Montville, *At the Altar of Speed*, xvii, xv, xvi.

49. For an insightful examination of American memorial spaces, consult Erika Doss, *Memorial Mania: Public Feeling in America* (Chicago: Univ. of Chicago Press, 2010), quote on 67.

50. *Statistical Abstract of the United States: 2001*, prepared by the U.S. Census Bureau (Washington, DC, 2002), 720.

51. Gordon Corcoran, "One Quarter-Mile from Heaven," in *Reinventing the Archetype*, ed. AnnMarie Avila, Jessica Lott, Kevin M. Mattix, M. Aaron Pelletier, and Megan Reigner (n.p.: After the Fall Productions, 2008), 61. Personal recollections of Earnhardt and reactions to his death have been collected in Tom Gillispie, *Angel in Black: Remembering Dale Earnhardt, Sr.* (Nashville: Cumberland House, 2008).

52. Timothy Jon Barrett, "The Man in Black," February 21, 2001, http://blk3gm.tripod .com/fancontrib/fancontrib.htm. A similar scenario appears at the end of *3* (directed by Russell Mulcahy, Santa Monica, CA: Orly Anderson Productions, 2012), an ESPN biopic about Earnhardt. After his crash at Daytona, the scene shifts (whether forward or backward in time is ambiguous) to a young Dale being embraced by his father Ralph.

53. For more information on Rice's life, see Charles Fountain, *Sportswriter: The Life and Times of Grantland Rice* (New York: Oxford Univ. Press, 1993); William A. Harper, *How You Played the Game: The Life of Grantland Rice* (Columbia: Univ. of Missouri Press, 1999); and Mark Inabinett, *Grantland Rice and His Heroes: The Sportswriter as Mythmaker in the 1920s* (Knoxville: Univ. of Tennessee Press, 1994).

6. To an Athlete Dying Old

1. Alfred Tennyson, "Tithonus," *Cornhill*, February 1860, 175.

2. Richard Ben Cramer, *Joe DiMaggio: The Hero's Life* (New York: Simon & Schuster, 2000), 80.

3. Quoted in Ira Berkow, *Red: A Biography of Red Smith* (New York: Times Books, 1986), 105.

4. Dave Anderson, ed., *The Red Smith Reader* (New York: Random House, 1982), 16, 15. For more on Stanley Woodward's life, see Stanley Woodward, *Sportswriter* (Garden City, NY: Doubleday, 1967). Journalist Seymour Krim joined Woodward's critique of the "gee-whiz" style. Writing in 1959, Krim observed that "sports journalism in our country remains a primitive backwoods mostly inhabited by second-rate word-slingers who have been trapped on the sports beat and feed the public a daily ration of mind-softening squash." Krim singled out Red Smith "as the number-one newspaper sportswriter in the country and a man who regards himself as a suave literateur" who was shockingly (to Krim, anyway) unfamiliar with the work of Dylan Thomas and E. E. Cummings. See Seymour Krim, "Sportswriting: Square and Avantgarde," in *Views of a Nearsighted Cannoneer* (New York: E. P. Dutton, 1968), 198, 199.

5. See Cramer, *Joe DiMaggio*, 193–94.

6. David Halberstam, *Summer of '49* (New York: William Morrow, 1989), 55.

7. Roger Kahn, *Joe and Marilyn* (New York: Avon Books, 1986), 127.

8. Ernest Hemingway, *The Old Man and the Sea* (New York: Charles Scribner's Sons, 1952), 17.

9. Quoted in Cramer, *Joe DiMaggio*, 80.

10. Red Smith, "Writing Less—and Better?" *New York Times*, January 11, 1982, C3.

11. Roger Kahn, *Memories of Summer* (Lincoln: Univ. of Nebraska Press, 1997), 216.

12. Halberstam, *Summer of '49*, 273.

13. Gay Talese, "The Silent Season of a Hero," in *The Gay Talese Reader: Portraits and Encounters* (New York: Walker, 2003), 109–10; the article originally appeared in *Esquire* in July 1966. David Halberstam and Glenn Stout named "The Silent Season of a Hero" as the best sports article written in the twentieth century. See Halberstam and Stout, eds., *The Best American Sports Writing of the Century* (Boston: Houghton Mifflin, 1999).

14. Robert Lipsyte, *An Accidental Sportswriter: A Memoir* (New York: HarperCollins, 2011), 24.

15. Talese, "Silent Season of a Hero," 93.

16. Cramer, *Joe DiMaggio*, 433.

17. Kasia Brody, *Boxing: A Cultural History* (London: Reaktion Books, 2008), 353.

18. Robert S. Boynton, ed., *The New New Journalism* (New York: Vintage Books, 2005), xi, xiii, xv. For Wolfe's manifesto on nonfiction writing, see Tom Wolfe, *The New Journalism* (New York: Harper & Row, 1973).

19. Tom Wolfe describes the revelatory effect that Talese's article about Joe Louis had on his view of nonfiction. See Wolfe, *New Journalism*, 10–11. Although Wolfe categorized Talese as a New Journalist, Talese rejects the label. "I just want to write about people in a way that is a short story with real names," Talese told a class of journalism students (Boynton, *New New Journalism*, 365).

20. David Halberstam, "History Is Their Beat: The New Journalist Historians," in *The Writing Life: Writers on How They Think and Work*, ed. Marie Arana (New York: Public Affairs, 2003), 283.

21. Cramer, *Joe DiMaggio*, 519, 520. In his acknowledgments, Cramer thanks "three reporters and authors who are as exemplary in my trade as DiMaggio was on a ballfield"— David Halberstam, Seymour Hersh, and Gay Talese (521). Not everyone was thrilled with Cramer's revisionist look at DiMaggio. One example is Wilfrid Sheed, "Baseball Was Very, Very Good to Him," *New York Times*, October 28, 2000, BR10. Novelist Jerome Charyn, in his recent biography of DiMaggio, takes exception to Cramer's treatment. "Cramer's book is itself a marvel that digs deep into the DiMaggio myth as it unmans him piece by piece," writes Charyn. "But its picture of the Jolter is far too reductive and bleak. DiMaggio was much more than the blind apparatus of a machine that spat out heroes and ruined them in the process. He wasn't as calculating as Cramer loves to think. He was like an idiot savant

whose magic was born on a baseball field and abandoned him once he left it." See Jerome Charyn, *Joe DiMaggio: The Long Vigil* (New Haven, CT: Yale Univ. Press, 2011), 3.

22. Cramer, *Joe DiMaggio*, ix, x.

23. In a nice turn of phrase that was clearly intended to be thrust into DiMaggio's back, Cramer writes of DiMaggio's "legendary disinclination to pay" for anything. See *Joe DiMaggio*, 450. Analyzing *Joe DiMaggio: A Hero's Life*, Robert Lipsyte wrote that Cramer "managed to diminish DiMaggio into a greedy, petty pig." See Lipsyte, *Accidental Sportswriter*, 130.

24. Cramer, *Joe DiMaggio*, 441.

25. Richard Bernstein, "Idol of Millions Yet a Bit of a Phantom," *New York Times*, October 18, 2000, E9.

26. Richard Sandomir, "Legends' Images Often Change in Death," *New York Times*, July 15, 2002, D2.

27. Cramer, *Joe DiMaggio*, ix.

28. Ibid., 471.

29. Stephen Jay Gould, "The Streak of Streaks," *New York Review of Books*, August 18, 1988.

30. "Mantle of Greatness," *Time*, March 14, 1969, 52.

31. Gerald Holland, "All Hail the Hero Mighty Mickey," *Sports Illustrated*, March 4, 1957, 53, 54.

32. Quoted in David Falkner, *The Last Hero: The Life of Mickey Mantle* (New York: Simon & Schuster, 1995), 176.

33. Roger Kahn, "Sports," *Esquire*, May 1971, 16. See also "Young Man on Olympus," *Time*, June 15, 1953, 64–70.

34. Maury Allen, *Memories of the Mick* (Dallas: Taylor Publishing, 1997), 141.

35. Merlyn Mantle, Mickey Mantle Jr., David Mantle, and Dan Mantle, *A Hero All His Life*, with Mickey Herskowitz (New York: HarperCollins, 1996), 12.

36. Quoted in Tony Castro, *Mickey Mantle: America's Prodigal Son* (Washington, DC: Brassey's, 2002), 175.

37. Jim Bouton, *Ball Four: The Final Pitch* (North Egremont, MA: Bulldog Publishing, 2000), 33; the Shoreham Hotel story appears on 41.

38. Falkner, *The Last Hero*, 200.

39. Pepitone may have been particularly eager to attack Bouton owing to the author's description of Pepitone as a comic figure, complete with two toupees—a large one to go out on the town and a smaller "game piece" that fit better under his cap. See Bouton, *Ball Four*, 178.

40. David Halberstam, "American Notes: Baseball and the National Mythology," *Harper's*, September 1970, 24, 25, 24.

41. Castro, *Mickey Mantle*, 290, 175.

42. Falkner, *The Last Hero*, 201.

43. Castro, *Mickey Mantle*, 238, 237 (italics in original), 250.

44. Mickey Mantle, "Time in a Bottle," with Jill Lieber, *Sports Illustrated*, April 18, 1994, 70.

45. *Medical News Report*, July 1995; copy in possession of the author.

46. Gina Kolata, "Transplants, Morality, and Mickey," *New York Times*, June 11, 1995, E5.

47. *Medical News Report*, July 1995.

48. Bob Costas, Eulogy for Mickey Mantle, Dallas, Texas, August 15, 1995, https://www.youtube.com/watch?v=Lr-tcB3L3g4.

49. Richard Hoffer, "Mickey Mantle," *Sports Illustrated*, August 21, 1995, 20, 25. Roger Kahn felt much the same way. He wrote, "When [Mantle] couldn't play ball anymore, a whole generation felt older. When he got cancer, a whole generation felt the fear of death" (quoted in Castro, *Mickey Mantle*, 285).

50. Allen, *Memories of the Mick*, 166.

51. Castro, *Mickey Mantle*, xii.

52. Falkner, *The Last Hero*, 245, 253–54 (italics in original).

53. Quoted in Allen, *Memories of the Mick*, 160.

54. Kahn, *Joe and Marilyn*, 182.

55. John Updike, "Hub Fans Bid Kid Adieu," *New Yorker*, October 22, 1960, 109–31.

56. Ibid., 109. Updike linked other literary characters to Williams as well. At one point, he argues that if the Red Sox were a tragedy, "then Williams was Hamlet." Later, Updike writes that Williams at the plate "was like having a familiar Leonardo appear in a shuffle of *Saturday Evening Post* covers." Presumably, lesser lights like Bobby Doerr and Dominic DiMaggio might have graced the cover of the *Post*.

57. Ibid., 116, 115, 109, 110.

58. Ibid., 109. Christ was not the only religious figure compared to Williams. Updike writes that Williams's involvement with the Jimmy Fund (charity for children with cancer) "gave him a civic presence somewhat like that of Richard Cardinal Cushing." Williams sided with no religious group (he was prodigiously profane), but "he and the Cardinal, when their good works intersect and they appear in the public eye together, make a handsome and heartening pair" (115). Richard Cardinal Cushing served as the archbishop of Boston from 1944 to 1970.

59. Ibid., 128, 131. As a side note, Leigh Montville, former writer at *Sports Illustrated* and author of the definitive biography of Williams, writes that Williams answered a letter that Montville wrote as a ten-year-old in 1953. He recalled the moment in the obituary of Williams that he wrote in 2002 for *Sports Illustrated*: "Even now I cannot think of another piece of mail that has made me feel happier, not college acceptances nor good reports from doctors, nothing. The Ted Williams postcard was unadulterated bliss, wholly equivalent to a letter straight from heaven." Apparently, unbeknownst to John Updike, God occasionally answered a letter. See Leigh Montville, *Ted Williams: The Biography of an American Hero*

(New York: Doubleday, 2004), 485. The original publication appeared as Montville, "Farewell, Teddy Ballgame," *Sports Illustrated*, July 15, 2002, 44–56 (quote on 46).

60. The Ted Williams Museum closed in 2006 and its baseball exhibits were moved to Tropicana Field in St. Petersburg, Florida.

61. Montville, *Ted Williams*, 448.

62. Ibid., 456.

63. Ibid., 436.

64. Tom Verducci, "What Really Happened to Ted Williams," *Sports Illustrated*, August 18, 2003, 68.

65. Rick Reilly, "Chillin' with the Splinter," *Sports Illustrated*, June 30, 2003, 104.

66. "This Week's Sign of the Apocalypse," *Sports Illustrated*, May 26, 2003, 28.

67. Kelley King, "Where Ted Lives Now," *Sports Illustrated*, March 10, 2003, 22.

68. Montville, *Ted Williams*, 477, 493.

69. Quoted in Geoffrey Wheatcroft, "Why Orwell Endures," *New York Times*, February 14, 2010, 27.

70. Voiceover from Philadelphia Eagles middle linebacker Tim Rossovich in *The New Breed* (Mount Laurel, NJ: NFL Films, 1971); quoted in Travis Vogan, *Keepers of the Flame: NFL Films and the Rise of Sports Media* (Urbana: Univ. of Illinois Press, 2014), 54.

71. Homer, *The Iliad*, trans. Robert Fagles (New York: Penguin, 1988), 296. The Greek version is spelled Tithonos and the Romanized variant is spelled Tithonus.

72. This translation of the Tithonos story appears in Susan C. Shelmerdine, trans., *The Homeric Hymns* (Newburyport, MA: Focus Publishing, 1995), 136–37. The idea that Tithonos eventually gets turned into a grasshopper or cicada is not original to the text but may have been added later by Hellanikos; see Timothy Gantz's commentary in *Early Greek Myth: A Guide to Literary and Artistic Sources* (Baltimore: Johns Hopkins Univ. Press, 1993), 36–37. I would like to thank David Lunt for bringing this material to my attention and helping me to flesh out these ideas.

73. Tennyson, "Tithonus," 175–76.

Selected Bibliography

The bibliography includes all of the sources cited in the notes with the exception of daily newspapers, archival records, and some online material. For those citations, please consult the notes.

Abreu, Christina D. "The Story of Benny 'Kid' Paret: Cuban Boxers, the Cuban Revolution, and the U.S. Media, 1959–1962." *Journal of Sport History* 38, no. 1 (2011): 95–113.

Alan, Jeff. "Shock. Disbelief. Sadness." Catchfence. Accessed August 12, 2003. http://www.catchfence.com (site discontinued).

Allen, Maury. *Memories of the Mick*. Dallas: Taylor Publishing, 1997.

Allen, Michael. "The Rise and Decline of the Early Rodeo Cowgirl." *Pacific Northwest Quarterly* 83, no. 4 (1992): 122–27.

Anderson, Dave, ed. *The Red Smith Reader*. New York: Random House, 1982.

Anderson, Eric. *In the Game: Gay Athletes and the Cult of Masculinity*. Albany: State Univ. of New York Press, 2005.

Ariès, Philippe. *The Hour of Our Death*. Translated by Helen Weaver. New York: Barnes & Noble, 1981.

Aristotle. *Poetics*. Translated by Malcolm Heath. London: Penguin, 1996.

Assmann, Aleida. "Transformations between History and Memory." *Social Research* 75, no. 1 (Spring 2008): 49–72.

Atwood, Margaret. *In Search of Alias Grace*. Ottawa: Univ. of Ottawa Press, 1997.

Bacon, Francis. *Bacon's Essays*. London: John W. Parker & Son, 1856.

Baender, Paul, ed. *A Hero Perished: The Diary and Selected Letters of Nile Kinnick*. Iowa City: Univ. of Iowa Press, 1992.

Baker, William J. *Playing with God: Religion and Modern Sport*. Cambridge, MA: Harvard Univ. Press, 2007.

Barnes, Simon. *The Meaning of Sport*. London: Short Books, 2006.

Baseball: Bottom of the Seventh Inning. Directed by Ken Burns. Walpole, NH: Florentine Films, 1999.

Becker, Ernest. *The Denial of Death*. New York: Free Press, 1973.

Bellow, Saul. *Humboldt's Gift*. New York: Viking Press, 1975.

Berkow, Ira. *Red: A Biography of Red Smith*. New York: Times Books, 1986.

Bodnar, John. "Pierre Nora, National Memory, and Democracy: A Review." *Journal of American History* 87, no. 3 (2000): 951–63.

Bouton, Jim. *Ball Four: The Final Pitch*. North Egremont, MA: Bulldog Publishing, 2000.

Boynton, Robert S., ed. *The New New Journalism*. New York: Vintage Books, 2005.

Bradlee, Ben, Jr. *The Kid: The Immortal Life of Ted Williams*. New York: Little, Brown, 2013.

Branch, Mark Alden. "The Ten Great Yalies Who Never Were." *Yale Alumni Magazine*, February 2003.

Breslin, Jimmy. "The Champion Who Can't Beat a Memory." *Saturday Evening Post*, December 8, 1962, 62–65.

———. "The Man Who Died for Notre Dame." *Real*, December 1955, 59–60.

Brody, Kasia. *Boxing: A Cultural History*. London: Reaktion Books, 2008.

Brossard, Chandler. "A Most Unusual Champion." *Look*, April 18, 1967, 54–60.

Broun, Heywood. "Dying for 'Dear Old—': A Study in Sportsmanship." *Harper's*, June 1925, 60–66.

Brown, Peter. *The Cult of the Saints*. Chicago: Univ. of Chicago Press, 1981.

Burbick, Joan. *Rodeo Queens and the American Dream*. New York: Public Affairs, 2002.

Cahn, Susan. *Coming on Strong: Gender and Sexuality in Twentieth-Century Women's Sports*. Cambridge, MA: Harvard Univ. Press, 1994.

Cannon, Lou. *President Reagan: The Role of a Lifetime*. New York: Simon & Schuster, 1991.

Castro, Tony. *Mickey Mantle: America's Prodigal Son*. Washington, DC: Brassey's, 2002.

Cavanaugh, Jack. *The Gipper: George Gipp, Knute Rockne, and the Dramatic Rise of Notre Dame Football*. New York: Skyhorse, 2010.

Charyn, Jerome. *Joe DiMaggio: The Long Vigil*. New Haven, CT: Yale Univ. Press, 2011.

Chelland, Patrick. *One for the Gipper: George Gipp, Knute Rockne, and Notre Dame*. Chicago: Henry Regnery, 1973.

Clavin, Tom, and Danny Peary. *Roger Maris: Baseball's Reluctant Hero*. New York: Touchstone, 2010.

Cobb, Ty. "They Don't Play Baseball Any More." *Life*, March 17, 1952, 136–53.

Cohen, Rich. "The Boys of Winter." *Harper's*, June 2002, 51–57.

Congress, Joint Committee on Printing. *Memorial Services in the Congress of the United States and Tributes in Eulogy of Ronald Reagan, Late a President of the United States*. Washington, DC: United States Government Printing Office, 2005.

Connor, Jeff. *The Lost Babes: Manchester United and the Forgotten Victims of Munich*. London: HarperSport, 2006.

Corcoran, Gordon. "One Quarter-Mile from Heaven." In *Reinventing the Archetype*, edited by AnnMarie Avila, Jessica Lott, Kevin M. Mattix, M. Aaron Pelletier, and Megan Reigner. n.p.: After the Fall Productions, 2008.

Costas, Bob. "Eulogy for Mickey Mantle." Dallas, Texas, August 15, 1995. https:// www.youtube.com/watch?v=Lr-tcB3L3g4.

Cousins, Norman. "Who Killed Benny Paret?" *Saturday Review*, May 5, 1962, 14.

Cowboy Up: Inside the Extreme World of Bull Riding. Directed by David Wittkower. Calabasas, CA: Lighthouse Productions, 2002.

Cox, James A. "Was 'the Gipper' Really for Real? You Can Bet He Was." *Smithsonian* 16, no. 9 (1985), 130–50.

Cramer, Richard Ben. *Joe DiMaggio: The Hero's Life*. New York: Simon & Schuster, 2000.

———. *What Do You Think of Ted Williams Now?* New York: Simon & Schuster, 2002.

Davies, Douglas J. *Death, Ritual, and Belief*. London: Continuum, 2002.

Davies, John. *The Legend of Hobey Baker*. New York: Little, Brown, 1966.

Davies, Richard O. *America's Obsession: Sports and Society Since 1945*. Belmont, CA: Wadsworth, 1994.

Deford, Frank. "Tragic Death of Dale Earnhardt and Trying to Understand the Popularity of Automobile Racing." Transcript of commentary delivered on National Public Radio, Morning Edition, Washington, DC, February 28, 2001, 1.

Doss, Erika. *Elvis Culture: Fans, Faith, and Image*. Lawrence: Univ. Press of Kansas, 1999.

———. *Memorial Mania: Public Feeling in America*. Chicago: Univ. of Chicago Press, 2010.

Dunphy, Don. *Don Dunphy at Ringside*. New York: Henry Holt, 1988.

Early, Gerald. "Three Notes toward a Cultural Definition of Prizefighting." In *Reading the Fights*, edited by Joyce Carol Oates and Daniel Halpern, 20–38. New York: Henry Holt, 1988.

Eig, Jonathan. *Luckiest Man: The Life and Death of Lou Gehrig.* New York: Simon & Schuster, 2005.

8 Seconds. Directed by Charlie McDade. New York: Harper, 1994.

Engelberg, Morris. *DiMaggio: Setting the Record Straight.* With Marv Schneider. St. Paul, MN: MBI, 2003.

Engle, Greg. "An Open Letter to Dale Earnhardt." Accessed August 25, 2004. http://www.ajnascarracing.com/earnhardt.htm (site discontinued).

———. "Where Do We Go From Here?" Accessed August 25, 2004. http://www.ajnascarracing.com/earnhardt.htm (site discontinued).

Evans, Christopher H. "Baseball as Civil Religion: The Genesis of an American Creation Story." In *The Faith of 50 Million: Baseball, Religion, and American Culture*, edited by Christopher H. Evans and William R. Herzog II, 13–33. Louisville, KY: Westminster John Knox Press, 2002.

Falkner, David. *The Last Hero: The Life of Mickey Mantle.* New York: Simon & Schuster, 1995.

Faust, Drew Gilpin. *This Republic of Suffering: Death and the American Civil War.* New York: Alfred A. Knopf, 2008.

Fountain, Charles. *Sportswriter: The Life and Times of Grantland Rice.* New York: Oxford Univ. Press, 1993.

Freedman, William. *More Than a Pastime: An Oral History of Baseball Fans.* Jefferson, NC: McFarland, 1998.

Freud, Sigmund. "Thoughts for the Times on War and Death." In *Civilisation, War and Death*, edited by John Rickman, 1–25. London: Hogarth Press and the Institute of Psycho-Analysis, 1915.

From Cheyenne to Pendleton: The Rise and Fall of the Rodeo Cowgirl. Directed by Steve Wursta. Bend, OR: Arctic Circle Productions, 2010.

Frost, Elsie. *Lane Frost: A Mother's Story.* Durant, OK: Victory Life Church, n.d.

Fuentes, Carlos. *The Buried Mirror: Reflections on Spain and the New World.* Boston: Houghton Mifflin, 1992.

Gantz, Timothy. *Early Greek Myth: A Guide to Literary and Artistic Sources.* Baltimore: Johns Hopkins Univ. Press, 1993.

Gatrell, Alan R. "It Only Takes a Tap." In *Cowboy and Cowgirl Poems*, 43. Bloomington, IN: AuthorHouse, 2007.

Gekas, George. *The Life and Times of George Gipp.* South Bend, IN: And Books, 1987.

"The Ghost of Washington Hall." *Notre Dame Alumnus* 10, no. 4 (January 1932), 114.

Giamatti, A. Bartlett. *Take Time for Paradise: Americans and Their Games.* New York: Summit Books, 1989.

Giffney, Noreen. "Introduction: The 'Q' Word." In *The Ashgate Research Companion to Queer Theory*, edited by Noreen Giffney and Michael O'Rourke, 17–26. Burlington, VT: Ashgate, 2009.

Gillispie, Tom. *Angel in Black: Remembering Dale Earnhardt, Sr.* Nashville: Cumberland House, 2008.

Gitlin, Todd. *The Sixties: Years of Hope, Days of Rage.* Rev. ed. New York: Bantam, 1993.

Glitz, Michael. "Mortal Combat." *Advocate*, April 26, 2005, 66.

Goldstein, Ruby. "The Middle Man." *Ring* 79, no. 3 (1999): 84, 87, 89.

Golenbock, Peter. *7: The Mickey Mantle Novel.* Guilford, CT: Lyons Press, 2007.

Gorman, Bob. "'I Guess I Forgot to Duck': On-Field Player Fatalities in the Minor Leagues." *Nine: A Journal of Baseball History and Culture* 11, no. 2 (2003): 85–96.

Gorn, Elliott J. *The Manly Art: Bare-Knuckle Prize Fighting in America.* Ithaca, NY: Cornell Univ. Press, 1986.

Gottschall, Jonathan. *The Professor in the Cage: Why Men Fight and Why We Like to Watch.* New York: Penguin, 2015.

Gould, Stephen Jay. "The Streak of Streaks." *New York Review of Books*, August 18, 1988, 10–16.

Guttmann, Allen. *From Ritual to Record: The Nature of Modern Sports.* New York: Columbia Univ. Press, 1978.

Halberstam, David. "American Notes: Baseball and the National Mythology." *Harper's*, September 1970.

———. "History Is Their Beat: The New Journalist Historians." In *The Writing Life: Writers on How They Think and Work*, edited by Marie Arana, 279–88. New York: Public Affairs, 2003.

———. *October 1964.* New York: Fawcett Books, 1995.

———. *Summer of '49.* New York: William Morrow, 1989.

———. *The Teammates.* New York: Hyperion, 2003.

Halberstam, David, and Glenn Stout, eds. *The Best American Sports Writing of the Century.* Boston: Houghton Mifflin, 1999.

Halpern, Dan. "Bull Marketing." *New York Times Magazine*, February 12, 2006, 56.

Hamill, Pete. "Blood on Their Hands: The Corrupt and Brutal World of Professional Boxing." *Esquire*, June 1, 1996, 92–99.

Harper, William A. *How You Played the Game: The Life of Grantland Rice*. Columbia: Univ. of Missouri Press, 1999.

Heller, Peter. *In This Corner . . . !* New York: Simon & Schuster, 1973.

Hemingway, Ernest. *Death in the Afternoon*. New York: Charles Scribner's Sons, 1932.

———. *The Old Man and the Sea*. New York: Charles Scribner's Sons, 1952.

Hemphill, Paul. *Wheels: A Season on NASCAR's Winston Cup Circuit*. New York: Simon & Schuster, 1997.

Hoffer, Richard. "Mickey Mantle." *Sports Illustrated*, August 21, 1995, 18–30.

Holland, Gerald. "All Hail the Hero Mighty Mickey." *Sports Illustrated*, March 4, 1957, 52–60.

Homer. *The Iliad*. Translated by Robert Fagles. New York: Penguin, 1988.

Hopkins, Gerard Manley. "Spring and Fall." In *Poems of Gerard Manley Hopkins*, edited by Robert Bridges. London: Humphrey Milford, 1918, 51.

Housman, A. E. *Collected Poems and Selected Prose*. London: Penguin, 1988.

———. "To an Athlete Dying Young." In *A Shropshire Lad*, 26–27. Portland, ME: Thomas B. Mosher, 1906.

Inabinett, Mark. *Grantland Rice and His Heroes: The Sportswriter as Mythmaker in the 1920s*. Knoxville: Univ. of Tennessee Press, 1994.

Israel, Jonathan. *Enlightenment Contested: Philosophy, Modernity, and the Emancipation of Man, 1670–1752*. Oxford: Oxford Univ. Press, 2006.

Jackson, H. J. *Those Who Write for Immortality*. New Haven, CT: Yale Univ. Press, 2015.

Johnson, Owen. *Stover at Yale*. Boston: Little, Brown, 1912.

Johnstone, Jeffrey, and Keith Ryan Cartwright. *Professional Bull Riders: The Official Guide to the Toughest Sport on Earth*. Chicago: Triumph Books, 2009.

Jordan, Tom. *Pre: The Story of America's Greatest Running Legend*. 2nd ed. Emmaus, PA: Rodale, 1997.

Kahn, Roger. *Joe and Marilyn*. New York: Avon Books, 1986.

———. *Memories of Summer*. Lincoln: Univ. of Nebraska Press, 1997.

———. "Sports." *Esquire*, May 1971, 16.

Kansteiner, Wulf. "Finding Meaning in Memory: A Methodological Critique of Collective Memory Studies." *History and Theory* 41, no. 2 (2002): 179–97.

Kennedy, Kostya. *56: Joe DiMaggio and the Last Magic Number in Sports*. New York: Sports Illustrated Books, 2011.

Kimball, Richard. "An Athlete Dying Young: Kenny Hubbs, Memory, and the Chicago Cubs." In *Sports in Chicago*, edited by Elliott J. Gorn, 197–208. Urbana: Univ. of Illinois Press, 2008.

King, Kelley. "Where Ted Lives Now." *Sports Illustrated*, March 10, 2003, 22.

King, Martin Luther, Jr. *Why We Can't Wait*. New York: Harper & Row, 1964.

Klosinski, Emil. *Gipp at Notre Dame: The Truth about "the Gipper."* Baltimore: PublishAmerica, 2003.

Krakauer, Jon. *Where Men Win Glory: The Odyssey of Pat Tillman*. New York: Anchor Books, 2010.

Krim, Seymour. *Views of a Nearsighted Cannoneer*. New York: E. P. Dutton, 1968.

Kurlansky, Mark. *1968: The Year That Rocked the World*. New York: Vintage Books, 2004.

Laegreid, Renee M. "'Performers Prove Beauty and Rodeo Can Be Mixed': The Return of the Cowgirl Queen." *Montana: The Magazine of Western History* 54, no. 1 (2004): 44–55.

———. "Rodeo Queens at the Pendleton Round-Up: The First Go-Round, 1910–1917." *Oregon Historical Quarterly* 104, no. 1 (2003): 6–23.

Lancaster, Roger N. "'That We Should All Turn Queer?' Homosexual Stigma in the Making of Manhood and the Breaking of a Revolution in Nicaragua." In *Conceiving Sexuality: Approaches to Sex Research in a Postmodern World*, edited by John H. Gagnon and Richard G. Parker, 97–115. New York: Routledge, 1995.

Leavy, Jane. *The Last Boy: Mickey Mantle and the End of America's Childhood*. New York: HarperCollins, 2010.

LeCompte, Mary Lou. *Cowgirls of the Rodeo: Pioneer Professional Athletes*. Urbana: Univ. of Illinois Press, 1993.

Lehmann-Haupt, Christopher. *Me and DiMaggio: A Baseball Fan Goes in Search of His Gods*. New York: Simon & Schuster, 1986.

Levy, Bernard-Henri. *American Vertigo*. New York: Random House, 2007.

Lidd, Thomas. *Nile*. Bloomington, IN: AuthorHouse, 2008.

Lipsyte, Robert. *An Accidental Sportswriter: A Memoir*. New York: HarperCollins, 2011.

Lunt, David. "Athletes, Heroes, and the Quest for Immortality in Ancient Greece." PhD diss., Pennsylvania State Univ., 2010.

"Magnified by TV." *Time*, April 6, 1962.

Mailer, Norman. *The Presidential Papers*. New York: G. P. Putnam's Sons, 1963.

Mantle, Merlyn, Mickey Mantle Jr., David Mantle, and Dan Mantle. *A Hero All His Life*. With Mickey Herskowitz. New York: HarperCollins, 1996.

Mantle, Mickey. "Time in a Bottle." With Jill Lieber. *Sports Illustrated*, April 18, 1994, 70.

"Mantle of Greatness." *Time*, March 14, 1969, 52.

The Man Who Shot Liberty Valance. Directed by John Ford. Los Angeles: Paramount Pictures, 1962.

Maraniss, David. *Clemente: The Passion and Grace of Baseball's Last Hero.* New York: Simon & Schuster, 2006.

Margolick, David. *Beyond Glory: Joe Louis vs. Max Schmeling, and a World on the Brink.* New York: Vintage Books, 2005.

Marquand, Ian. "Covering America's Heroes." *Quill* 89, no. 7 (2001): 13.

Massaquoi, Hans J. "Should Boxing Be Abolished?" *Ebony*, June 1962, 45–48, 50–52.

McGinnis, Vera. *Rodeo Road: My Life as a Pioneer Cowgirl.* New York: Hastings House, 1974.

McKenzie, Shelly. *Getting Physical: The Rise of Fitness Culture in America.* Lawrence: Univ. Press of Kansas, 2013.

McRae, Donald. *A Man's World: The Double Life of Emile Griffith.* London: Simon & Schuster, 2015.

Miller, Madeline. *The Song of Achilles: A Novel.* New York: Ecco, 2012.

Montaigne, Michel de. *The Essays of Michel de Montaigne.* Translated by M. A. Screech. London: Penguin, 1991.

Montville, Leigh. *At the Altar of Speed: The Fast Life and Tragic Death of Dale Earnhardt.* New York: Doubleday, 2001.

———. "Farewell, Teddy Ballgame." *Sports Illustrated*, July 15, 2002, 44–56.

———. *Ted Williams: The Biography of an American Hero.* New York: Doubleday, 2004.

Moore, Kenny. *Bowerman and the Men of Oregon: The Story of Oregon's Legendary Coach and Nike's Cofounder.* Emmaus, PA: Rodale, 2006.

Mugnier, Andrea. "Ridin', Ropin', and Rodeoin': Champion Cowgirls of Professional Rodeo, 1930–1945." *Nevada Historical Society Quarterly* 44, no. 2 (2001): 166–74.

Mumford, Lewis. *Technics and Civilization.* New York: Harcourt, Brace, 1934.

"Murder by TV." *Christian Century*, April 18, 1962, 482.

Nagy, Gregory. *The Ancient Greek Hero in 24 Hours.* Cambridge, MA: Belknap Press, 2013.

Neal-Lunsford, Jeff. "Sport in the Land of Television: The Use of Sport in Network Prime-Time Schedules, 1946–50." *Journal of Sport History* 19, no. 1 (1992): 56–76.

The New Breed. Mount Laurel, NJ: NFL Films, 1971.

Newcombe, Jack. "A Man Greater Than the Legend." In *The Glory of Notre Dame*, edited by Fred Katz. New York: Bartholomew House, 1971.

Newman, Roberta. "The American Church of Baseball and the National Baseball Hall of Fame." *Nine: A Journal of Baseball History and Culture* 10, no. 1 (2001): 46–63.

New Testament: New International Version. Crete, IL: The Bible League, 1984.

Nichols, Nikki. *Frozen in Time: The Enduring Legacy of the 1961 U.S. Figure Skating Team.* Cincinnati: Clerisy Press, 2006.

Nora, Pierre. "Between Memory and History: Les Lieux de Mémoire." *Representations* 26 (Spring 1989): 7–24.

Novak, Michael. *The Joy of Sports: End Zones, Bases, Baskets, Balls, and the Consecration of the American Spirit.* Rev. ed. Lanham, MD: Madison Books.

Oates, Joyce Carol. *On Boxing.* Garden City, NY: Dolphin/Doubleday, 1987.

Oriard, Michael. *Dreaming of Heroes: American Sports Fiction, 1868–1980.* Chicago: Nelson-Hall, 1982.

———. *King Football: Sport and Spectacle in the Golden Age of Radio and Newsreels, Movies and Magazines, the Weekly and the Daily Press.* Chapel Hill: Univ. of North Carolina Press, 2001.

Page, Norman. *A. E. Housman: A Critical Biography.* London: Macmillan Press, 1983.

Parfit, Michael. "Rodeos: Behind the Chutes." *National Geographic* 196, no. 3 (September 1999): 104–25.

Patchett, Ann. "Southern Comforts." *New York Times Magazine,* December 30, 2001, 40.

Pellegrini, Frank. "They're Crying over Dale Earnhardt Now." *Time,* February 23, 2001, http://content.time.com/time/pow/article/0,8599,100437,00.html.

Peter, Josh. *Fried Twinkies, Buckle Bunnies, and Bull Riders: A Year inside the Professional Bull Riders Tour.* New York: Rodale, 2005.

Pierce, Daniel S. *Real NASCAR: White Lightning, Red Clay, and Big Bill France.* Chapel Hill: Univ. of North Carolina Press, 2010.

Pilkinton, Mark C. *Washington Hall at Notre Dame: Crossroads of the University, 1864–2004.* Notre Dame, IN: Univ. of Notre Dame Press, 2011.

Price, Joseph L. "Dying to Win: America's Grieving for Athletes." *Journal of American and Comparative Cultures* 25, no. 3–4 (2002): 405–11.

The Pride of the Yankees. Directed by Sam Wood. 1942. New York: HBO Home Video, 1988.

Quakenbush, Robert. *The Gipper's Ghost.* Chicago: O'Connor Publishing, 1985.

Raftery, Heather. "The Bronc Busters Wore Lipstick." *RANGE,* Winter 2010, 28–31.

Reagan, Ronald. *Ronald Reagan: An American Life.* New York: Pocket Books, 1990.

———. *Where's the Rest of Me?* With Richard G. Hubler. New York: Karz Publishers, 1981.

Reilly, Rick. "Chillin' with the Splinter." *Sports Illustrated,* June 30, 2003, 104.

Riess, Steven A. "Only the Ring Was Square: Frankie Carbo and the Underworld Control of American Boxing." *International Journal of the History of Sport* 5, no. 1 (1988): 29–52.

Ring of Fire: The Emile Griffith Story. Directed by Dan Klores and Ron Berger. Troy, MI: Anchor Bay Entertainment, 2005.

"A Ring Requiem." *America.* April 21, 1962, 73.

Rinker, Harry L. "There Is Nothing Wrong with It, Except It Just Does Not Seem Right." *Antiques & Collecting,* July 2001, 47.

Roberts, Randy. "The Wide World of Muhammad Ali: The Politics and Economics of Boxing." In *Muhammad Ali, The People's Champ,* edited by Elliott J. Gorn, 24–53. Urbana: Univ. of Illinois Press, 1995.

Roberts, Randy, and James S. Olson. *Winning Is the Only Thing: Sports in America Since 1945.* Baltimore: Johns Hopkins Univ. Press, 1991.

Robinson, Ray. *Rockne of Notre Dame.* New York: Oxford Univ. Press, 1999.

Rockne, Knute. *The Autobiography of Knute M. Rockne.* Indianapolis: Bobbs-Merrill, 1931.

———. *Coaching: The Way of the Winner.* New York: Devin Adair, 1929.

Rogin, Michael Paul. *Ronald Reagan, the Movie.* Berkeley: Univ. of California Press, 1987.

Rondinone, Troy. *Friday Night Fighter: Gaspar "Indio" Ortega and the Golden Age of Television Boxing.* Urbana: Univ. of Illinois Press, 2013.

Rosenblatt, Roger. "Baseball: The Light of Winter Coming." *Time,* August 19, 1996, 76.

Ross, Ron. *Nine . . . Ten . . . and Out! The Two Worlds of Emile Griffith.* New York: DiBella Entertainment, 2008.

Salvini, Emil R. *Hobey Baker, American Legend.* Minneapolis: Hobey Baker Foundation, 2005.

Sammons, Jeffrey T. *Beyond the Ring: The Role of Boxing in American Society.* Urbana: Univ. of Illinois Press, 1988.

Santos, Kendra. "A World Champion in Life." *ProRodeo Sports News,* August 11, 1999, 28.

Schultz, Jaime. "The Legend of Jack Trice and the Campaign for Jack Trice Stadium, 1973–1984." *Journal of Social History* 41, no. 4 (2008): 997–1029.

"Scorecard." *Sports Illustrated,* April 16, 1962, 4.

Scott, Joan Wallach. "Gender as a Useful Category of Historical Analysis." In *Conceiving Sexuality: Approaches to Sex Research in a Postmodern World,* edited by John H. Gagnon and Richard G. Parker, 57–75. New York: Routledge, 1995.

Senna. Directed by Asif Kapadia. Universal City, CA: Universal Pictures, 2010.

Sheed, Wilfrid. "Find Me a Writer." *Harper's,* February 1984, 21–22.

Shelmerdine, Susan C., trans. *The Homeric Hymns.* Newburyport, MA: Focus Publishing, 1995.

Shields, David. *The Thing about Life Is That One Day You'll Be Dead.* New York: Alfred A. Knopf, 2008.

Shuttleworth, Paul. *Poems to the Memory of Benny Kid Paret.* West Lafayette, IN: Sparrow Press, 1978.

Slusher, Howard. *Man, Sport, and Existence: A Critical Analysis.* Philadelphia: Lea & Febiger, 1967.

Smith, Gary. "The Shadow Boxer." *Sports Illustrated,* April 18, 2005, 58–68.

Sowell, Mike. *The Pitch That Killed: The Story of Carl Mays, Ray Chapman, and the Pennant Race of 1920.* Chicago: Ivan R. Dee, 1989.

Spencer, Lee. "Black Sunday." *Sporting News,* February 26, 2001, 17.

Sperber, Murray. *Onward to Victory: The Crises That Shaped College Sports.* New York: Henry Holt, 1999.

———. *Shake Down the Thunder: The Creation of Notre Dame Football.* Bloomington: Indiana Univ. Press, 1993.

Stump, Al. *Cobb: A Biography.* Chapel Hill, NC: Algonquin Books, 1996.

———. "The Gipper Didn't Die." *Esquire,* October 1952, 103.

Sullivan, Robert. "Dale Earnhardt, 1951–2001: The Last Lap." *Time,* March 5, 2001, 60–69.

Swanson, Mark. "Intimidator Goes out Protecting His Own." *CBS Sportsline,* February 18, 2001. Accessed August 12, 2003. http://www.cbssportsline.com (site discontinued).

Swift, E. M. "Whoopee Ty Yay!" *Sports Illustrated,* December 24, 1990, 49.

Talese, Gay. "The Loneliest Guy in Boxing." In *The Silent Season of a Hero: The Sports Writing of Gay Talese,* edited by Michael Rosenwald. New York: Walker, 2010.

———. "The Silent Season of a Hero." In *The Gay Talese Reader: Portraits and Encounters.* New York: Walker, 2003.

Tennyson, Alfred. "Tithonus." *Cornhill Magazine,* February 1860, 175.

Thay, Edrick. *Ghost Stories of Indiana.* Edmonton: Ghost House Books, 2001.

"This Week's Sign of the Apocalypse." *Sports Illustrated,* May 26, 2003, 28.

Thompson, Hunter S. "Death in the Afternoon." ESPN. Last modified February 19, 2001. http://www.espn.go.com/espn/page2/story?id=1095213.

3. Directed by Russell Mulcahy. Santa Monica, CA: Orly Anderson Productions, 2012.

Touré. *Never Drank the Kool-Aid*. New York: Picador, 2006.

Turner, Gil. "Benny 'Kid' Paret." *Broadside Ballads No. 1*. New York: Folkway Records, 1963.

Twombly, Wells. *Shake Down the Thunder! The Official Biography of Frank Leahy*. Radnor, PA: Chilton Books, 1974.

United States Senate Committee on the Judiciary. Professional Boxing. Hearings before the Subcommittee on Antitrust and Monopoly of the Committee on the Judiciary. United States Senate, Eighty-sixth Congress, second session, Parts 1–4. Washington, DC: United States Government Printing Office, 1960–64.

Updike, John. "Hub Fans Bid Kid Adieu." *New Yorker*, October 22, 1960, 109–31.

Verdery, Katherine. *The Political Lives of Dead Bodies: Reburial and Postsocialist Change*. New York: Columbia Univ. Press, 1999.

Verducci, Tom. "What Really Happened to Ted Williams." *Sports Illustrated*, August 18, 2003, 68.

Vogan, Travis. *Keepers of the Flame: NFL Films and the Rise of Sports Media*. Urbana: Univ. of Illinois Press, 2014.

Walker, Jeff. *The Last Chalkline: The Life and Times of Jack Chevigny*. Shelbyville, KY: Wasteland Press, 2012.

Walton, Theresa A. "Steve Prefontaine: From Rebel with a Cause to Hero with a Swoosh." *Sociology of Sport Journal* 21, no. 1 (2004): 61–83.

Waltrip, Darrell. *Sundays Will Never Be the Same*. With Nate Larkin. New York: Free Press, 2012.

Waltrip, Michael. *In the Blink of an Eye: Dale, Daytona, and the Day That Everything Changed*. With Ellis Henican. New York: Hyperion, 2011.

Ward, Arch. *Frank Leahy and the Fighting Irish*. New York: G. P. Putnam's Sons, 1947.

Wargin, Kathy-Jo. *Win One for the Gipper: America's Football Hero*. With illustrations by Bruce Langton. Chelsea, MI: Sleeping Bear Press, 2004.

Warren, Louis S. *Buffalo Bill's America: William Cody and the Wild West Show*. New York: Vintage Books, 2006.

Watterson, John Sayle. *The Games Presidents Play*. Baltimore: Johns Hopkins Univ. Press, 2006.

Williams, Brian. "No. 3 and Me." *Time*, March 5, 2001, 67.

Williams, Peter. "Every Religion Needs a Martyr: The Role of Matty, Gehrig, and Clemente in the National Faith." In *From Season to Season: Sports as American Religion*, edited by Joseph L. Price, 99–111. Macon, GA: Mercer Univ. Press, 2001.

Williams, Ted. *My Turn at Bat: The Story of My Life*. With John Underwood. New York: Simon & Schuster, 1988.

Wills, Garry. *Reagan's America*. Garden City, NY: Doubleday, 1987.

Wolfe, Tom. *The New Journalism*. New York: Harper & Row, 1973.

Woodward, Stanley. *Sportswriter*. Garden City, NY: Doubleday, 1967.

Yalom, Irvin D. *Existential Psychotherapy*. New York: Basic Books, 1980.

"Young Man on Olympus." *Time*, June 15, 1953, 64–70.

Young, Neil, and Crazy Horse. "My My, Hey Hey (Out of the Blue)." *Rust Never Sleeps*. Burbank, CA: Reprise Records, 1979.

Index

Richard Ian Kimball is an associate professor of history at
Brigham Young University.